940.44   Tanks and weapons
of World War One.

75-62471

TANKS & WEAPONS
OF WORLD WAR I

BEEKMAN HOUSE, NEW YORK

TANKS & WEAPONS
OF WORLD WAR I

BEEKMAN HOUSE, NEW YORK

Introduction

The outbreak of war in 1914 found the bolt-action rifle at the peak of its development and the machine-gun being used in large numbers for the first time. No infantry charge could hope to succeed in the face of such concentrated firepower, and from Switzerland to the sea a system of trenches appeared which made nonsense of the theories of warfare current in the pre-war years.

The first reaction of the generals was to use longer and heavier artillery barrages in a futile attempt to break the deadlock—with the result that trenches were dug deeper and shell-holes made the ground even more impassable. On other fronts this pattern was repeated, and until the advent of the tank there seemed no hope of any solution to the stalemate.

In this book we present the full story of the weapons of the First World War. Artillery, tanks and infantry weapons, as well as gas, flame and other methods of destruction, are described in detail, and illustrated by a superb combination of action photographs and detailed drawings of the weapons themselves.

Edited by Bernard Fitzsimons

Phoebus, London.

This edition © BPC Publishing Ltd.
1973

First published in Purnell's History of
the First World War

First published in this form 1973

ISBN 0-517-130874

Printed in Belgium - H. Proost & Cie p.v.b.a. Turnhout - Belgium

Contents

Much capital has been made in the half-century following the First World War of the fact that in the period of lively military speculation which preceded its outbreak the only theorist fully to appreciate what its nature was likely to be was a civilian – Bloch, a Polish banker and economist writing in 1897. His thesis was that the development of industrialism had fundamentally altered the character of war. He claimed that 'the outward and visible sign of the end of war was the introduction of the magazine rifle. The soldier, by natural evolution, has so perfected the mechanism of slaughter that he has practically secured his own extinction'. The picture he painted of what actually was to happen in 1914 and 1915 on the Western Front turned out to be startlingly accurate. *At first, he wrote, there will be increased slaughter on so terrible a scale as to render it impossible to get troops to push the battle to a decisive issue. They will try to, thinking they are fighting under the old conditions, and they will learn such a lesson that they will abandon the attempt. The war, instead of being a hand-to-hand contest in which the combatants measure their physical and moral superiority, will become a kind of stalemate, in which, neither army being able to get at the other, both armies will be maintained in opposition to each other, threatening each other, but never being able to deliver a final and decisive blow. Everybody will be entrenched in the next war; the spade will be as indispensable to the soldier as his rifle.*

Fifty years later it can be seen that these were the deductions which the General Staffs and defence philosophers of all the belligerents should have drawn from their studies, ardently pursued before 1914, of the American Civil War, the Franco-Prussian War, the South African War and the Russo-Japanese War. The effect of rifle fire at Gettysburg, Gravelotte and Saint Privat indicated that the defence had become the stronger form of war. The two gallant but abortive French cavalry charges at Wörth showed that the day of the *'arme blanche'* was over: never again would armies be able to justify the large amount of railway rolling stock their forage absorbed. The great potential of modern artillery was already apparent. The development of railways with the inevitable risks arising from being tied to fixed lines of supply had been shown to be both an advantage and a disadvantage. British experience in the South African War had emphasised the great potential of the skilled marksman firing from cover and consequently that of the machine gunner: it had also brought out the need for more mobile and intelligent infantry exercising their initiative to the full.

These then were the facts of life which the armies were to discover by bitter experience on the Western Front in 1914 and 1915. It is therefore surprising, in view of the emphasis that had been laid on the study of military history, that the French, German and British military leaders should have gone to war in 1914 steeped in doctrines which flouted to a considerable degree the lessons of the immediate past.

In view of their obsession with Napoleon and their tradition since Waterloo of arriving at the wrong conclusion by apparently faultless logic, the French pre-war theories must be considered first. Foch, Grandmaison and Langlois were disciples

40
War Office
2932

[*Crown Copyright Reserved.*

FIELD SERVICE REGULATIONS
PART I.

OPERATIONS.
1909.
(*Reprinted, with Amendments,* 1914.)

GENERAL STAFF, WAR OFFICE.

LONDON:
PRINTED UNDER THE AUTHORITY OF HIS MAJESTY'S STATIONERY OFFICE
By HARRISON AND SONS, 45-47, ST. MARTIN'S LANE, W.C.,
PRINTERS IN ORDINARY TO HIS MAJESTY.

To be purchased, either directly or through any Bookseller, from
WYMAN AND SONS, LTD., 29, BREAMS BUILDINGS, FETTER LANE, E.C., and
54, ST. MARY STREET, CARDIFF; or
H.M. STATIONERY OFFICE (SCOTTISH BRANCH), 23, FORTH STREET, EDINBURGH; or
E. PONSONBY, LTD., 116, GRAFTON STREET, DUBLIN;
or from the Agencies in the British Colonies and Dependencies,
the United States of America and other Foreign Countries of
T. FISHER UNWIN, LONDON, W.C.

Price Sixpence.

THE NEW WARFARE

As the belligerent powers surveyed the events of 1915, they looked with dismay at the mistakes they had made, the opportunities they had lost. Nevertheless, both sides hoped for a successful conclusion to the war in 1916
Major-General H. Essame
Above: Sixpenny handbook for the troops at the front

of Clausewitz who taught that the secret of success in war was offensive action and the concentration of superior force in terms of bayonets at the decisive point and time. They were further greatly influenced by Colonel Ardent du Picq's *Études sur le Combat* which stressed that morale was the most important factor in war, which indeed has always been true, but did not necessarily imply that a solid phalanx of heroes in red trousers was the best answer to the bullet and the shell. Foch even went so far as to claim that 'a battle lost is a battle one thinks one has lost; for a battle cannot be lost physically'. He went on to state that future improvements would increase the effectiveness of the attack. Above all, the French envisaged a short and mobile war in which the mystic quality of *élan,* which they believed they possessed to a higher degree than all other nations, combined with the threat of the long bayonet (*Rosalie*), would triumph. The artillery would merely be an auxiliary arm. In the attack they pictured an advance supported by controlled fire to within 400 yards of the enemy; thereafter they considered that aimed fire by the enemy would become impossible and that a mass of infantry in depth charging with the bayonet would carry all before it.

The German theorists prescribed opening the attack with a dense infantry firing line followed by an advance with artillery support until a position about 600 yards from the enemy was reached. At this stage they thought a struggle for fire superiority would develop which, when won, would enable the infantry to move forward until, on reaching a position about 100 yards from the enemy, they would be able to deliver the final assault on classic lines.

Both nations had studied the battles of Mukden and Port Arthur and had realised the need for increased artillery support for the infantry attack. In the case of the French, this took the form of increased emphasis on the rôle of their excellent 75-mm field gun. The Germans mobilised under Corps control four heavy batteries of 5.9-inch guns per division in addition to the normal divisional artillery.

The British tactical approach to the coming war was understandably influenced by the experience of the South African War. After this war, Roberts had given General Henderson the task of producing a tactical manual. This appeared in 1905 and was entitled *Combined Training.* In it, Henderson embodied not only his own deductions from the South African War but also what were thought to be the lessons of the Russo-Japanese War – the importance of entrenchment, the problems raised by barbed wire obstacles, the need for attack in depth at the enemy's weakest point and the value of indirect artillery fire. *Field Service Regulations (Volume 1),* which superseded this manual in 1909, reproduced much of what Henderson had thought. By this time, however, there had been a good deal of cross-fertilisation of ideas with the French. The results of this liaison are evident in the section entitled *The Decisive Attack,* where concentration of all available artillery and machine gun fire and the building up of a firing line are envisaged. The section goes on to say: *The climax of the infantry attack is the assault which is made possible by superiority of fire to be gained by the artillery, machine guns and infantry. The fact that superiority of fire has been obtained will usually be first observed from the firing line; it will be known by the weakening of the enemy's fire. The impulse for the assault must therefore come from the firing line and it is the duty of any commander in the firing line who sees that the moment for the assault has arrived, to carry it out and for all other commanders to co-operate. Should it be necessary to give the impulse from the rear, all available reinforcements will be thrown into the fight and as they reach the firing line will carry it with them and rush the position.* Its companion volume, *Infantry Training (Volume 1 1914),* was even more explicit: *The action of the infantry in attack must therefore be considered as a constant pressing forward to close with the enemy. When effective ranges are reached there must usually be a fire fight, more or less prolonged according to the circumstances, in order to beat down the fire of the defenders. The leading lines will be reinforced and as the enemy's fire is gradually subdued, further progress will be made by bounds from place to place, the movement getting renewed force at each pause until the enemy can be assaulted with the bayonet.* This manual, the bible of the vast New Armies, goes on to stress the need for close liaison with the supporting artillery and places responsibility for communication with them on the infantry.

Field Service Regulations (Volume 1)

also implied that at the crisis of the battle the chances of successful cavalry intervention *en masse* would increase—something Henderson had never said and probably now inserted as a result of the influence of Haig, Director of Staff Duties at the relevant time, and the coterie behind the *Cavalry Journal*, brought privately into being in 1906 to ensure that the well bred horse occupied a distinguished place on the battlefield—a concept which even managed to survive the First World War.

Thus so far as their approach to battle was concerned, all the belligerents in August 1914 had this much in common: all paid lip service to mobility and thought in terms of a short and highly mobile war; all stressed the importance of offensive action; all gave the impression that if the assault

They fell for what seemed to them the obvious solution—overwhelming bombardment. They would now crush all resistance by sheer weight of shell.

was determined enough it must succeed; all agreed on the importance of close co-operation between the artillery, machine guns and infantry, in order to gain superiority of fire and thus enable the infantry to close with the bayonet. Furthermore, all implied that cavalry had still a future as an assault arm and none fully appreciated the great strength of defensive systems in depth based on entrenchments, wire, interlocking arcs of machine gun fire and artillery defensive fire. As a result of years of brainwashing drill on barrack squares all were wedded to the ideas of units attacking in straight lines thus producing perfect targets for machine guns firing in enfilade.

The first three months of the war were to show that in armament and organisation, although the Germans had the

John Batchelor

Above: French St Chamond 400-mm rail gun, the largest land gun used in the First World War. *Total traverse:* 12°. *Elevation:* −15° to +73°. *Maximum range:* 17,500 yards. It had three different types of shells, weighing 1,410 pounds, 1,960 pounds and 1,980 pounds respectively.

Below: French Batignolles 320-mm rail gun. *Muzzle velocity:* 2,630 feet per second. *Maximum range:* 2,950 yards. There were several different types of shells, varying between 790 pounds and 1,100 pounds in weight

John Batchelor

advantage in heavy howitzers and numbers of machine guns, this was counterbalanced by the French 75s and the British outstanding superiority in rifle marksmanship vividly demonstrated at Mons and Le Cateau. It has been claimed that if French had not allowed his divisions to drift to battle and had made a more vigorous and determined attempt to capture the Chemin des Dames in the Battle of the Aisne he might have ended the war in 1914. This is doubtful; his army had neither the technique nor the equipment.

At the First Battle of Ypres in the following month the rapid and accurate rifle fire of the British army in the opening engagement had virtually the stopping effect of machine gun fire. In this bitter struggle—a 'soldiers' battle' if ever there was one—the fallacy of prewar theory was finally demonstrated. The defence, for the time being at any rate, had shown itself to be much the stronger form of war. A whole generation of British regular officers and men had been destroyed in the process: consequently they would not be available to train the New Armies. For the future, the blind must lead the blind. Virtually a whole generation of young Frenchmen had also sustained such losses that the national morale would never be quite the same again. With the onset of winter, the front finally congealed: trench warfare began. Tactical and strategical stalemate on the Western Front was complete.

The Allies and Germans now contemplated a deadlock. Meanwhile, by trial and error, they would all learn their lessons, item by item, by costly instalments. For the Allies there was no alternative to offensive action: the Germans were on French and Belgian soil and public opinion unanimously demanded their removal with the greatest possible speed.

The battles of the Aisne and Ypres had resulted in a demand for artillery ammunition far exceeding anything anticipated by the British War Office before the outbreak of war and in consequence an acute shortage developed during the winter. This led those preparing for the renewal of the offensive in the spring to think that overwhelming artillery bombardment—to swamp the German machine guns and cut the enemy wire with shrapnel—would provide the key to success. These ideas dominated the meticulous preparations for the battle of Neuve Chapelle in March 1915, the aim of which was to capture Aubers Ridge. In this battle, after a brief but intense preliminary bombardment, lasting only 35 minutes, four infantry brigades advanced to the attack on a total frontage of only 2,000 yards. Complete surprise was achieved, the German front line was overrun and the infantry advanced about 1,200 yards. Thereafter communications between the infantry and the artillery collapsed and between commanders below the divisional level as well. It was not until late in the afternoon that anything in the nature of serious exploitation was attempted—obviously too late. Further attempts on the succeeding days came to nothing. Such success as this battle achieved was due to the surprise effect of the preliminary bombardment lasting only 35 minutes. Obviously the front of attack was too narrow. The battle further accentuated in dramatic form a complex problem—that of communications between the forward infantry and the supporting artillery. Tele-

'The soldier, by natural evolution, has so perfected the mechanism of slaughter that he has secured his own extinction'

phone lines were found to be and continued to be almost hopelessly vulnerable.

The success of the short and sharp preliminary bombardment at Neuve Chapelle encouraged Haig to try a similar technique when he was ordered to make a further attempt to take Aubers Ridge on May 9, in conjunction with a French offensive under Foch north of Arras. This time there was to be a 40-minute preliminary bombardment to cut the wire, swamp the Germans' forward troops and cut off their reinforcements. Haig planned two converging attacks 6,000 yards apart hoping to cut off some six or seven German battalions. To ensure continuous artillery support, specific batteries were detailed to follow the advancing troops and batteries of mountain artillery were placed in close support of attacking battalions.

Unfortunately, the Germans too had learnt something at Neuve Chapelle, notably the need for solidly constructed fortifications in depth. The British bombardment was a failure, much wire remained uncut when the infantry advanced to find the German defences to be immensely strong. Twenty-foot breastworks and bomb-proof shelters protected the garrisons and enabled them to line their parapets with rifles and machine guns the moment the bombardment lifted. According to an officer survivor of the 2nd East Lancashire Regiment: 'the artillery entirely failed to shake the enemy, who maintained heavy rifle fire and machine gun fire throughout the bombardment.'

Casualties among the attacking troops were as high as 75%.

In his next offensive at Festubert a month later Haig, encouraged by the French who had had some success in attacking after four days' intensive shelling, arranged for a 36-hour artillery preparation to be followed by a night attack to gain a footing in the first two German lines. It was then proposed to exploit the penetration next day. Although the Germans were not taken by surprise, this gambit at first had some success but the artillery support proved inadequate, ammunition ran out, no reserves were available when the crisis came and troops already tired were driven forward to assault once more. The attack soon expired in the teeth of greater machine gun fire than had ever previously been encountered. Haig concluded however from the experience gained in the battle that provided the preliminary bombardment was long enough, heavy enough and meticulously prepared an advance to a depth of about 1,400 yards could be guaranteed.

'Miserable offensive'
The British wanted no more major offensives in 1915. The shell shortage was now at its height and it would take the new ammunition factories in the United Kingdom and the United States at least a year to reach peak production. Delay, however, did not suit the French who demanded and finally obtained British assistance in the build-up area about Lens and Loos on the immediate left of Foch's September offensive towards Namur. French and Haig could see little future to operations in this area of coal mines and industrial slums but were overruled in what were thought to be the interests of the Alliance. Haig, now committed to the policy of prolonged artillery preparations, had only sufficient ammunition to support two of the six divisions available for this battle. He therefore decided to make good the deficiency by using gas discharges from cylinders operated by Special Companies of the Royal Engineers. As the German gas attack at Ypres in April had already shown, success depended on the vagaries of the wind: on the day of the attack there was virtually none. Nevertheless the attacking troops did succeed in capturing the German first line and in advancing beyond it. Now, however, there was delay in bringing forward the reserves who were controlled by French himself, and the Germans were able to stabilise the battle. Haig continued this dismal offensive for a further miserable 17 days. It was the first experience of the New Armies and despite their outstanding courage and high grade human material it emphasised not only the lack of training of the troops but also of their commanders and staffs as well. It also showed that the Germans once again were a step ahead: they now catered for a second line of defence out of range of any bombardment the Allies could mount.

At Loos, Haig had been right in asking for control of the reserves and French wrong. French therefore was removed. His replacement in somewhat dubious circumstances by Haig involved no dramatic leap forward in tactical thought. In the planning and conduct of the battle he had failed to find a means of keeping his finger on the pulse of it. After zero hour the battle so far as he was concerned had virtually

France's older guns, brought out once again in the hour of crisis

French Model 1878 120-mm gun
Weight limbered up: 8,250 pounds. *Length of barrel:* 27 calibres. *Range:* 8,975 yards. *Muzzle velocity:* 1,590 feet-per-second. *Weight of shell:* 40¼ pounds

French Model 1878 90-mm gun
Weight limbered up: 4,400 pounds. *Length of barrel:* 25.3 calibres. *Range:* 7,550 yards. *Muzzle velocity:* 1,494 feet-per-second. *Weight of shell:* 17½ pounds

French Model 1898 155-mm howitzer
Elevation: from −5 degrees to +60 degrees. *Range:* 7,660 yards. *Weight of shell:* 88 pounds

'Infantry alone does not possess effective offensive power against obstacles defended by gunfire'

Right: A German supply party carries billy-cans of food up to the troops on the front line.
Below: French troops take over a former German strongpoint. They are equipped with the Chauchat 8-mm light machine gun with its characteristic moonshaped magazine.

fought itself. Experience gained up to the end of 1915 had convinced him that the heavier the bombardment, the greater the chances of success, even if it inevitably involved the sacrifice of surprise. He proceeded to create senior artillery appointments at every level of command. In the development of tactics, Major General Birch, at first Rawlinson's and later Haig's principal artillery adviser, was henceforth to exert ever increasing influence. He and Haig saw the coming battles as series of step by step advances, each stage covered by an elaborate fire plan. This procedure, they thought, would eventually so demoralise the enemy that the waiting cavalry divisions could gallop through his shattered defences.

On the Eastern Front the operations had on the whole conformed to the mobile type envisaged by Allied and German prewar theory. Here, the cavalry divisions had played a prominent part both in Russia and the Balkans, largely on account of their mobility. The general incompetence of the Russian commanders at all levels, the virtual absence of an efficient logistic system, the acute shortage of munitions, had combined with the vast distances and featureless terrain to give the Germans comparatively easy victories. Politically, the Germans intended to embody Belgium in the *Reich*; it therefore sufficed in 1915 to stand on the defensive on the Western Front and in the process concentrate on economising in manpower by the ever increasing use of wire, machine guns and deep dugouts. The end of active operations in 1914 had left the Germans, unlike their opponents, in tactically sound defensive positions. Throughout 1915 they had pushed ahead with the construction of well-drained and well-revetted trench systems with an industry which put the efforts of the British in this respect to shame. Their prewar theory had stressed the importance of depth in defence and provision for counterattack. Constructed in accordance with these principles, their defensive systems by the end of 1915 were formidable: four to six miles deep, crisscrossed by interlocking arcs of machine gun fire, dead ground covered by artillery defensive fire and protected by everincreasing belts of wire. By the end of 1915 they had put an amazing amount of work into the construction of shellproof and weather-proof accommodation, thus enabling them to keep their troops for long periods in the forward defences without undue discomfort and with small loss of life.

Falkenhayn, like Joffre and Haig, saw the coming battles of 1916 in terms of fire rather than of large scale movement, but with greater subtlety. He planned to attack with very light forces after an intense bombardment, thus forcing the French to counterattack straight into the maw of his massed artillery and machine guns. By this means he hoped to bleed them to death.

Weighed down

It is surprising that so little thought was given in the early years of the First World War to the tactics needed once the much desired breach in the German defences had been blasted by the artillery. One consideration, which the prewar regulations had stressed, was that the infantryman would have to show great initiative and be highly mobile. Instead, throughout

1915 his mobility had been continuously reduced. In August 1914 his load had been 59 pounds 11 ounces, by Christmas 1915 this had risen to 66 pounds. Apart from his weapons, he had to carry into the attack a pick or shovel, wire cutters, sandbags, an anti-gas respirator and 170 rounds of ammunition. To this had to be added his personal necessities – a heavy greatcoat, a ground sheet, three pairs of thick socks, a spare woollen undervest and long underpants, a cardigan, a spare shirt and his iron ration of a one pound tin of corned beef, tea and sugar and two packets of cement-hard biscuits. The steel helmets issued in this year were of solid steel and very heavy, often causing headaches. Each man also had a heavy mess tin, a waterbottle, a knife, fork and spoon, an enamel mug and washing and shaving kit including a cut-throat razor. In winter, thigh gum boots and leather jerkins were added for good measure. In an attack the infantryman was expected to carry on for days on hard rations washed down with such tea as he could brew for himself in his mess tin with solidified paraffin. At all times his food included an inordinate amount of cheese – a constipating factor which the almost continuous shell fire did something to mitigate. The infantryman was thus almost always overloaded and inadequately sustained by hot food.

The short Lee-Enfield rifle carried by each man was an accurate and simple weapon capable, in skilled hands, of producing 15 aimed rounds a minute.

Thus to a limited extent platoons and companies, although overloaded, had the means to get forward on their own in a fluid situation once clear of the enemy's main defences. Despite the bias of the prewar manuals to what they called open warfare and the stress on it as the ultimate aim, little or no thought at the higher levels of command was given to it after 1914. As late as spring 1916 the Infantry Officers' Basic Course of one month at the School of Musketry at Hythe was devoting a complete week to firing the rifle in the standing position. Platoon tactics received two hours in the whole course – two sections of instructors advancing by alternate rushes from the 800-yard firing point to the butts. A high proportion of training time was devoted to bayonet fighting. So important was this subject deemed to be that all troops passing through the Base at Étaples were rushed through an institution known as the Bull Ring. Here instructors in red jerseys showed how 'easy' it was. You stabbed your opponent in the stomach, stirred your bayonet round a bit, then pulled it out smartly.

Also available within brigades was the Stokes Mortar which had a maximum range of about 400 yards. It consisted of a plain steel tube with a spike at the bottom end. The crew attached a sporting cartridge to the base of the shell, slid it down the barrel onto the spike and hoped for the best. It was advisable to wait for the departure of one round before inserting the next: increased range could be obtained by adding rings of ballastite to the cartridge. The main drawback to this weapon was its weight, particularly that of the base plate. Nevertheless, it does seem that these drawbacks could have been eliminated quickly if more attention had been given to the problem at GHQ.

More than half a century later it is not

easy to explain the shortsightedness of the Allied High Command in tactical matters in 1915. It may have sprung from the fact that most of them had never in their lives had to fight on foot as infantrymen. It may well be that from sheer inexperience and lack of imagination they literally could not understand that it was virtually impossible for a battalion commander in the attack to control his companies and maintain touch with his supporting artillery. Now that the tactical problem by which they were confronted had taken an unmistakable form they fell for what seemed to them the obvious solution – overwhelming bombardment. They would now crush all resistance by sheer weight of shells. Accordingly they proceeded to pile gun on gun, substitute high explosive for shrapnel and bring in ever increasing numbers of heavy artillery batteries with calibres ranging from 6 inches to 18. In almost all their eyes, the developments inspired by Swinton and Churchill which would eventually completely change the character of land warfare had no significance.

The views expressed by Robertson, at the time Chief of the General Staff of the BEF, in his memorandum to Asquith on November 6, 1915, may be taken as epitomising the official attitude. He wrote: *Experience has taught us that, given sufficient guns and ammunition, any front system can be broken. It is the depth of the enemy's defences and the power of bringing intact reserves up quickly to occupy rear lines which make attack difficult on the Western Front.* He later went on to state that the main lessons of the attacks in 1915 had been that *given adequate artillery support there is no difficulty in overwhelming the enemy's forces in front line and support. The principles are that sufficient force should be employed to exhaust the enemy and force him to use up his reserves, and then, and then only, the decisive attack which is to win victory, should be driven home. There are therefore no grounds for considering that the prospects of a successful offensive next spring are anything but good.*

Further Reading
Edmonds, Sir James, *Military Operations France and Belgium* (HMSO)
Falkenhayn, E. von, *General Headquarters and its Critical Decisions* (Hutchinson 1919)
Fuller, Maj-Gen. J. F. C., *Decisive Battles of the Western World* (Eyre and Spottiswoode 1957)
Liddell Hart, Sir Basil, *The Tanks* Vol. 1. (Faber 1959)
Montgomery, Viscount, *A History of Warfare* (Collins 1968)
Sixsmith, E. K. G., *British Generalship in the 20th Century* (Arms and Armour Press)
Weller, J. A. C., *Weapons and Tactics* (Vane 1966)

MAJOR-GENERAL H. ESSAME served as an Infantry Officer from early 1915 to 1949. In the First World War he fought at the battles of the Somme, Third Ypres and Passchendaele and was present at the March retreat of 1918 and the final advance to the Armistice Line. He was awarded the Military Cross. Between the wars, he graduated at the Staff College, Quetta and in the Second World War he commanded the 214th Infantry Brigade from Normandy to the Baltic. Since his retirement he has been active as a radio commentator, military television adviser, lecturer, freelance journalist and as a writer on military historical subjects. His literary works include: *The 43rd Wessex Division at War* (Clowes), *Battle for Germany* (Batsford) and *Normandy Bridgehead* (Ballantine).

The guns of the 'Great Retreat'

Light and medium field pieces of both sides

Above: British 18-pounder Mark I. *Calibre:* 3·3-inches. *Barrel length:* 28 calibres. *Weight of shell:* 18 pounds. *Maximum range:* 7,000 yards. *Elevation:* −5 degrees to + 16 degrees. *Weight of gun and carriage:* 3,800 pounds

Left: French 75-mm field gun. *Calibre:* 75-mm. *Weight of shell:* 16 pounds (shrapnel). *Maximum range:* 7,440 yards. *Elevation:* −10 degrees to + 19 degrees. *Weight:* 2,657 pounds. *Rate of fire:* 6 rounds-per-minute normally, but up to 20 rounds-per-minute when necessary

Above: British 4·5-inch howitzer. *Barrel length:* 13·33 calibres. *Weight of shell:* 35 pounds. *Maximum range:* about 7,000 yards. *Elevation:* −5 degrees to + 45 degrees. *Weight of gun and carriage:* 3,000 pounds

Left: German 7·7-cm field gun. *Length of barrel:* 27 calibres. *Weight of shell:* 15 pounds. *Maximum range:* 9,200 yards. *Elevation:* −13 degrees to + 15 degrees. *Weight of gun ready to fire:* 2,240 pounds. *Muzzle velocity:* 1,523 feet-per-second

Below: German 10·5-cm 1913 model howitzer (made by Krupp). *Length of barrel:* 20 calibres. *Weight of shell:* 35·34 pounds. *Maximum range:* 9,733 yards. *Elevation:* −4 degrees to +43 degrees. *Muzzle velocity:* 1,410 feet-per-second

John Batchelor

One of the most heroic actions fought by the BEF during the retreat from Mons to the Marne was that at Néry, a village near Compiègne, where on September 1 a single battery of the Royal Horse Artillery which, with the 1st Cavalry Brigade, was covering the withdrawal of III Corps, held off for several hours the whole of the German *4th Cavalry Division*. The battery, which in 1914 was equipped with six 13-pounders, is now known as 'L' (Néry) Battery, RHA

NÉRY

'L' Battery, Royal Horse Artillery, following in the wake of its Cavalry Brigade to Néry, reached it after the other units had begun to shake down into their quarters. The allotment of the village was as follows: at the northern end were the 5th Dragoon Guards with their horses in the open; the 11th Hussars were billeted on the eastern face and up the east side of the village street, the men and horses being under cover – in houses, yards, barns, sheds, or lean-to's. On the west side of the village street, and in the fields behind the village on this side, were the Queen's Bays, one squadron being in a field further to the south; all their horses were in the open.

'L' Battery on arrival was given a field to the south to bivouac in, and the sugar factory was allotted to it as its headquarters. In the north-west corner of the field were some haystacks.

While the battery was completing its arrangements for the night the Battery Commander proceeded to Cavalry Brigade Headquarters, situated in the main street, to ascertain what protective arrangements had been made to cover the bivouac of his battery.

He received orders that 'L' was merely required to block the two roads which led east and south from the sugar factory. He was also told that the force would continue the march at 0430 hours on September 1. Major Sclater-Booth returned to his battery, and the necessary posts were found by 'L' to cover the southern end of the billeting area.

Gradually the work was finished and, wearied with the day's march under the hot August sun, men and horses settled down to rest. Silence brooded over the little village and the surrounding bivouacs that nestled around it on the western slope and at the bottom of the narrow valley, which was shut in to east and west by its guardian heights. Day broke cool and very misty, and when the march should have been resumed it was quite impossible to see objects more than 150 to 200 yards away. Orders were, therefore, issued that units should stand fast until 0500 hours.

The battery, which was standing halted in mass with the teams hooked in, took advantage of this delay to let down the poles and water the horses by sections at the sugar factory. Generally, it may be said, 'the only desire of our force in Néry at this moment was to get outside an excellent breakfast'. This very natural desire was to be roughly frustrated. The mist was nearly as thick as ever when, just before 0500 hours Major Sclater-Booth, with his officers, walked down from the sugar factory to the north-west corner of the battery field, where the haystacks stood. Leaving the others here, the Battery Commander walked on up the main street of the little village to Brigade Headquarters in order to get the latest instructions as to the resumption of the march.

Going into the house he found the Brigadier and his Brigade Major. Hardly had he entered when a high-explosive shell burst over the village, and a roar of gun and rifle fire broke out from the heights overlooking the eastern side of Néry.

At the same moment Lieutenant Tailby, who had been sent with a patrol to reconnoitre the high ground north of Néry, reached headquarters and reported that he had ridden into a body of German cavalry in the mist and had been chased back. It was now about 0505 hours and the 1st Cavalry Brigade had been taken completely by surprise.

Despite the disadvantage at which the British Cavalry and Horse Artillery were taken, and despite the heavy artillery, machine gun and rifle fire pouring into the open bivouacs around the village, steps were taken by all units to offer an effective resistance and hold on till assistance arrived from neighbouring troops.

Imperial War Museum

A British crew poses beside their gun – a 13-pounder, the standard equipment of the RHA

As soon as firing broke out the Brigade-Major went out to see that the necessary action was being taken. Major Sclater-Booth also went out into the street with the Brigadier, and then left at once to return to his battery. Suddenly a mob of maddened horses came galloping wildly down the main street. They were the horses of the Bays, stampeded by the enemy's fire. At the same moment a high-explosive shell burst among the surging mass of animals and rendered the road impassable. Crossing over to the western side of the street the Battery Commander ran behind the houses and so came to the field where 'C' Squadron of the Bays had bivouacked during the night. From here the battery field was open to view, and Major Sclater-Booth saw that three guns had been unlimbered and brought into action to answer the fire of the German battery, the flashes of which could be seen stabbing through the slightly thinning mist. Apparently the German guns were in action on the heights to the eastward a short half-mile away. The din was terrific. There was one incessant roar of gun and rifle fire, punctuated by the violent detonations of 'Universal' shells bursting over the battery.

As he ran forward to reach his battery

Bayer. Hauptstaatsarchiv München Abt.

a shell burst immediately in front of him, knocked him down, and put him out of action for the rest of the fight.

An inferno of shells
At the moment the surprise was effected, Captain Bradbury and the other officers of the battery were standing near the haystacks. Suddenly, with no previous warning, a shell burst over the battery, and immediately afterwards the bivouac came under very heavy rifle fire from the ridge. Captain Bradbury shouted out 'Come on! Who's for the guns?' and running out from behind the haystacks, made for them, followed by all the other officers. Meanwhile, in the exposed battery, horses and men were falling fast. Joined by those men who were engaged in steadying the horses in the inferno of bursting shells, the officers got three guns unlimbered and swung round to face the German battery. Captain Bradbury, Sergeant Nelson, and others took one gun; Lieutenant Giffard took another; while Lieutenants Campbell and Mundy were at a third. The ammunition wagons were 20 yards away, and over that death-swept open space the ammunition had to be brought up. Hardly were the three guns in action when one of them,

Flyweight guns at Néry

The heroic action of 'L' Battery at Néry, which resulted in the award of three VCs. *Inset:* Superior in numbers and calibre, the German guns nevertheless suffered heavy casualties under Lieutenants Campbell and Mundy, was knocked out by a direct hit; the other two guns opened fire on the enemy.

These two guns of 'L' carried on an unequal struggle. A few rounds only had been fired when Lieutenant Giffard, in charge of one of the guns, was severely wounded and all the detachment either killed or wounded. This left only one gun — under Captain Bradbury — still in action.

Lieutenants Campbell and Mundy, when their gun was knocked out, at once ran to the gun where Captain Bradbury and Sergeant Nelson were working, while Gunner Darbyshire and Driver Osborn crossed and recrossed the shell-swept zone behind the gun to bring up the necessary ammunition from the wagons.

Almost immediately after the two subalterns joined Captain Bradbury's detachment Lieutenant Campbell was killed, and the distribution of the duties at the gun became as follows: Lieutenant Mundy in position close to the gun, acted as Section Commander, while Captain Bradbury carried out the duties of layer, and Sergeant Nelson those of range-setter. The gun appeared to bear a charmed life and remained untouched. Also it was clear that its fire was not without result, for the German guns were being badly mauled.

When the action began the German guns seem to have been in two groups—one battery in action on the heights, and now busily engaged with 'L' Battery, and two more batteries, unlimbered farther to the north almost opposite the centre of the village and firing on it.

Drawn by the fire kept up by 'L', the Germans now apparently decided to mass all their guns, and the two batteries in action abreast of the centre of the village moved round to join that engaged with 'L'.

The solitary gun of the latter was now opposed to heavy odds; for the hostile guns were under 800 yards away and in a commanding position. The action broke out with renewed fury and the massed German batteries made a determined effort to crush the single undaunted gun. Lieutenant Mundy was now seriously wounded, and the tale of casualties began to mount up, until at last at 0715 hours there remained only Captain Bradbury, still unhit, and Sergeant Nelson, who had been severely wounded. They kept up the best rate of fire they could, but naturally it became very desultory. A reinforcement now reached the little detachment, in the person of Battery-Sergeant-Major Dorrell, and on his arrival Captain Bradbury, knowing that the ammunition up with the gun was running low, went back to fetch up more from the wagons. As he left the gun he was hit by a shell and mortally wounded. There now remained only the Battery-Sergeant-Major and the wounded Sergeant Nelson. With these two to serve it, the gun fired its last remaining rounds and was silent. The end had come.

But it had not been fought in vain, for, as its last discharge boomed and echoed, reinforcements of all arms reached the field and the result it had fought so hard to attain was achieved.

'L' Battery's casualties amounted to 45 officers and men killed and wounded out of a strength of 170. Among the killed was Captain Bradbury, who was awarded posthumously the Victoria Cross: it was also awarded to Sergeant Nelson and Battery-Sergeant-Major Dorrell. The German cavalry division lost more heavily, was driven into the surrounding forests, did not emerge from hiding until late next day and was still unfit to move on September 4.

[From the Royal Artillery War Commemoration Book 1914-1918, reprinted by permission of the Royal Artillery Institution.]

BOLIMOW AND THE FIRST GAS ATTACK

Since the beginning of the war, the idea of using poison gas as a weapon had been regarded with suspicion by soldiers of the front line. But Germany's scientists had nevertheless continued their research into various forms of offensive chemicals and by January 1915 a new gas was ready for use. *Ian Hogg*

Christmas 1914 found the armies on the Eastern Front locked solidly together, entrenched in the ice, snow and bitter cold of the Polish winter, as static as the opposing forces on the Western Front. In an endeavour to break this deadlock and get the German army rolling once more on the road to Warsaw and beyond, Hindenburg planned an attack in the central sector. If it succeeded, the momentum would carry the Germans on to Warsaw; if it failed, at least it would have caused a big enough diversion to occupy large numbers of Russian defenders and keep them occupied while his northern armies deployed from their positions in East Prussia in a flanking attack towards Bialystok. The problem was to overcome the inertia at the beginning of the attack—the same problem which confronted the commanders on both sides in Flanders. Some new approach, some new technique, some new weapon was called for.

Although the war was only five months old, there had already been talk of poison gas as a weapon. The subject had recently been given a public airing in 1908, when *The Panmure Papers* were published. These were a volume of reminiscences by Lord Panmure, and revealed in it were copies of letters between Panmure, Palmerston and Admiral Lord Dundonald which showed that the admiral had, during the Crimean War, suggested the use of sulphur fumes to overcome the defenders of Sebastopol. The authorities of the time, while admitting the idea showed promise, turned it down on the grounds that 'no honourable combatant would use such means'.

At about the same time as the publication of these papers was causing a mild stir, the French army developed a rifle grenade charged with a small quantity of tear-gas. This was intended for the attack of casemates and fortifications by firing the grenade through the loopholes and so incapacitating the defenders. These grenades were brought into the public view when they were used in 1912 by the military and police authorities when the notorious Bonnot Gang—the Motor Bandits—was trapped in a house at Choisy-le-Roi.

After the war had begun, the German army was alert to the possibility of these grenades being used against them, though there appears to be no record of their use. Any suspicious smell was treated with respect; cases of asphyxiation after artillery bombardment were at first thought to be due to the use of gas, and chemists were sent to make checks in the front line. It was found that the casualties were due to carbon monoxide poisoning, the gas being generated by incomplete detonation of high explosive shells of faulty design in confined spaces such as dug-outs. Then in late September 1914 the Allied press featured stories of a new French shell filled with a mysterious substance called Turpinite, and once more the gas bogey arose in German minds. But Turpinite was no more than a liquid explosive of doubtful efficiency which the French army employed for a short time to overcome shortages of the more usual shell fillings, and which had suffered a change in the over-heated prose of the newspapermen.

These incidents, minor in themselves, served to keep the poison gas idea alive in some minds, particularly in German minds. They were ever-alert for signs that gas was being used against them.

Towards the end of October 1914, the Kaiser Wilhelm Institute for the Advancement of Science, in Berlin, was approached by the German army with an unusual request. Due to the shortage of steel, a number of artillery shells had been made from cast iron; because of the relative weakness of the metal, the shell walls had to be much thicker than those of a steel shell in order to withstand the stress of firing. This meant that the space within the shell for high explosive was so small that the effect of the shell's detonation was merely to split the shell into one or two large chunks, instead of the shower of fine, lethal fragments desired. The Institute was asked to examine these shells and see if it could suggest some form of chemical filling which would give them back their lethal effect. After a violent explosion in a laboratory, which killed one professor and severely injured another, this particular investigation was quietly dropped, but the 'chemical warfare' idea had taken root in the Institute.

The first serious suggestion for using some form of offensive chemical agent came from a Professor Nernst, who proposed placing an irritant substance among the bullets of shrapnel shells. His idea was accepted, and he was given the task of supervising the production of a batch of these shells. In October 1914 some were used at the front, in an attack near Neuve Chapelle. It speaks volumes for their lack of effect that nobody on the Allied side knew that such a weapon had been used, and it was not until after the war that the facts became known. It is said that Professor Nernst's shells were abandoned after General Falkenhayn's son had won a case of champagne by betting he could remain inside a cloud of this 'irritant substance' for five minutes, unprotected and unharmed.

The next move was by a Dr von Tappen, also of the Kaiser Wilhelm Institute. His brother was Operations Chief at OHL, and through this convenient channel, Tappen suggested the use of a shell carrying a charge of xylyl bromide; this was a lachrymatory (tear producing) compound which Tappen had studied extensively for a research degree. Professor Haber, head of the

Institute, also interested himself in this proposal, to such an extent that he eventually became director of all German chemical warfare research. Tappen's shell was tested on the artillery ranges at Kummersdorf in December 1914 with reasonable success, and opinion began to form that here was the sought-for weapon which could break the deadlock on the fronts, flush the enemy out of his trenches, and get the war mobile and fluid once again. After the trial, General von Tappen was placed in charge of a programme to produce quantities of 15-cm howitzer shells charged with high explosive and xylyl bromide; Haber suggested using powerful mortars to fling large canisters of gas; and someone, never identified, suggested putting gas in cylinders and simply turning the tap when required, an idea which was seized upon and given to Professor Haber to turn into a workable proposition.

It is worth looking closer at Tappen's shell and its contents; this was a pioneering effort, based on nothing but faith and a certain knowledge of chemistry. The shell itself was the standard 15-cm high explosive type, filled from the base—a common German design feature—with TNT. Into a cavity in this TNT was placed a lead canister containing the xylyl bromide, so that when the shell detonated on striking the ground, the blast of the explosion would break open the lead canister and disperse the chemical in a fine mist. It would then vaporise and give rise to severe irritation of the eyes and nose of anyone unfortunate enough to breathe it. Indeed, xylyl bromide—or *T-Stoff* as it was code-named—could be lethal if inhaled in a heavy enough concentration, but Tappen appreciated that such concentrations were out of the question with artillery shells as the delivery system, and was quite satisfied that the irritant effect would sufficiently incapacitate the Allied troops to allow the German attackers to overrun them. By way of protection, the German troops were to be provided with a simple face mask, a pad of cotton waste tied in front of the nose and mouth with tapes, and moistened with a chemical solution carried in a bottle and reapplied when necessary. In view of the known tear-producing effect of xylyl bromide, such a mask seems a trifle optimistic.

While manufacture was getting under way, a more difficult job had to be done—the soldiers had to be persuaded that the proposal was worth consideration. This was to be the first example of a difficulty which was to persist throughout the war in all the armies. While the scientists were full of ideas, particularly in the chemical warfare field, the front-line troops were more than a little opposed to their proposals. Very little was known about the effect of chemical agents, while a great deal had been discovered about the effects of shrapnel shells, machine guns, wire and bayonets. Gas was a mystery, and nobody liked the idea of going forward with nothing but a mystery to sustain him.

Eventually Hindenburg was persuaded to use the new *T-Stoff* shells in his forthcoming attack on the Eastern Front, and supplies were shipped to ammunition dumps near Łódź. Some sources aver that large quantities of explosive rifle bullets were also supplied for this attack, but this is open to considerable doubt. After the war, the Germans took great pains to point out that the wording of the Hague Convention—*d'employer du poison ou des armes empoisonnées* (to use poison or poisoned weapons)—was never intended to apply to war gases; that gas did not cause undue suffering by comparison with other weapons; that their use was not excluded by the convention's phrase *d'employer des armes, des projectiles ou des matières propres à causer des maux superplus* (to use weapons, projectiles and materials likely to cause the utmost injury); and that since the *T-Stoff* shells carried a large charge of TNT they were not contrary to the convention. In view of all this it is difficult to believe that they would deliberately employ explosive small arms bullets whose use was most definitely proscribed by the same convention paragraphs. It seems likely that these reports were simply atrocity propaganda of the type both sides engaged in.

By the end of January 1915, Hindenburg's position in the centre of the Eastern Front straddled the road and rail lines from Łódź to Warsaw. Just north of the railway is the village of Bolimow, and the line in this sector rested its left flank on the River Bzura and ran southwards along the line of the Riva Rawka, through forests and farmland. The opposing Russian line rested its northern flank on the village of Sochaczew and ran south through the villages of Borzymow, Humin and Wola-Szydlow to a point on the Rawka where it loops to the east below the railway line. It was here that Hindenburg proposed to demonstrate his new weapon.

On the high ground west of the Rawka, Mackensen's army artillery was massed, upwards of 600 guns across the seven-mile front, a gun density of one gun for every 20 yards or so. This was, for January 1915, a considerable concentration. The majority of these guns were of 7.7-cm and 10-cm, the usual field pieces for the close support infantry, but there was a considerable leavening of 15-cm heavy howitzers spread across the front, and it was these guns which received the supplies of *T-Stoff* shells. On Sunday January 3, the bombardment of the Russian positions began with a rain of high explosive and shrapnel shells together with the new threat of lachrymatory gas.

While the bombardment thundered on, seven divisions, almost 100,000 men, were concentrated ready for the attack. Their three main objectives were the Russian positions round the three villages of Borzymow, Humin and Zduńska Wola. One of these three must crack, and the breach thus made would allow the main weight to pour through, turn, and take the remaining defensive positions in the rear. Contemporary newspaper accounts spoke of these troops as 'Divisions of Death', a highly-coloured phrase coined in an attempt to convey their determination and contempt for casualties. The seven divisions had been carefully assembled from selected regiments of high morale and proven fighting ability, since a great deal hung on the result of this attack, and the physical condition of the battlefield was sufficient to deter all but the hardiest; waist-deep snow, intense cold in which tree branches snapped like glass and unprotected hands froze to bare metal, harsh east winds and the numbing dry cold of the Polish plains.

Early on Monday the attack began, after an intensified artillery bombardment

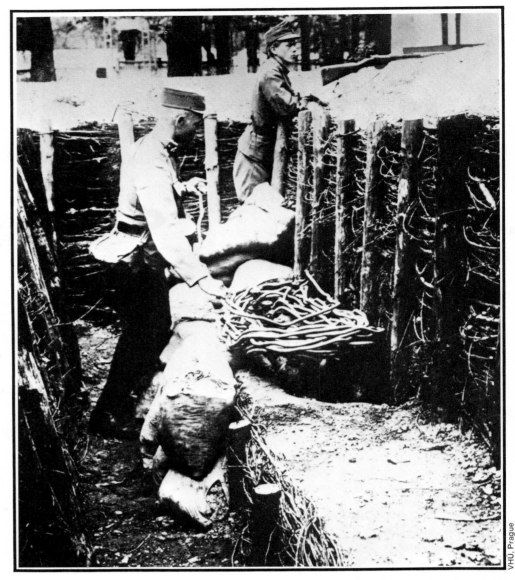

VHU, Prague

which included more gas. There are no records of what the climate did to the primitive liquid-soaked respirators of the German troops, if indeed any were worn. In that climate, such a mask would freeze in seconds and effectively suffocate the wearer. In the event, the attackers had no trouble from the after-effects of their own gas bombardment. But having fought across the icy Rawka and through the snow to the Russian defensive line, it seemed to have had no effect on the defenders either. There were no crowds of weeping men beside their arms, no defensive positions in which men were so bemused by tears and sneezing that they were unable to man their weapons. The reception was harsh and deadly, and it was a long and bitter struggle before the Russians yielded their positions, fell back into the forests behind them, and enabled the Germans to take the three villages almost simultaneously.

Falling back, the Russian defence was still cohesive and gave the Germans no chance to make the breakthrough their plans had envisaged. But by falling back into the forest, and widening the front, the Russian move caused the German attack to lose formation, and the attacking divisions were split into smaller groups as they took up the pursuit. As the Russians vanished into the forests, they filtered through a mass of field guns and machine guns disposed ready for just this situation, and as the dispersed German groups reached the forest edge, the trap was sprung.

A withering fire of shrapnel and machine gun bullets tore the heart from the attacking force, and dispersed the groups into smaller and smaller parties, more interested in staying alive than forcing the forest barrier. Rough defensive positions were formed and a new line of battle struck as the German armies regrouped and prepared for a fresh assault. Artillery moved forward, observers were deployed, and a fierce artillery duel now broke out while the infantry slowly hammered their way into the forests. The battle now degenerated into a frozen slogging-match, every yard disputed and every tree a strong-point.

On the southern end of the attacking line, the Germans crossed the railway and managed to advance as far as Bednary, some six miles from the start line, by Wednesday. The remainder of the line barely reached the River Sucha, a matter of three or four miles of ground taken. The Russian resistance was so fierce that no sector could be stripped of troops to reinforce the southern push in the hopes of making a break-through at Bednary, and the advance got no further. On Thursday the issue was still in doubt, but on Friday the doubt was removed by the appearance of reserves of Siberian troops on the Russian side. By this time the Germans were depleted and exhausted, and in no condition to withstand the onslaught of fresh troops, who, moreover, were more accustomed to the climate conditions than were the attackers. With increasing speed, and

Above: The site of Hindenburg's demonstration of his new weapon — xylyl bromide gas. The German attack on Russian positions near Bolimow relied on a massive concentration of artillery: 600 guns positioned across a seven-mile front. *Left:* The system of releasing gas in artillery shells used at Bolimow was not the only method of dispensing it. Here, Austrian soldiers prepare chlorine gas in steel bottles.
Below right: A French contemporary cartoon depicts a 'true to life portrait of the pioneers of civilization and culture'

Right: The new German 15-cm *T-Stoff* gas shell
1 Fuse pocket
2 3·3 lbs explosive
3 Paraffin wax
4 Shell
5 Lead container
6 7·0 lbs liquid gas
7 Felt wad
8 Copper driving band
9 Lead washer

John Batchelor

mounting casualties, the attack was stopped and then rolled back. By Friday the Russian troops had recovered the three villages and had ejected the German advanced troops in Bednary. By Saturday they had driven the whole German line back across the Rawka to their starting point, and by Sunday both sides were licking their wounds. The battle was over. After six days of intense effort and sacrifice, the Divisions of Death were back where they had started, leaving over 20,000 dead behind them. Hindenburg's long awaited demonstration had failed as an attack, but, at a cost, had succeeded in occupying the defenders while the attack in the north got under way.

And what of the gas shells? What effect had the new weapon which had promised to flush out the enemy from his defensive positions at no cost to the attacker? In this, their first battle, they were utterly useless. It is possible to appreciate the desperate attitude which led to their employment on this particular occasion; the Russians were a stubborn enemy, and anything which promised to ease the attackers' task was worth trying. It is also possible that the Eastern Front was used for the first employment of gas so as to preserve some element of surprise for the Western Front and still be able to try the new weapon in combat. But it is impossible to avoid pointing a finger and saying that somewhere, someone did not do his homework. The simple fact which seems to have escaped those responsible for the proposal was that xylyl bromide was unsuited to the climate; the object of the shell was to disperse the liquid in fine droplets by the explosion of the TNT charge, so that it

Bapty

could evaporate and give rise to the irritant effect. But due to the sub-zero temperature at the time of the battle, the liquid was thick and turgid, failing to break down into fine enough drops, and when distributed, froze instead of evaporating. Indeed, the whole effect could be called negative, since the space in the shells taken up by the gas canisters was wasted, where it might have been used to carry more TNT and thus do more damage in the conventional fashion. It was at least realised by the Russians that gas had been used in the action, contrary to the British experience at Neuve Chapelle. But con-

temporary accounts failed to mention it, and it was not until a few months later that it came to light in Western reports. Even then, it was credited with being chlorine gas; since this was the cloud gas used in Flanders, it can be accepted that the writers simply assumed that no other war gas had been discovered at that time. If it did nothing else, the employment of gas at Bolimow alerted the Russians and enabled them to begin provision of rudimentary gas-masks before the Germans had perfected the technique. But as far as its tactical effect on the battle is concerned, gas at Bolimow was a failure.

Further Reading
Fries and West, *Chemical Warfare* (New York: McGraw-Hill, 1921)
Foulkes, C. H., *'Gas!'; the Story of the Special Brigade* (Blackwood 1934)
Hanslian, *Der Chemische Krieg* (Berlin: Mittler, 1939)
Lefebure, V., *The Riddle of the Rhine* (New York: Chemical Foundation, 1923)
Meyer, J., *Der Gaskampf und die Chemischen Kampstoffe* (Leipzig: Hirzel, 1926)

IAN HOGG was born in 1926 in Durham City, enlisted in the Regular Army during the war, and is now a Master Gunner in the Royal Artillery. After serving in Europe and the Far East, including duty with a Field Regiment during the Korean War, he became a member of the Instructional Staff of the School of Artillery, Larkhill. He is at present employed in the Ammunition Branch of the Royal Military College of Science as an Assistant Instructor. He has made a study of the history and development of modern artillery equipment for several years, with particular emphasis on ammunition.

Top left: The German Model 1917 gas mask, made of heavily oiled leather. It was not proof against high concentrations of gas, however, and was stuffy, as the wearer had to breath both in and out through the drum containing the chemicals. *Above right:* The Italian Modello Piccolo No. 2 mask. *Above:* The German Model 1916 mask, made of rubberised fabric. It was again stuffy, and the eye pieces were prone to misting up

GAS

Gas was introduced to the arsenal of the First World War in 1915, and quickly adopted by all the other belligerents. There were two methods of launching a gas attack, from cylinders or by projectiles. The cylinder attack entailed bringing a large number of cylinders of compressed gas up to the line, laying pipes from these as far forward into No-Man's Land as possible and releasing the gas in a dense cloud when the wind was from the right quarter to blow the cloud of gas down onto the enemy's front line. The need for the right wind was a distinct disadvantage for the Germans on the Western Front,

Left: The British 1917 pattern Small Box Respirator. This had splinterless eye pieces and a breath-outlet valve, and was therefore more comfortable to wear than its German counterpart. It was the best mask of the war, proof against all gases except, of course, mustard gas. *Centre:* The Russian box respirator, with the box attached to the nose piece. *Right:* The British 1916 Respirator, with an extra filter on the box

Above: A bellows-operated resuscitator. There was always the chance that if uncontaminated air could be given quickly to a man who had been only slightly gassed, he might make a far better recovery

Top row left: The British 1915 Veil Respirator, an impregnated mouth pad. *Centre:* The British 1916/17 Phenate-Hexamine-Goggle helmet. *Right:* The British tank-crew respirator and goggles (left) and anti-lachrymator gas

THE ODOUR OF DEATH

where the prevailing wind was a westerly one. The other disadvantages were the labour involved in installing the equipment and the vulnerability of the cylinders to shell-fire. The main gases used were phosgene and chlorine. The other method of gas attack was by means of projectiles fired from guns or trench mortars. The advantages of this system were independence of the wind, simplicity and the ability to attack rear areas. The disadvantages were the need for heavy bombardments, as each shell carried so little gas, and the need for windless conditions to keep the gas from dispersing

goggles (three on right). *Bottom row left:* The Maw civilian mask of 1917. *Centre left:* The British 1915 Hypo Helmet. *Centre right:* The British 1916 Phenate-Hexamine helmet. *Right:* An unrubberised German fabric helmet

British gas casualties in France, 1915–1918
from British official sources

	Casualties	Deaths
APRIL AND MAY 1915 Cloud attacks with chlorine	7 000 *	350 *
MAY 1915–JULY 1916 Lachrymator gas shell	?	—
DECEMBER 1915–AUGUST 1916 Cloud attacks	4 207	1 013
JULY 1916–JULY 1917 'Lethal' gas shell	8 806	532
JULY 1917–NOVEMBER 1918 (Mustard gas period) Gas shell	160 526	4 086
DECEMBER 1917–MAY 1918 PROJECTOR ATTACKS	444	81
TOTAL	180 983	6 062

German cloud gas attack April 30 1916

FRONT LINES
BRITISH
GERMAN
GAS STRONGLY FELT, HELMETS WORN
GAS SLIGHTLY FELT
PLACES WHERE CATTLE WERE KILLED
0   400 YARDS

CASUALTIES

DEATHS

* Approx figures for casualties admitted to medical units only; many died on the field or were taken prisoner.

Gas casualties in the First World War

	Non-fatal injuries	Deaths	Total
BRITISH EMPIRE	180 597	8 109	188 706
FRANCE	182 000	8 000	190 000
UNITED STATES	71 345	1 462	72 807
ITALY	55 373	4 627	60 000
RUSSIA	419 340	56 000	475 340
GERMANY	191 000	9 000	200 000
AUSTRIA-HUNGARY	97 000	3 000	100 000
OTHERS	9 000	1 000	10 000
TOTAL	1 205 655	91 198	1 296 853

Note: These figures, apart from the American ones, are only approximate. In many cases they differ from the official published figures, which, since they do not include men who died on the battlefield, tend to be far too low.

Production of poison gases during the First World War (in tons)

	Lachrymators	Acute Lung Irritants	Vesicants	Sternutators	Totals
BRITAIN	1 800	23 335	500	100	25 735
FRANCE	800	34 000	2 140	15	36 955
UNITED STATES	5	5 500	170	—	6 215
ITALY	100	4 000	—	—	4 100
RUSSIA	150	3 500	—	—	3 650
GERMANY	2 900	48 000	10 000	7 200	68 100
AUSTRIA-HUNGARY	245	5 000	—	—	5 245
TOTALS	6 000	123 335	13 350	7 315	150 000

Poison Gases used during the First World War

	date of introduction	approx concentration to incapacitate a man in a few secs. (in parts per 10m)	approx concentration which, if breathed for more than 1 or 2 mins, would cause death	used by: British, French, Germans, Austrians
ACUTE LUNG IRRITANTS				
Chlorine	1915	1 000	1 000	British French Germans Austrians
Phosgene	1915	100	200	British French Germans Austrians
Chlormethyl-chloroformate	1915	100	1 000	British French Germans
Trichlormethyl-chloroformate	1916	50	200	British French Germans
Chloropicrin	1916	50	200 ▲	British French Germans Austrians
Stannic chloride	1916	—	1 000	British French
Phenyl-carbylamine-chloride	1917	50	1 000	Germans
Cyanogen bromide	1918	—	300	Austrians
Dichlor-methyl-ether	1918	1 000	1 000	Germans
LACHRYMATORS (tear producers)				
Benzyl bromide	1915	5	—	Germans
Xylyl bromide	1915	5	—	Germans
Ethyl-iodoacetate	1916	5 to 2	200	British
Bromacetone	1916	5	1 000	British French Germans Austrians
Monobrom-methyl-ethyl-ketone	1916	2	2 000	French Germans
Dibrom-methyl-ethyl-ketone	1916	2	2 000	Germans
Acrolein	1916	—	—	French
Methyl-chlorsulphonate	1915	—	—	French Germans
PARALYSANTS				
Hydrocyanic acid	1916	5 000 ●	5 000	British French
Sulphuretted hydrogen	1916	10 000 ●	1 000 ■	British French
STERNUTATORS (sensory irritants of eyes, nose and chest)				
Diphenyl-chlorarsine	1917	1	200	Germans
Diphenyl-cyanarsine	1918	1	200	Germans
Ethyl-dichlor-arsine	1918	20	500	Germans
Ethyl-dibrom-arsine	1918	—	—	Germans
N.ethyl carbazol	1918	—	—	Germans
VESICANTS (blister producers)				
Dichlor-ethyl-sulphide (Mustard gas)	1917		10 ○	British French Germans

▲ Cumulative   ● Immediately fatal   ■ Affects eyes and lungs   ○ With 60-minute exposure

Chris Barker.

Above: Gas casualties, production and types in the First World War. It is worth noting that the most effective type was not one of the so-called lethal types, but one of the incapacitators, mustard gas

AUSTRIA ON THE DEFENSIVE

Along the Isonzo valley, the Austrians held excellent natural defensive fortresses. Thrown time and time again against these, the Italian infantry was cut down in its tens of thousands — as much for political as strategic reasons.
Below: An Austrian crew prepares to fire a 15-cm howitzer

Far left: An Austrian tunnelling machine in action on the Galician Front.
Right: A Krupp-made Russian 15-cm howitzer, Model 1880. Little is known about this gun except that it had a crew of 5 and a rate of fire of 3 rounds-per-minute.
Centre left: An Austrian 22.5-cm mortar in travelling position. Little is known about this gun also except that it had a crew of 4 and a rate of fire of 2 rounds-per-minute.

Centre right: A Russian 25-cm coastal gun. Little is known about this gun too except that it had a crew of 22 and a rate of fire of 1 round every five minutes.
Bottom left: An Austrian 10-cm light field howitzer, Model 1899. *Weight:* 2,250 lb. *Range:* 6,015 yards. *Rate of fire:* 5 rounds-per-minute. *Crew:* 6.
Bottom right: A German 25-cm heavy minenwerfer. *Weight:* 1,362 lb. *Range:* 992 yards

John Batchelor

Top: Loading an Austrian 12-cm trench mortar.

Above: The breech swung back into place: the mortar ready for firing. In the trenches in Italy as in those on the Western Front, trench mortars came to play an increasingly important rôle in defence as they were handy weapons and could be used right up in the front line.

△ Austrian 15-cm heavy field howitzer M 99.
Range: 6,780 yards. *Weight in action:* Two
tons 8.5 cwt. *Weight limbered:* Two tons 14.6
cwt. *Weight of shell:* 156 lbs. *Muzzle velocity:*
960 feet-per-second. *Elevation:* −2 degrees/
+45 degrees. *Crew:* Eight. *Rate of fire:* Two
rounds-per-minute
◁ Austrian 15-cm heavy field howitzer M 14.
Range: 8,858 yards. *Weight in action:* Two
tons nine cwt. *Weight of shell:* 28 lbs.
Muzzle velocity: 1,120 feet-per-second.
Elevation: −5 degrees/+70 degrees. *Crew:*
Eight. Motor transport was frequently employed
▽ Austrian 10.4-cm field gun. *Range:* 13,670
yards. *Weight in action:* Two tons five cwt.
Muzzle velocity: 2,230 feet-per-second.
Elevation: −10 degrees/+30 degrees. The gun
was made of nickel steel, and the shrapnel
shell had 70 bullets

▽ The *feld grau* uniform of the Austrian
infantry, introduced in late 1915. Shown is the
Austrian-style steel helmet with a ventilation
hole in the top, although usually a cap rather
than a steel helmet was worn. He is carrying a
tornister (calf-hide full pack), a bread bag on
his hip, and the M 1895 Mannlicher 8-mm rifle

Below left: An enormous flash as an Austrian 30.5-cm howitzer is fired. *Right top:* Culled from every available source, Austrian reserves rush to the front near Doberdo. *Right centre:* A few of the droves of Italian infantry cut down in the almost hopeless battles along the Isonzo. *Right bottom:* An Italian 75-mm mountain gun in the Alps

Kriegsarchiv/Vienna

Imperial War Museum

Museo del Risorgimento/Turin

ROMMEL IN THE ARGONNE

Bibliothek für Zeitgeschichte

In the summer of 1915, a figure later to play a rôle of the greatest importance in the Second World War was a captain, commanding an infantry company in the Argonne in France. This was the future *Feldmarschall* Erwin Rommel, who described his varied career in the First World War in a book entitled *Infantry Attacks*. *Left:* The young Erwin Rommel

Although General Joffre's summer offensives were usually concentrated on selected sectors of the Western Front in the hope that their impact would achieve far-reaching strategic results, this in no way inhibited his army commanders projecting strong attacks elsewhere to absorb German resources. But to be successful these subsidiary attacks had to be directed at some place where a breakthrough—no matter how unlikely—would threaten some vital German artery. The southern Argonne was one such place, for this heavily forested and hilly terrain lay on the flank of the crucial fortress zone of Verdun and of the bitterly contested St Mihiel salient, and was held on many important heights by the Germans, and here the French persisted in trying to repel the Germans, while developing their own counter threat towards Metz and along the Moselle into Germany.

Here, where the Germans could apply their defensive strategy in a most economical manner, they could also momentarily afford to concentrate their relatively meagre local artillery reserves for a counteroffensive, and it was towards the end of June that they provoked a struggle which was to bring only marginal changes in possession, at a totally unreasonable loss of life on both sides. Yet from amid the squalor of this fighting there came an enlightening account by a young professional German officer who was to achieve great fame in later years—an account which accurately described the battle techniques as well as catching the horrific atmosphere. The officer's name was Erwin Rommel (then a company commander in the 124th *Infantry Regiment), who, having recovered from a wound received in 1914, had rejoined his unit in January 1915. Thereafter he had partaken in fierce fighting in the Argonne. In May his unit moved into a fresh sector.*

At Bagatelle there were few indications that the Argonne was a dense forest, for the French artillery fire had cleared the trees thoroughly, and for miles all that remained visible were stumps.

As was our custom, we deepened the trench at once and built dugouts for ourselves. Sudden and violent bursts of French artillery and mortar fire, accompanied by hand grenade fights all along the line, kept us from having dull moments. In the warm weather the frightful stench of corpses wafted into the position. Many French dead still lay in front of and between our positions, but we could not bury them because of the French fire.

The nights were really exciting. Hand grenade battles went on for hours along a broad front and became so confused that we never knew whether or not the enemy had broken through at some place or had worked his way behind our front line. Added to this, various French batteries chimed in from the flanks. This was repeated several times nightly, and we soon found it a strain on our nerves.

Below: The devastating and bloody attacks on the French Central I and Central II positions. The close quarter fighting, combined with the use of large catapulted bombs, entailed heavy casualties and very great destruction. *Above right:* Some of Rommel's crack troops. Rommel had nothing but praise for the outstanding bravery and initiative of his men at this time

PDA: Robertson/Rees

The heat was unbearable during those days. One day Ensign Möricke, an especially fine soldier, visited me. I was down in my dugout, and we had to talk to each other through the shaft because there was not room for two in my warren. I told Möricke I was convinced that we were not safe from the damned flies even when we were 12-feet underground. Möricke said it was no wonder since the edge of the trench was simply black with them. He got a pick and started to dig there, and at the first swing the half-decayed, blackened arm of a Frenchman came to light. We threw chloride of lime on it and left the dead man.

We managed to weather the ten days, and on our return to our regimental sector we were shoved back into the front line. We found that every effort had been made to render trench warfare more unpleasant, for the French had added mining to an increased volume of artillery and trench mortar fire. The opposing outposts were only a few yards apart in half-covered sap trenches heavily reinforced with wire, and the night was full of lively hand grenade battles which from time to time brought the entire garrison to its feet. Each side tried to destroy the other's advance tunnels and positions and hardly a day passed without an explosion.

Swept by machine guns

Our attempts to capture the nearby French sentry posts usually ended in considerable losses. These posts and the sections of trench leading to them were completely enclosed with barbed wire. At the slightest noise, the French in the blockhouses would sweep the obstacles with machine gun fire. These conditions soon became exasperating and we hoped to remedy them by storming 'Central'.

Following a three and a half hour artillery and trench mortar preparation, we were to seize the French strongpoints of Labordaire, Central, Cimetière and Bagatelle. Close behind the front line in shell-proof emplacements, medium and heavy mortars had been sited. Day and night, reserve companies brought up supplies, dismantled mortars and ammunition through the narrow communication trenches. The French harassing fire had increased in violence, and many a carrying party had been hit. Toward the end of June and after a few days in the rest camp, the *9th Company* headed back into the line. We were amazed to see a large quantity of medium and heavy artillery emplaced and camouflaged in the vicinity of Binarville. It was pleasant to note that adequate ammunition seemed to be available. This time we moved up into position in the best of spirits.

The regiment prepared detailed plans for the five assault companies. During the preparation, my platoon remained in reserve about two-thirds of a mile north of Central. Shortly before the jump-off, we were to move up behind the line of departure, follow the assault echelon closely, and keep it supplied with grenades, ammunition, and entrenching equipment.

At 0515 hours on June 30, the artillery opened up with everything it had including 8.3- and 12-inch mortars. The effect of the shells was unbelievable. Earthen geysers shot into the air, craters suddenly appeared before us. The strong French earthworks were smashed apart as if hit by gigantic trip hammers. Men, timbers, roots, obstacles and sandbags flew into the air. We wondered how the French felt, for we had never seen such heavy fire before.

One hour before the assault, the medium and heavy mortars opened up on the blockhouses, wire entanglements and breastworks. The French massed their artillery fire to break up the assault, but their efforts were futile. Our forward line was thinly held and was too close to the main hostile position. The French guns ploughed up the dirt farther to the rear.

I kept looking at my watch. We had 15 minutes to go. A blue-grey pall of smoke from the bombardment obscured vision as both sides increased their volume of fire.

The communication trench assigned us was exposed to strong hostile fire, and I decided to deviate from my orders in displacing to the side for about 100 yards. We ran for our lives across the open stretch of ground and found shelter down in the hollow; then, through the communication trench, we rushed into the front line with French standing barrages bursting all around. The storm troops were lying side by side, and across from us the last gun and mortar shells were bursting.

0845 hours, and our assault moved forward over a wide front. French machine guns poured out their fire; the men jumped around craters, over obstacles and into the enemy position. The assault echelon of our company was hit by machine gun fire from the right and a few fell, but the bulk rushed on, disappearing in craters and behind embankments. My platoon followed. Each man had his load, either several spades or else sacks filled with grenades or ammunition. The French machine gun to the right was still hammering away. We passed through its field of fire and climbed over the walls on which the *9th Company* stood on January 29. The position was a mass of rubble. Dead and wounded Frenchmen lay scattered through the tangle of revetments, timbers and uprooted trees.

To the right and in front of us hand grenade fights were in progress and from rearward positions French machine guns swept the battlefield in all directions and forced us to take cover. The sun was hot. We moved off to the left and then, hard on the heels of our company's assault echelon, pressed on to a communication trench leading to the second position.

Our artillery had shifted its fire to the second French line (Central II), located 160 yards to the south, which was to be captured on July 1 only after renewed artillery and mortar bombardment. The assault echelons of the regiment not engaged in mopping up Central I were pushing on toward Central II.

About 30 yards ahead of us a violent hand grenade fight raged, and beyond that we could see the outlines of Central II some 90 yards distant. French machine gun fire made it impossible to move outside the communication trench, and our own assault group up forward seemed to be stalled. Its young leader, Ensign Möricke, was lying in the trench severely wounded with a bullet in his pelvis! I wanted to carry him back, but he said that we should not worry about him. Stretcher bearers took charge. One last hand-clasp and I assumed the command up front. The ensign died the next day in the hospital.

The French flee

We engaged the garrison of Central II. Our own artillery had ceased firing. A few salvoes of hand grenades followed by a charge, and we were in Central II. Part of the garrison ran down the trench, others fled across the open fields, and the rest surrendered. While part of the unit worked to widen the trench, the bulk of the assault force kept pressing south. We moved through a ten-foot-deep communication trench and had the luck to surprise and capture a French battalion commander with his entire staff. About 100 yards down the line the trench opened on a large clearing. In front of us the terrain dropped sharply down to the valley at Vienne-le-Château, which was obscured from view by the woods. We lost contact on both flanks and to the right. On the edge of the forest some 200 yards away we saw a considerable number of the French. We opened fire and after a sharp fire fight they withdrew into the woods. While this was going on I established contact on my left with elements of the *1st Battalion* who had advanced this far; and I also reorganised my command, which by this time included elements of all units of the *3rd Battalion*, and deployed it in a defensive position some 350 yards south of Central II. Because of our exposed right flank and since we still heard the sounds of bitter fighting behind us, I felt it inadvisable to continue the advances to the south.

A reconnaissance detachment reported that the unit on our right had been unable to clear Central I. This meant we must prepare blocking positions to protect our newly-won positions against attacks from the west. To bolster the defence I put my best veterans in line and was glad of it, for during the next few hours the French launched a series of violent counterattacks to regain their lost positions. I kept the battalion commander informed of developments.

On the left some companies of the *1st Battalion* had advanced down the valley as far as Houyette gorge. Combat outposts reported strong French forces in the woods on the slope 330 yards ahead. I discussed the situation with Captain Ullerich, the commander of the *1st Battalion,* and he decided to have the *1st Battalion* dig in on the left of the *9th Company.*

We wasted no time in getting to work. I kept one platoon in reserve and used it to bring up ammunition and hand grenades and for work on the flank position in Central II. French reconnaissance detachments were probing our front, but we drove them off without trouble.

Digging was easy, and in a short time our trench was more than three feet deep. Since the start of the attack the French artillery had been rather quiet, but now it opened up on Central II with every weapon at its disposal. The French appar-

ently believed we occupied the place in force, for their ammunition expenditure was very heavy. The net result was to smash up their old position and cut our communications to the rear. Supplies ran a gauntlet of fire, and our lone telephone wire was soon knocked out. We did succeed in emplacing one heavy machine gun platoon in the company sector.

By evening our trench was five feet deep, and the French artillery was still falling behind us. Suddenly bugle calls rang out in the woods; and the French, in their usual massed formation, rushed us from the woods an eighth of a mile away. However, our fire soon drove them to earth. There was a slight fold in the ground, and as a result we picked up targets from our trench only when they came to within 90 yards of our position. Perhaps a position farther back near Central II would have been better. We certainly would have had a good field of fire; but, on the other hand, the French artillery would have punished us severely. The French attacked with vigour, and hand grenade fights continued all over the place even after it became quite dark. Our supply of grenades was limited and we did most of our fighting with rifles and the heavy machine gun. The night was black and the smoke from

Strong trenches and heavy guns — defence and aggression in the wooded Argonne

Left: Trench construction in the summer of 1915. These troops do not seem to be unduly concerned with their task, but on their efforts and their thoroughness at this time would depend their lives if and when the French attacked, particularly if heavy artillery or the much-feared flying bombs were used.
Right: It was essential for the troops to get all the rest they could, even when they were at the front, and so the trenches criss-crossing Europe saw the proliferation of all sorts of locally devised methods of making the men more comfortable, such as this hut in the German line. The superscription over the door reads 'Into the Lions' Den'. *Below left:* A French 155-mm gun. Against guns of this calibre, good trenches stood some sort of chance, but Rommel's men had to contend with these and much heavier artillery, as well as flying bombs, which fell in a more vertical trajectory.
Below: A German 21-cm howitzer. These heavy howitzers, together with even heavier ones, wrought great destruction on the French trenches before Rommel's attack went in. Their shells produced 'great earthen geysers'

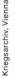

Südd Verlag

Kriegsarchiv, Vienna

Imperial War Museum

bursting grenades reduced the effectiveness of our rocket flares. Grenades burst all around us, for the French were within 50 yards of our position. The fight waxed and waned all night, and we beat off all attacks. At daybreak we made out a sandbag wall some 50 yards away and all sounds indicated that the French were busily engaged in digging in behind their improvised shelter. The French infantry kept us on the go during the night and their artillery then took over the morning shift. Fortunately the bulk of artillery fire landed in Central I and II with only a small fraction striking close to our position, and a hit in the front line was a great rarity. So we felt comparatively secure and did not envy the carrying parties who had to move rations and other supplies up through the shell-plastered ammunition trenches.

We spent the succeeding days in improving the position. The trench was soon six feet deep; we constructed small wood-lined dugouts, installed armoured shields, and sandbagged firing points. The front line losses from artillery fire were few, but we lost men daily in the shell-torn communication trenches leading to the rear.

The strong artillery concentrated for the June 30 offensive moved to another front, and our weak organic artillery lacked

sufficient ammunition to give us worthwhile support. However, an artillery observer was always up front, and we in the infantry appreciated this very much.

During the early days of July the French began to wreck our trenches daily with flying mines delivered from positions that permitted a certain degree of enfilade fire. These flying-mine projectors are of simple construction and provided but little lateral dispersion; consequently they obtained a high percentage of direct hits, and it was not always possible to evacuate the dangerous localities in time to avoid losses. Our casualties from these mines were considerable, seven men being killed by the blast effect of the 220-pound bomb alone.

During July I began a five weeks' assignment as substitute of the commander of the *10th Company* in a sector where relief was furnished by the *4th* and *5th Companies*. We company commanders worked on a unified plan for construction of shell-proof

Positions entirely flattened by the guns

The French pounded the German trenches in the Argonne with 220-pound flying mines

multi-entrance dugouts 26 feet under ground. This work went on day and night with several parties working on one dugout from different directions. The officers pitched in, and we found that sharing the work helped morale.

Frequently an entire position was flattened by artillery inside an hour. When this happened we saw our lightly timbered dugouts collapse like cardboard boxes. Fortunately the French bombardment followed a rigid plan. Usually they began on the left and traversed right. To remain under heavy fire proved too expensive; so whenever it started I evacuated the trench and waited until they moved their fire laterally or lifted it to our rear area. If French infantry had followed their artillery and attacked us, then we would have thrown them out with a counterattack. This did not bother us because, man to man, we felt ourselves to be superior.

(The battles, which took place in the Argonne between June 20 and July 14, cost the French over 32,000 casualties: they also cost General Sarraill, the Commander of Third Army, his job. And nothing of value had been achieved.)

[Reprinted from *Infantry Attack* by Erwin Rommel.]

Mortars firing —
a painting by the German war artist Frost

▽ Krupp 120-mm howitzer, in use with the Russians. *Weight:* 26 cwt. *Crew:* 5—6. *Rate of fire:* 4—5 rounds-per-minute. *Range:* 7,400 yards. *Weight of shell:* 46 pounds.

The German-made **42-cm howitzer**, popularly known as **Big Bertha**, or more accurately Fat Bertha, was the largest gun yet to be seen in war. *Weight:* 75 tons. *Crew:* a two gun battery had a complement of 280 men. *Rate of fire:* ten rounds-per-hour. *Range:* 15,530 yards. *Weight of projectile:* 2,052 lbs

Howitzers and mortars, vital for dropping shells into entrenched positions

◁ **The British 1886 6-inch howitzer**
This howitzer weighed about 44 cwt and could fire a high explosive shell weighing between 100 and 122 pounds

△ **The German 21-cm *Mörser* (mortar)**
Little is known about this gun other than its bore, equivalent to 8.3-inches, and its range, which varied from 10,280 yards with the 1914 short shell to 11,155 yards with the 1896 long shell

Below: The Russian light field howitzer, model 1909. This 12·2-cm gun was of French design and probably required a crew of six men. *Barrel:* 13 calibres long. *Shell:* 23 kilograms. *Range:* 7,500 metres. *Elevation:* −3° to + 45°. *Traverse:* 4°. *Rate of fire:* 6 RPM

Bundesarchiv

Imperial War Museum

Far left: 21-cm howitzers *(top)* firing from the German trenches. The black smoke produced by the exploding shell earned them the nickname 'Jack Johnsons' after the prewar negro prizefighter. German 25-cm trench mortars *(bottom)* maintained a crippling bombardment of British front lines. *Left:* A German 15-cm L/40 navy gun, originally designed as a secondary armament for pre-dreadnought battleships. *Total weight:* 25,400 lb. *Weight of barrel:* 10,300 lb. *Length of barrel:* 19¾ ft. *Elevation:* −8° to +32°. *Traverse:* 27° left and right. There were two types of shells, with maximum ranges of 14,000 yds and 19,000 yds

Artillery — ancient and modern

Compared with the venerable Cohorn mortar *(bottom left)* the new model Light Minenwerfer *(top left and bottom right)* was a most efficient weapon. Here it is shown *(top left)* on its flat trajectory carriage for mobile use, and *(bottom right)* on trench mounts. *Maximum range:* 1,422 yards (on trench mounts), 955 yards (on carriage). *Weight in action:* 312 lbs (on trench mounts), 550 lbs (on carriage). The Cohorn was made of brass, with a wooden base. The fact that this ancient weapon, which dates back to at least the Battle of Culloden 1746, was still in use in 1914 bears witness to the paucity of British artillery rather than to the Cohorn's technical performance

John Batchelor

Right: Schneider 155-mm French howitzer, 1917 model. There were two types of shell: one an 1890 model, with a maximum range of 10,500 yards; the other a 1915 model, with a maximum range of 12,000 yards. *Weight of shell:* 95 lbs, both types. *Rate of fire:* Two rounds per minute, although this could not exceed the rate of 30 rounds per hour. *Total weight:* 3 tons, 7 cwt in action; 3 tons on the road. *Traverse:* 3° left to 3° right. When horse-drawn the gun could be moved at a speed of 3 mph; when motor-carried, at 7½ mph. It took approximately quarter of an hour to prepare the gun for action or to withdraw it.

▷ A Russian 15-cm howitzer, the 1884 model. Russian industry could not meet the army's needs and the Russians bought artillery from many other countries

Right: The **Japanese 150-mm Howitzer** used to bombard the German trenches at Tsingtao. *Weight:* 6,160 lbs. *Length:* 20 feet 9 inches. *Elevation:* 65 degrees. *Crew:* 6 or 7. *Rate of fire:* Four rounds-per-minute (maximum). *Range:* 10,464 yards. *Muzzle velocity:* 1,344 feet-per-second. *Projectile weight:* 80 lbs.

▽ The Rimailho 155-mm howitzer, the French equivalent of the German 5.9-inch German howitzer, and the only modern piece of heavy artillery in the French army at the outbreak of the war. It saw much use in the artillery duel at Verdun

The Austrian-made **Skoda 30.5-cm howitzer** played a vital rôle in crushing the Liège forts. *Weight:* 28 tons. *Crew:* variable, but usually 12. *Rate of fire:* ten rounds-per-hour. *Range:* 13,124 yards. *Projectile weight:* 846 lbs

AMMUNITION SCANDAL

The blindness of those in command to the real demands of the war machine led, during the first year of the war, to a critical shortage of ammunition. As the factories in Britain struggled to meet the new demands, the press laid the blame for the crisis at Kitchener's door
Major Henry Harris

It is generally considered beyond question that at the outbreak of war in 1914 none of the combatant nations foresaw either the lengthy duration of the war or the form it would take.

Field-Marshal Lord Kitchener, the lonely, formidable, Irish-born Englishman, who was brought into the Liberal government to fill the vacant post of Secretary of State for War (the first serving soldier to hold the job since Monk), had been one of the few to predict that the war would be a prolonged one. But not even he had foreseen that the lines would become static and that the artillery, the standard counter, would be used so extensively and would go on firing continuously day and night, using up enormous quantities of ammunition.

In anticipation of besieging Belgian and French fortresses, Germany was at first better prepared for heavy ammunition expenditure than her foes, but by the spring of 1915 she too was deficient in the types of guns and ammunition which experience was showing to be necessary.

And the pattern of warfare which had emerged now called for an unprecedented number of guns and enormous reserves of ammunition, not only of existing calibres and types, but also of new weapons more suited to trench conditions. Of these, high explosive shells for all calibres of guns were to be the most critical. By early October 1914 there was general concern among the Staff and the Ordnance in the BEF about the ammunition shortage. So meagre was the supply that every round had to be rationed. At the First Battle of Ypres, the allocation for 18-pound shell had to be reduced first from 20 to ten rounds per gun per day and towards the end of that month's fighting to two rounds per gun per day; the 4.5-inch howitzers were on two rounds and the 6-inch howitzers on six rounds per gun per day. Reports of daily stocks at railheads were telephoned to a senior Ordnance Officer at GHQ who prepared a tabulated statement for the QMG, BEF. From this, allocations on a priority basis were made. At times this meant not more than six rounds per gun per day, or less for some if the situation was worse than usual in another sector. To provide some flexibility, the Ordnance kept certain types of ammunition on special trains, which could be diverted from one army railhead to another in accordance with operational needs. During the 1915 battles nothing was left in depots and ammunition was being brought up to the guns straight from the ships. At Ypres in 1915 the British Second Army demands for howitzer ammunition had to be refused.

Shared responsibility
In 1914 the British War Office's Army Council included two military and one civilian member concerned with supply — the Quartermaster-General (QMG), the Master-General of the Ordnance (MGO) and the Finance Member.

The QMG and the MGO shared the chief responsibility, the latter being concerned with artillery supplies and technical munitions. The MGO's principal officer for material was the Director of Artillery whose branches dealt with all types of field and fixed guns, their pattern, design, manufacture, inspection and employment. The total staff of this Directorate was only 40. The MGO also had various technical bodies, such as the Ordnance Board and

Above: Kitchener visits France for talks during the ammunition crisis. The Press, in their campaign against him, underestimated his popularity and found themselves boycotted by major institutions. Kitchener survived the crisis and public faith in him remained unshaken. *Opposite:* Men and women at work in a shell filling factory. The system of tenders governing shell production was largely inefficient and led to inflated prices

the Small Arms Committee, as well as the production establishments of the Royal Ordnance Factories (ROFs) at Woolwich Arsenal, Waltham Abbey and Enfield Lock. The QMG had a principal officer, the Director of Equipment and Ordnance Stores (DEOS), whose duties included receiving, storing, issuing and repairing artillery equipment and ammunition.

Under the Finance Member was the Director of Army Contracts, in charge of the Contracts Branch born out of the British troubles in the Crimea. This was responsible for purchasing the total requirements of all departments of the army, but could order nothing without the concurrence of the military branch concerned. It had a staff of eight in August 1914. The size of the army being determined by Parliament and scales of equipment approved, the ordering followed a well-defined pattern through two main channels.

A large amount of artillery equipment and ammunition was obtained from the ROFs under direct MGO control. ROF contracts were regulated so as to keep them busy, but when necessary outside orders were placed to prevent civilian firms from closing through lack of work. Shells were ordered from 'the trade' so as to give the firms concerned experience of such work in the event of war. ROF work also acted as a check on contractors' prices.

To obtain such work, civilian firms had first to get on the List of Contractors. There were rigid rules on eligibility for this list — fair wages, no sub-letting, cutting out agents and middlemen, financial and quality control criteria and inspection of plant — all to be satisfied before a manufacturer could be put on the list. There were arrangements and facilities for firms

to inspect 'sealed patterns' and obtain specifications of equipment which was highly standardised.

Supplies were invited by tender. Tendering was a formal and leisurely business; the tenders came in by a fixed date in sealed envelopes and were dropped through a slit in a metal tender box, the key of which was held by a specially nominated officer. At an appointed hour this box was ceremonially opened and the tenders listed, signed and witnessed by those attending. Tenders were afterwards tabulated and considered, the basis being the most favourable price, though some note would be taken of the competence of individual firms. The procedure which laid down that 'The established principle of public purchase is competition and the acceptance of the lowest offer' was designed to ensure fairness between rivals and to avoid suspicions of favouritism or collusion. In normal times the system ensured reasonable prices for standardised articles.

But the supply requirement in August 1914 was far from normal. The supply departments realised this, but with no precedents to guide them, their steps to cope with the new situation were slow and hesitant, based on the existing machinery. Had the demands escalated immediately, the fundamental reorganisation on a national rather than a localised basis might have taken place earlier. But the gradual build-up obscured the fact that the current organisation for supply was only capable of limited expansion.

The defects were not immediately apparent, even to Kitchener who considered the Liberal government guilty of the collective sin of irresponsibility, and himself took on the burden of raising and equipping new armies of unprecedented size, and supervising the conduct of British military strategy throughout the world. Apart from lack of shells, shortages of all kinds were immediately apparent within a couple of weeks of the outbreak of war. Some requirements, such as clothing and footwear, harness and saddlery, could be met by large scale purchases of certain non-standard patterns.

When shortages became crucial and it was widely known that, contrary to his orders, many recruits were without boots and other necessities, Kitchener dismissed the Director of Army Contracts.

But guns and ammunition could not be obtained by speedy resort to trade patterns. No action by Kitchener — or anyone else — could redress for many months the prewar blindness and indifference of the British people and their leaders. But the demand for more heavy guns had to be met. In September 1914 a Siege Committee of officers from the War Office and GHQ, BEF recommended the provision of 140 heavy howitzers 'for use against fortresses on the Rhine', as well as anti-aircraft guns and weapons for use in trenches. Kitchener immediately authorised these but when the MGO (Lieutenant-General von Donop) demurred about the size and cost of the order which ran to £3,000,000 Kitchener had it checked with the French War Ministry. When they replied that they thought these were essential, he overruled von Donop and gave peremptory instructions for their purchase.

In the early days of the war, shells were put to tender to the approved firms, and the ROFs put on full capacity production.

These first orders, totalling 500,000 rounds (mainly shrapnel), were contracted for by separate components and assembled at Woolwich Arsenal. But unplaced demands began to accumulate as early as August 12. Kitchener invited US manufacturers to send representatives over to discuss production and the War Office placed some orders in Canada and India. Troubles and misunderstandings were to hold up deliveries of these overseas orders; there were variations in meanings between US and British technical terms, and the British were ignorant of US methods and vice versa. So keen were US firms to get orders that one company signed a contract a month before they knew what they were going to make! Another firm quoted for an entirely different article from that which they were expected to supply. Canadian production was to be particularly disappointing as a result of the difficulties in organising manufacture among a large number of inexperienced firms.

One of the first relaxations of the supply procedure was to permit sub-contracting—as this was recognised as giving training to firms inexperienced in munitions work—but the main contractors were held fully responsible. But lack of Inspecting Officers to visit the new firms led many to ask for and receive orders they were unable to fulfil. The most that could be done by the overworked inspection staff was to show samples and give advice to would-be contractors who came to Woolwich.

'To get them and hold them'

Unnoticed and unrealised by the government, a grave shortage of skilled labour developed. The initial and temporary breakdown of trade impelled many men to enlist rather than face the miseries of unemployment. The engineering trade alone lost 12% by October 1914 (this was to go up to 20% by July 1915). In the scramble for orders, firms began to poach each other's labour, inducing tradesmen who were already on war work with other employers to join them. Some firms, wishing to give their men on war work some recognition, suggested special badges. Churchill agreed to this and ordered one for Admiralty Service but it was initially vetoed by the Treasury. Full peacetime Treasury control (prior approval of all expenditure) was not completely relaxed for munitions until February 1915.

Employers made various other proposals; the Chief Superintendent of the Ordnance Factories suggested that suitable skilled men be given two to three year contracts of employment—'the only way to get them and hold them'. Messrs Vickers proposed bringing over Belgian workers and implementing large scale employment of women. It was also suggested that the French system of industrial mobilisation should be adopted, under which workmen were conscripted by the government into their jobs and moved about as munitions production required. This was fiercely resisted by the trade unions. Some of the drain off into the army was checked by telling Recruiting Officers not to enlist men from certain firms without their employers' consent. But despite these measures, by the end of the year the munitions programme was in deep trouble.

The tendering system created artificial scarcities and inflated prices. All the tendering firms went after the same raw materials at the same time, the net demands multiplying several times over in the market. Two hundred firms would put in for orders which involved the use of 2,000 tons of raw materials. Only 20 firms would get the orders but all 200 would have obtained options on 2,000 tons each. This caused chaos in the markets and forced options up to fictitious and unwarranted levels. Calling for tenders also led to the War Office revealing its total requirement to everyone in the trade and the relation of such demands to probable supply was quickly and accurately gauged by most. The War Office, being in a hurry, accepted high tenders in the hope that disappointed firms would reduce their prices next time.

The abandonment of many standard patterns and specifications for 'trade pattern' substitutes made inspection for quality control and other checks difficult, with innumerable queries arising. Most of this work was done physically after delivery, in the labyrinthine Peninsula-period accommodation of Woolwich Arsenal. Delays occurred often, with masses of items lying around in confusion until decisions could be made.

The most frequent excuse for failing to keep to delivery dates was shortage of machine tools. The UK output was insufficient and US orders were not delivered on time. One firm working on shells, Cammell Laird, in two months had only obtained 26 machines out of over 200 ordered, and had to put off their planned expansion. Gun contractors were also badly affected, and by the end of 1914, though their production had only just begun, they were finding it impossible to live up to their promises.

The greatest amount of delivery failures occurred among sub-contractors, who, despite their initial experiences, continued to give too optimistic a picture of their powers of production. They were harder hit by labour shortages than the big firms and were also hampered by delays in obtaining samples, drawings, specifications and of course in delivery of machine tools.

The War Office machinery for dealing with this situation was itself in poor shape. There was confusion in the offices as a result of over-crowding, the staffs' long hours (some worked 14 hours a day) and the ordinary civil servants' ignorance of commercial matters clashing with the contempt shown by the businessmen brought in to assist. Despite the addition of these 'expert buyers and advisers' in the Army Contracts Department, the old-fashioned purchasing procedure was little altered, some 'expert buyers' often being subjects of suspicion on grounds of gaining unfair advantage over their competitors.

In October the government set up a Cabinet Shells Committee. It was presided over by Kitchener and met six times up to December 1914. On December 21 there was a 'Shells Conference' which debated all the munitions troubles (in this month the government had considered it imperative to ship munitions to Russia to avert a military collapse there) and on December 23 the Cabinet agreed to co-ordinate the supply of labour in the following ways:
● substitute Belgian for British workers;
● divert labour from less urgent industries 'such as the railways'; and
● put pressure on firms not on munitions work to release their men.

To strengthen the War Office, an additional civilian member was appointed to the Army Council, and a general officer added to the MGO's Branch to visit and report on the flood of untried firms offering their services (as a result of an appeal by the Board of Trade) and whose production capacity was unknown.

From this point on, the responsibilities of the War Office were shared by other government agencies, and certain interests in and outside Parliament began to feel uneasy about the way munitions production was being directed. But the government still maintained that no drastic revision of policy was necessary except for machinery to deal with the delays in deliveries. The Board of Trade's efforts included attempts to obtain relaxation of trade union restrictive practices, and a drive against drinking by workers.

Unfair load

A large section of the engineering industry was dissatisfied with the War Office's methods of contracting, feeling that more direct contracting would help to reduce the loss of workers. Cammell Laird and Vickers were two firms to put this view when revising downwards their delivery dates. Demands for direct contracts by sub-contracting firms were stimulated by the steady loss of their work force. But it was not easy, as shown above, to give orders direct to untried firms and the policy of organising supply through firms already on the Contractors List had much in its favour. In 1914-15 these were the only firms with experience of such work; with little or no higher organisation to instruct and supervise, ordinary firms were quite incapable of going on to such work at short notice. To a great extent, the 'education' firms received as sub-contractors enabled them to organise themselves better in the summer of 1915. But apart from delays, deliveries in early 1915 were often defective. The ROFs were compelled to carry an undue share of the load at the expense of more specialised manufacture and every branch of the Arsenal was congested with work in hand and for inspection. Kitchener tried to conceal these troubles from his Cabinet colleagues, although he informed Asquith, who told him that *any* form of conscription (including industrial conscription, which Bonar Law was advocating) would wreck the government. Kitchener therefore addressed himself anew to enlisting private firms into making munitions.

But by March it was no longer possible to conceal that, as far as the immediate future was concerned, adequate supply was not assured. Kitchener abandoned his usual reticence in a speech in the House of Lords on March 15, 1915. He admitted that 'progress in equipping the new armies and forces in field is hampered by failure to obtain sufficient labour and by delays in production of plant, largely due to enormous demands', and went on to say: 'Labour has a right to say that their patriotic work should not be used to inflate the profits of directors and shareholders and we are arranging a system under which the important firms come under Government control. Men working long hours in the shops by day and night, week in and out, are doing their duty for King and Country the same as those on active service in the field.'

By now, Lloyd George and others had decided that a radical reorganisation was vital but Kitchener opposed this. He did, however, accept the Munitions of War Committee which was set up on April 12 under Lloyd George and he was represented on it by the MGO. But he refused to delegate any War Office responsibility for munitions, and also, on security grounds, to provide the committee with information about the numbers of men being put into the line by particular dates. Lloyd George claimed they were unable, as a result, to prepare accurate estimates of quantities required by specific dates.

Britain's other enemy

Lloyd George, though Chancellor of the Exchequer, was active on many other matters at this time in addition to munitions supply. He was giving advice on strategy (with Churchill he had strongly advocated an attack on Turkey), industrial unrest and the problems of drink. He was particularly keen to deal with 'the lure of the drink' which he felt was detrimental to good work and the cause of many serious production delays. He announced that: 'If we are to settle with Germany we must first of all settle with drink.' He induced the King to set an example by banning all alcoholic liquor from Royal establishments and sought a law to control or close public houses near where war work was being done. He claimed that it was 'proved quite clearly that excessive drinking in the works [sic] connected with (munitions) operations is seriously interfering with output'. During March the government negotiated an agreement with trade union leaders with recommendations to workers including eschewing of strikes, the use of negotiating machinery and temporary relaxation of demarcation and dilution rules. Most moderate trade unionists welcomed this and readily co-operated with local munitions committees in 'delivering the goods' and 'doing their bit'. But Lloyd George was not satisfied with these steps and felt he had a duty to play a more direct part in munitions supply. He considered it proper to invite the megalomaniac Lord Northcliffe to take up the munitions question in the press and so compel Kitchener and the government to act. Northcliffe, who considered Kitchener an impediment to victory over the Germans, naturally favoured a campaign against this overburdened titan, based on information obtained from Sir John French.

At this time things were not going very well for the British on the Western Front and Sir John French was induced to lend his name to the campaign. He appears to have done so willingly after his defeat at Neuve Chapelle, claiming that a shortage of ammunition robbed him of victory. But there was in fact no shortage during that four-day battle; ammunition was fired off at an unprecedented rate, described by Kitchener as 'irresponsible'. Shortages had hampered French on other occasions, mainly because of his refusal to accept the logistic situation and curtail offensive operations until supplies were adequate for his plans. Such appreciations were not well understood by that generation of Commanders and Staffs. However, on April 14, Kitchener told Asquith that 'French says that with the present supply of ammunition he will have as much as his troops will be able to use in the next for-

ward movement.' The 'next forward movement' was Festubert, a week before which French told Kitchener that 'the ammunition will be all right'. But on the first day of the battle, Kitchener had had to reserve 20,000 shells on paper for Gallipoli – an earmark which was cancelled the next day but it was enough to upset Sir John French and spark off the crisis.

In the preceding weeks, press comments on munitions had become more pointed. On April 7, *The Times* (a Northcliffe paper), writing about Kitchener's Armaments Output Committee, criticised the 'extraordinary failure of the Government to take in hand in business-like fashion the provision of full and adequate supply of munitions. The War Office has sought to do too much and been jealous of civilian aid. It should chiefly devote itself to the organisation of the armies and should state its supply requirements and leave to others the far more complex task of organising industry.' On April 10, *The Times* stated that *the primary reason why Sir John French is unduly short of munitions is not drink at all. It is that in our previous wars the War Office has been accustomed to rely for all such supplies on the MGO as a sort of Universal Provider. In this unprecedented war the Government ought to have insisted on instant organisation of the whole of our national resources, leaving the War Office to state its requirements and raise its armies.* But Lloyd George was saying that it was *obviously better to get your men under the direct supervision and control of those who for years have been undertaking this kind of work, obviously better than going to those without experience. The failure [of the Board of Trade to get men through Labour Exchanges] drove us to other courses – to introduce the Defence of the Realm Act to equip War Office and Admiralty with powers to take over engineering works.*

In mid-April the Prime Minister set up the Munitions of War or Treasury Committee under Lloyd George. He announced that the decision to do so had been taken a month earlier but the ground had had to be prepared for its activities. Kitchener was not a member of it and by its terms of reference it superseded his Armaments Output Committee. One of its schemes was for National Shell Factories and it was in effect the embryo of the Munitions Ministry.

The Battle of Aubers Ridge of May 9 resulted in heavy British casualties and on the 14th *The Times* printed a telegram from its correspondent in Northern France, stating that the 'attack had failed because of want of unlimited supply of HE (High Explosive)'. This correspondent was Colonel Repington, a retired officer, who had been staying at GHQ as French's personal guest. Kitchener had cautioned French about having Repington with him as it was a breach of orders, but French replied: 'Repington is an old friend and stayed for a day or two in an entirely private capacity – I really have no time to attend to these matters.' French gave Repington access to the papers on munitions and said all his efforts were crippled by lack of shells. He also sent copies of the papers to the opposition leaders, unknown to Asquith and Kitchener.

A week after *The Times* reported Repington's telegram, the *Daily Mail* (another Northcliffe paper) opened a direct attack intended to hound Kitchener from office

with the banner headline 'The Shells Scandal – Lord Kitchener's Tragic Blunder'. But Northcliffe had underestimated the nation's belief in its idol and the ceremonial burning of the paper containing the headline outside the Stock Exchange was but one reaction. Clubs and other institutions cancelled subscriptions to the *Daily Mail* and the general public indignantly boycotted it to such an extent that sales became seriously affected. After a few weeks, Northcliffe dropped the campaign, ruefully admitting his failure to a fellow press lord – Beaverbrook.

The press campaign, described by Churchill as 'odious and calculated' and by Haig as 'reptilian', had, if anything, increased public faith in Kitchener, and the King made him a Knight of the Garter. In the reconstruction of the government on a coalition basis, Asquith therefore had no choice but to retain him, but his position was weakened. In the new coalition National Government formed on May 26, Kitchener remained as secretary of State for War and Lloyd George went from the Exchequer to the new Ministry of Munitions. In the latter's words, this was *from first to last a businessman's organisation. Its most distinctive feature was the appointments I made to chief executive posts of successful businessmen to whom I gave authority and personal support that enabled them to break through much of the aloofness and routine which characterised the normal administration of Government Departments.* These businessmen had powers to take over any land or buildings they required, to engage such labour as they needed and to make conditions of work binding for the war period. Strikes and lockouts were forbidden, profits were limited, but workers were encouraged to earn as much as they could by piece work. But despite all these powers (and an increase of staff from 137 to 2,350 in five months) the time needed from creation of new capacity to delivery of bulk outputs differed little from that experienced by the War Office. The shortage of shells – the prime reason for handing over supply to a new department – was brought about by arrears of deliveries, not lack of orders, and these could be remedied by time alone.

Further Reading
Magnus, Sir Philip, *Kitchener, Portrait of an Imperialist* (Murray 1958)
Maurice, *Life of Haldane* (Faber & Faber)
Maurice, *British Strategy* (Constable)
Official History of the Great War Vols. I to III (Macmillan)

MAJOR HENRY HARRIS, a retired British Army Officer, is well known in historical circles for his lectures to the Military History Society of Ireland, of which he is a founder member. He has contributed articles on military matters to the *Irish Times*, the *Irish Army Defence Journal*, the *Army Quarterly* and *Brassey's Annual*. He has written two histories of the British Ordnance and has contributed 50 monthly articles on the 'Lost Generation' of 1914-1918 to the *British Ordnance Gazette*, chiefly on logistic and administrative aspects of the First World War. His *Model Soldiers*, based on his collection to be seen in Curragh, Kinsale, London and Camberley, has appeared in four languages. He is working on four more books, including a dictionary of Irish battles and one on the Anglo-Norman invasion of Ireland in 1169.

The fire power that French industry laboured to produce; what could not be made at home had to be imported

Below: The French 270-mm mortar, model 1885. *Length of barrel:* 6 calibres. *Elevation:* 30°. *Range:* 5 miles. *Projectile weight:* 204-384 lbs. *Crew:* 11 men. **1** The French 8-mm Hotchkiss machine gun, the principal machine gun of the French army during the First World War. Although it was rather heavy (gun 55 lbs, tripod 60 lbs) it was very reliable. **2** The French 8-mm Chauchat light machine gun, model 1915. This gun was reputedly unreliable and the standard of its manufacture was poor, nevertheless it was used extensively during the First World War. *Opposite page, top:* The French 220-mm mortar, model 1901 (modified). *Elevation:* 40°. *Rate of fire:* 1 round per minute. *Range:* 5 miles (approx). *Projectile weight:* 200 lbs. *Crew:* 4-5. **3** *Top:* The Lebel

8-mm rifle, model 1886. *Centre:* Dandeteau 6.5-mm rifle, model 1895 (not widely used). *Bottom:* Single shot rolling block Remington rifle, chambered for the 8-mm Lebel cartridge. Many of these obsolete rifles were purchased by France during the early part of the war.
4 *Left:* 8-mm Modèle d'Ordonnance 1892 revolver. *Centre:* The 11-mm revolver, model 1873. *Right:* A Spanish-made pistol poorly made but typical of many of the pistols purchased by the French during the war.
5 Flare pistols—the top one is a modification of the 1886 model R35 carbine. **6** *Left to right:* 'Hair brush grenade', grenade projector. *Top:* 'Vivien Bessier' grenade, assault grenade. *Bottom:* 37-mm cannon shell, bomb for pneumatic mortar

John Batchelor

3

4

5

6

Jack Pia

THE FIRST FLAME ATTACKS

The necessary basis of this first flame attack was proximity of the trench lines, but this basis vanished immediately the Germans advanced

After an ominous silence in the early hours of the morning the Germans released the terror of a new weapon: from the nozzles of six flame throwers they launched jet upon jet of liquid fire at the British trenches at Hooge. Although it was a very minor action, the new weapon achieved a spectacular success. *Michael Dewar*

The idea of the modern flamethrower was first conceived by one Richard Fiedler, a Berlin engineer, in 1900. Fire had, of course, been employed as a means of warfare for hundreds of years, but it was Richard Fiedler who converted this art into a science. In 1901, the German army tested two models, both submitted by Fiedler. The smaller *Flammenwerfer,* which was sufficiently light to be carried by one man, used gas pressure to send forth a stream of flaming oil for a distance of about 20 yards. The larger version, which was more cumbersome to transport and operate, had a range of some 40 yards, and fuel enough for 40 seconds continuous firing.

It is the smaller version with which we are chiefly concerned. It consisted of a steel cylinder resembling a milk churn in shape and filled with an inflammable liquid. The interior of the cylinder was divided into two parts, the lower containing a compressed gas to provide the pressure, and the upper, the inflammable liquid. To one side of the cylinder was fitted a rubber hose, six feet in length, with a long steel nozzle at the end. This whole apparatus was attached to the back of the operator by padded metal arms.

The principle upon which the *Flammenwerfer* worked was extremely simple: a valve released the gas in the lower chamber which pushed the liquid in the upper chamber into the rubber pipe. Two other valves held the fluid in check before it reached the device for igniting it at the nozzle. This device consisted of a small tube containing a spring, a detonator, some gun cotton, and a wick soaked in paraffin. When the gas pressed the fluid against the spring, the wick ignited, and a jet of flame projected from the nozzle for 20 yards or more. To add to the effect, volumes of black smoke were also produced. The flame had a total duration of approximately two minutes. However, should bursts of a shorter duration be required, a firing tube had to be fixed into the end of the steel nozzle for each separate ignition.

Numbers *23*, *24* and *25 Pioneer Battalions* were issued with this equipment in 1911. In 1912 the first *Flammenwerfer Regiment* was formed, namely the *3rd Guard Pioneer Regiment*, consisting of 12 flamethrower companies. This unit was commanded by *Major der Landwehr* Reddermann, and was subsequently to see action on both the Western and Eastern Fronts, and from the *Flammenwerfer Regiments* were formed the *Sturmbatallions*.

An ominous silence

The Official French History of the First World War records a flame attack by the Germans as early as October 1914: 'In Malancourt wood, between the Argonne and the Meuse, the enemy sprayed one of our trenches with burning liquid, so that it had to be abandoned. The occupants were badly burned.' However, it is not clear whether this was a *Flammenwerfer* attack, or simply a spray of pure petrol, later ignited by incendiary bombs, another technique used by the Germans. *Flammenwerfer Apparate,* however, were definitely used against the French on February 26, 1915, near Verdun. *Major* Reddermann of the *3rd Guard Pioneer Regiment* commanded this particular flame attack. In retrospect, it would seem that this attack was a dress rehearsal.

The larger version of the German flame thrower. The smaller version could be carried by one man

The tactical situation at Hooge in July 1915 was as follows. Two actions had taken place recently in the area, but on July 18 the Germans still held the line of brick heaps which had once been Hooge Château, while the stables remained in the hands of the British. From that point the British line ran westwards, crossing and recrossing the Ypres-Menin road through the ruins of Hooge village. On July 19 a mine was exploded by the British and the resulting

Stupefying in its effect, the 'flame' was like a thick smoke incandescent at the centre and stretching for approximately 20 yards

crater which was 120 feet wide and 20 feet deep, was occupied. Hereabouts, No-Man's Land was some 70 to 150 yards wide, but in the vicinity of the Hooge crater it was as little as 15 yards. In fact at one point what had become a German communication trench led from the German line right into the British line: it was barricaded at the British end, but by means of a periscopic arrangement the German sentry could be seen on the other side of the barricade precisely five yards away. On July 22 two further attempts, involving, in each case, two platoons, supported by bombers and an RE detachment, were made to seize parts of the German lines near Hooge. Both failed, breaking down under heavy German fire.

The Hooge sector was held by the 41st Brigade of the 14th Division. On the night of July 29 the 8th Battalion of the Rifle Brigade and the 7th Battalion of the King's Royal Rifle Corps replaced the 7th Battalion of the Rifle Brigade, and the 8th Battalion of the King's Royal Rifle Corps. The Rifle Brigade held the front at the Hooge crater, and the King's Royal Rifle Corps was situated on their right. They were total strangers to the front.

The Germans knew exactly what was taking place. They knew that the new troops were comparatively inexperienced, and that they found the crater and mining operations difficult. They almost certainly knew not only the identity of the division and the fact that it belonged to the New Army, but also the composition of the brigades, and even the names of the commanding officers, gaining this information by means of 'listening sets', which enabled them to intercept all British telephone messages. Consequently they could act with full prior knowledge of British movements, and previous British attacks had failed for precisely this reason.

An ominous silence pervaded the Hooge sector of the front on the night of July 29-30. A few bombs, thrown into the German trenches, provided no reply. Then, at 0315 hours on July 30, came the carefully planned German stroke. From the nozzles of six *Flammenwerfer Apparate* placed unobtrusively over the parapets of their trenches, they launched jet upon jet of liquid fire, simultaneously dropping a three-minute intense artillery bombardment on the British line. A sudden hissing sound was heard by 2nd Platoon, A Company of the Rifle Brigade who were situated on the left of the crater and a platoon of C Company on the right of the crater. Seconds later they were hit by a deluge of flame. Intense small arms fire swept the 300 yards of open ground between the British front and support lines in Sanctuary and Zouave woods. Then the Germans attacked in force.

The Rifle Brigade dispositions were too tightly packed, and also lacked depth. They had inherited an unsatisfactory position, which they had had neither the time nor opportunity to improve. The unoccupied Hooge crater dominated the centre of their position and was a positive invitation to disaster. The German attack broke through at the crater, and fanned outwards left and right, bombing along the trenches. 'Exactly what took place,' says Reginald Berkeley, 'will never be known, for there is no one alive to speak.' One can only surmise that the Germans occupied the trenches on either side of the Hooge crater with comparative ease as there can have been no real opposition remaining. Brigadier-General Oliver Nugent, commander of the 41st Brigade at Hooge, says of the attack: 'Those that were on the flank of the flame attack speak of the great heat generated by the flame, and their evidence tends to indicate that it was in the nature of thick smoke, incandescent in the centre and up to about 20 to 25 yards from the nozzles of the projectors rather than an inflammable gas.'

'A sudden hissing sound'
Perhaps the most accurate firsthand account is provided by Lieutenant G. V. Carey, who was in A Company at Hooge. He gives the following extremely interesting account: *There was a sudden hissing sound, and a bright crimson glare over the crater turned the whole scene red. As I looked I saw three or four distinct jets of flame, like a line of powerful fire hoses spraying fire instead of water, shoot across my fire trench. How long this lasted it is impossible to say, probably not more than a minute, but the effect was so stupefying that I was utterly unable for some moments to think correctly. About a dozen men of Number 2 platoon were all that I could find. Those who faced the flame attack were never seen again.*

Most of the 8th Battalion of the Rifle Brigade were overwhelmed and fell back. The Germans did not follow, but consolidated in the trenches either side of the Hooge crater. All but a small sector of the King's Royal Rifle Corps' trenches were also lost. The Germans brought up their *Flammenwerfer* again, but they were unable to use them since there were no targets sufficiently close. Moreover, rapid fire was directed upon the crews by the remainder of A Company, who had now recovered sufficiently from their initial surprise to offer organised resistance. By 0900 hours all that remained of the 8th Battalion, reinforced by one company of

the King's Royal Rifle Corps, held a line along the northern edge of Zouave wood.

The Germans had achieved complete surprise, and the employment of flame-throwers was not only totally effective within the limited area in which they were used, but also terrorized the troops in the peripheral area of the attack. Colonel Carey, the only witness to the attack surviving today, states that the numbers actually killed by the flame were comparatively small. Most were able to duck the flame, but the German infantry were so close on its heels that they were able to bayonet the British troops while they were still sheltering from the effects of the flame. He says, 'If the flame is being discharged from 15 yards range, there is every possibility of someone with a bayonet jumping on top of you before you have time to get up. No doubt this happened at Hooge.'

The events in the vicinity of Hooge crater, and the German success in that area, formed only part of what was a much larger attack. German troops were launched against the whole front held by the 41st Brigade. But the only sector in which they succeeded in taking any substantial area of ground was either side of the Hooge crater, and there they drove the British back to Zouave and Sanctuary woods. The trenches lost by the British were some hundreds of yards in length, for the Germans had worked their way into part of the line held by the King's Royal Rifle Corps on the right. They had succeeded in gaining a footing on a commanding ridge, and the division decided that the ground must be retaken without delay, otherwise the position in Zouave wood might become untenable.

It was determined that the assault should be made by the 8th Battalion of the Rifle Brigade attacking from Zouave wood, and by the 9th Battalion of the King's Royal Rifle Corps from Sanctuary wood, with the 7th and 9th Battalions of the Rifle Brigade in support. The objective was Hooge and the trenches in its neighbourhood.

Against the advice of the brigade commander, the attack took place that afternoon. Artillery preparation was limited to three-quarters of an hour's bombardment. At 1500 hours the four battalions duly went over the top and were swept out of existence by an enemy whose machine guns there had been no time to locate, and on whom the meagre artillery bombardment had made no impression. Many were caught on the British wire, and none got more than 50 yards beyond the edge of Zouave wood. The utilisation, in the forefront, of the 8th Battalion of the Rifle Brigade, a spent force, was a serious error of judgement. Consequently, the casualties on July 30 were extremely heavy.

Unwarranted criticism
The flame attack at Hooge was in itself only a small part of an attack which was aimed at the front of a whole brigade. Thus it was an episode of limited importance, but because of the nature of the attack, Hooge has assumed a special place in the history of the First World War. Hooge serves as an example of the ingenuity of the German military mind, and of the tenacity and courage of these representatives of the New Army. Despite the obvious disadvantage of facing a new and terrifying weapon, the British troops at Hooge recovered from

their initial surprise remarkably quickly, and offered a spirited resistance. A certain degree of unwarranted criticism was levelled at the British troops at Hooge. It was pointed out that a man using a *Flammenwerfer* which carries only about 20-30 yards, is bound to be a vulnerable target, and that a rifle or a machine gun brought up on a flank will make short work of him. This is true provided, firstly, that the trench of the flamethrower is more than 30 yards away and secondly, that his opponent has flanks which can be utilised. In this case the Germans had no need to leave their trenches in order to discharge the flame, and A Company had no flanks for offensive purposes, for the right flank was left 'in the air' by the crater, and on the left flank the trench bent back towards the support line. The same facts applied to C Company's sector.

Hooge was, in many ways, the ideal place to prove the effectiveness of the *Flammenwerfer* in battle. The apparatus had been used before, but with little effect, and a success was needed if the weapon was to be retained. The *Flammenwerfer* could only be used effectively in certain limited conditions. It was cumbersome, and therefore could only be operated safely from the security of a trench. Since the German trench systems were seldom less than 40 yards from those of the French and British, there were few places where the *Flammenwerfer* had any potential use. But at Hooge, not only was the British position weak, but the two front lines were sufficiently close to be within the limited range of the *Flammenwerfer*. There was every chance that an attack with *Flammenwerfer* might yield the success which the weapon so sorely needed. For these very simple reasons, the Germans specifically chose Hooge for their experiment. The success at Hooge undoubtedly explains the retention of the weapon for future operations. But the same combination of favourable circumstances was seldom presented to the Germans, which explains why *Flammenwerfer* failed to achieve a success as spectacular as Hooge on the Western Front again. The British and French, for their part, ensured that their trench systems remained, where possible, beyond the range of the German *Flammenwerfer*.

Further Reading
Das Ehrenbuch der Deutschen Pionere (Germany 1923)
Flammenwerfer und Sturmtruppen (Germany 1921)
Hare, Steuart, *Annals of the King's Royal Rifle Corps*
King's Royal Rifle Corps Chronicle, The KRRC Club Ltd (London 1915)
Military Operations, France and Belgium 1915, Vol II, Official History of the War (Macmillan & Co 1928)
The Rifle Brigade 1914-1918, The Rifle Brigade Club Ltd (London 1927)
Roberts, A. A., *The Poison War*

MICHAEL DEWAR was born at Fulmer in Buckinghamshire in 1941, and was educated at Downside, RMA Sandhurst and Pembroke College, Oxford, where he obtained an Honours Degree in History and specialised in Military History. He saw active service with his regiment, the 3rd Royal Green Jackets, during the Malaysian-Indonesian confrontation in Borneo in 1965-66. He now instructs at the RMA Sandhurst and writes for military history publications in his spare time.

Mainstay of the Infantry: The Bolt-Action Rifle

Of the millions of men who fought in the First World War, the majority were infantrymen whose personal weapon was a rifle. The First World War was fought at a time when the bolt-action magazine rifle had reached a peak of development upon which no subsequent improvements have been made. From the comparatively crude Dreyse Needle Gun of the Austro-Prussian war, the modern rifle gradually took shape, but no improvements would have been possible without the one outstanding feature of the Needle Gun: the combination of projectile, propellant and detonator. From this improvement all others sprang.

The principle of the bolt action is as follows:

The bolt, in outline resembling an ordinary door bolt, contains a long, spring-loaded, firing pin. On sliding the bolt towards the breech, the bullet is inserted into the breech, the spring, making contact with the trigger mechanism via the cocking piece, is compressed, thus withdrawing the firing pin, and the bolt is locked into the breech mechanism. The most effective of the locking systems is by dual lugs which revolve into recesses in the breech; these can be either vertical or horizontal. Other locking systems are of a

wedge type in the breech or by a rear lug. This last system, which is employed in the British Short Magazine Lee-Enfield, has been subjected to criticism because it allows too much 'play' in the bolt and, in general, is not as strong as the front locking system. Various methods of triggering the mechanism to release the firing pin have been developed. Essentially, however, the process is the same — by squeezing the trigger the resistance to the cocking piece is released and the firing pin makes contact with the percussion cap. With a turn-bolt, the locking mechanism is engaged by turning the bolt handle down when the bolt has been fully pushed home. The straight-pull bolt has an internal spiral system which automatically revolves the lugs into place as the bolt slides forward.

The box magazine, variations of which were employed by the majority of rifles of the period, is an extremely simple mechanism; it consists of a metal box incorporating a spring-loaded platform. The magazine is situated, forward of the trigger guard, below the mechanism. The capacity of the various designs varied from 3 to 10 rounds. For the most part, the magazines were an integral part of the rifle but there were several removable designs. In some instances,

The Short Rifle, Magazine Lee-Enfield (Mark III), showing the Lee action and box magazine

The Russian M1891 Moisin-Nagant rifle with Moisin action and the Belgian Nagant magazine

The magazine and action of the Austro-Hungarian Model 1895 straight-pull rifle

The action and tubular magazine of the French Lebel Model 1886 rifle

The action and magazine of the German Model 1898 rifle and carbine

the cartridges were staggered within the box, in others they were in-line. Cartridges were injected into the magazine by means of a clip. Clips assumed a variety of different shapes, but the principle was the same in all. They consisted of open-ended slides or cases within which a number of cartridges, 3, 5, or 6, were gripped whether by the spring metal of the case or a spring incorporated in the base. When the bolt was withdrawn, the clip was positioned between the bolt-head and the breech, and the cartridges were usually pressed down into the magazine by the thumb. The subsequent forward movement of the bolt ejected the clip and pushed the first round into the breech. The major deviation from this method was that adopted by Mannlicher for most of his designs. The Mannlicher system involved placing the clip with the cartridges into the magazine, a spring then pushing the cartridges up *within* the clip. When the last round was in the breech, the clip would fall through an aperture in the bottom of the magazine.

Without doubt the German contribution to small arms design has been the greatest. In particular the rifles of Peter Paul Mauser demonstrated a remarkable ingenuity and have influenced rifle design throughout the world. The Mauser Gewehr 98 was probably the most successful rifle of its kind ever designed.

Second only to Mauser was Mannlicher. A frequently under-estimated inventor, he was often badly used. It is significant, however, that his designs and elements of his designs have been incorporated in the weapons of many different countries.

The United States claims, with some justification, much credit for advances in small arms design. Most of these advances, however, applied to weapons of eras before and after that which concerns us here. The biggest single contribution from America was that of the Lee box magazine and Lee, although he worked in America, was born in Scotland.

Britain's contribution was in the field of rifling. Before the introduction of the smokeless 'cordite' propellant, the Metford system of rifling was general; the new propellant, however, necessitated a different system and the Enfield system was almost universally adopted and is still used. Illustrated overleaf are the genealogies of the major design features of the First World War's rifles and carbines, with the colour coding showing the provenance of each weapon's cartridge, bolt system and magazine. A few further points about some of the weapons follow. The Italian Mannlicher-Carcano is sometimes called the Mauser-Paravicino and has been described, erroneously, as dangerous to fire. The Mauser Gewehr 88 was Germany's answer to the French introduction of smokeless powder with the 1886 Lebel rifle. The Gewehr 98 was a development of this, and can be claimed to be the world's most successful bolt-action rifle ever. The Mauser M1889 was Belgium's first modern rifle, and was the first rifle to utilise the Mauser magazine charger. The Turkish M1893 rifle was basically the same as the Spanish 7-mm weapon of the same date. Both introduced the Mauser staggered-row magazine. The Springfield M1903 was an adaptation of the Mauser ▷

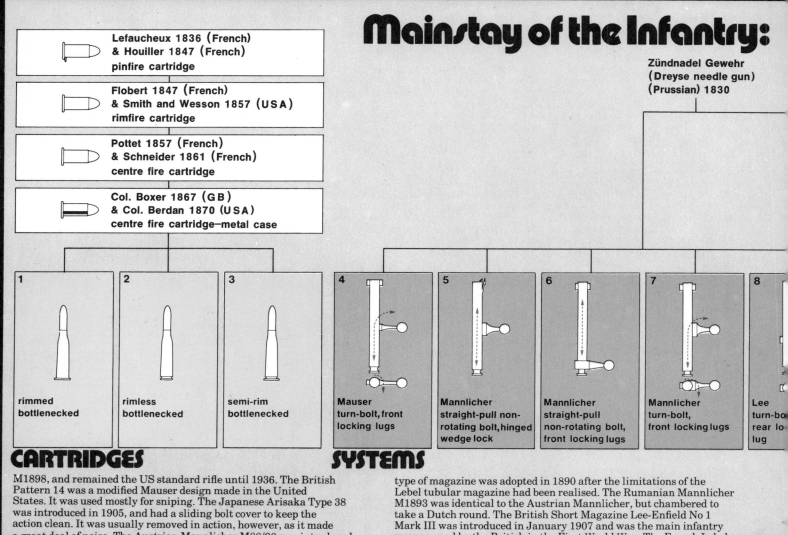

Mainstay of the Infantry:

Zündnadel Gewehr
(Dreyse needle gun)
(Prussian) 1830

Lefaucheux 1836 (French)
& Houiller 1847 (French)
pinfire cartridge

Flobert 1847 (French)
& Smith and Wesson 1857 (USA)
rimfire cartridge

Pottet 1857 (French)
& Schneider 1861 (French)
centre fire cartridge

Col. Boxer 1867 (GB)
& Col. Berdan 1870 (USA)
centre fire cartridge—metal case

1 rimmed bottlenecked

2 rimless bottlenecked

3 semi-rim bottlenecked

4 Mauser turn-bolt, front locking lugs

5 Mannlicher straight-pull non-rotating bolt, hinged wedge lock

6 Mannlicher straight-pull non-rotating bolt, front locking lugs

7 Mannlicher turn-bolt, front locking lugs

8 Lee turn-bolt, rear locking lug

CARTRIDGES

SYSTEMS

M1898, and remained the US standard rifle until 1936. The British Pattern 14 was a modified Mauser design made in the United States. It was used mostly for sniping. The Japanese Arisaka Type 38 was introduced in 1905, and had a sliding bolt cover to keep the action clean. It was usually removed in action, however, as it made a great deal of noise. The Austrian Mannlicher M88/90 was introduced in 1890 to take advantage of the new and more powerful smokeless powder. Otherwise the rifle was identical to the Model 1886. An unusual feature was the fact that the magazine charger clip was ejected from the bottom of the magazine when the latter was empty. The M90 carbine introduced the rotating bolt to the Austrian army. The M95 was the main Austrian rifle of the First World War and was used also by the Italians, Bulgarians, Serbs and, to a lesser degree, by the Greeks. The Mannlicher-Berthier rifles were, with the Lebel, France's standard rifle until well into the 1930s. The Mannlicher

type of magazine was adopted in 1890 after the limitations of the Lebel tubular magazine had been realised. The Rumanian Mannlicher M1893 was identical to the Austrian Mannlicher, but chambered to take a Dutch round. The British Short Magazine Lee-Enfield No 1 Mark III was introduced in January 1907 and was the main infantry weapon used by the British in the First World War. The French Lebel was the world's first modern, mass-produced magazine rifle, and also introduced smokeless powder to the armies of the world. The Lebel's round was, however, of a design unsuitable for automatic weapons, and future French rifles reverted to a more conventional design of magazine and round. Finally, the Russian Moisin-Nagant, which was introduced in 1891. It was designed for a conical-nosed bullet, but the adoption of the Spitzer pointed round in 1908 necessitated no more than a change in the rear sight to accommodate the new ballistics.
Owen Wood

6·5-mm Mannlicher–Carcano M1891
Italy
| 2 | 4 | 14 |

7·92-mm Mauser Gewehr 88
Germany
| 2 | 4 | 14 |

7·92-mm Mauser Gewehr 98
Germany
| 2 | 4 | 11 |

7·65-mm Mauser M1889
Belgium
| 2 | 4 | 11 |

7·65-mm Mauser M1893
Turkey
| 2 | 4 | 13 |

·30-in Springfield 1903
USA
| 2 | 4 | 13 |

·303-in Pattern 14
Britain
| 1 | 4 | 13 |

6·5-mm Arisaka Type 38
Japan
| 3 | 4 | 13 |

The Bolt-Action Rifle

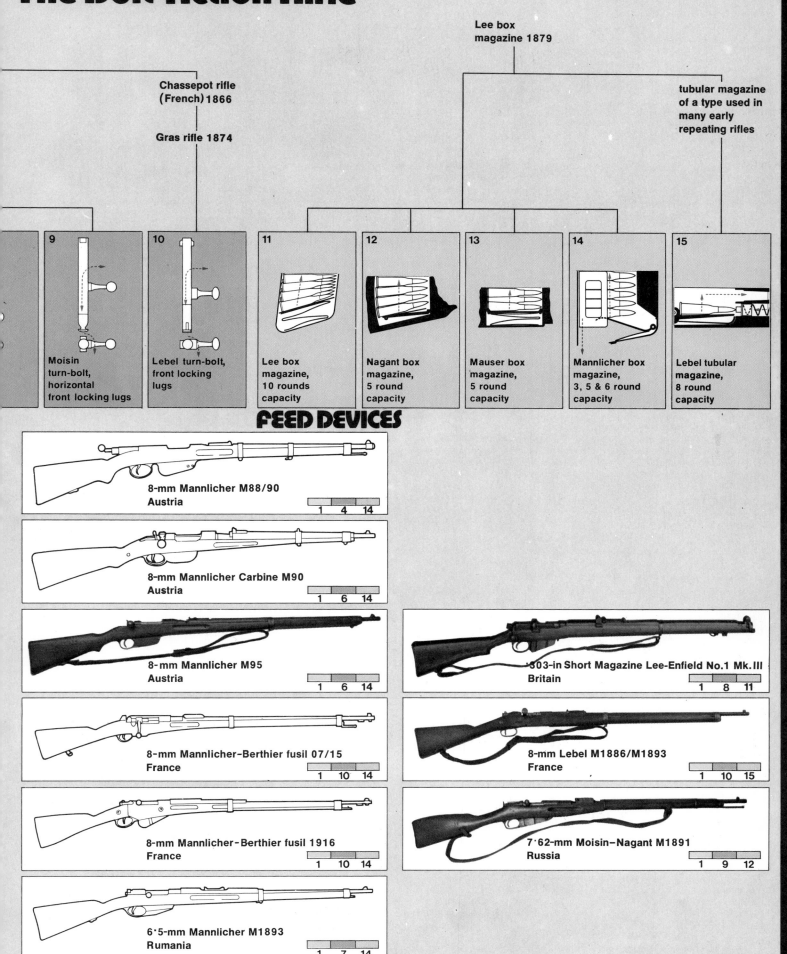

Lee box magazine 1879

Chassepot rifle (French) 1866

Gras rifle 1874

tubular magazine of a type used in many early repeating rifles

9 Moisin turn-bolt, horizontal front locking lugs

10 Lebel turn-bolt, front locking lugs

11 Lee box magazine, 10 rounds capacity

12 Nagant box magazine, 5 round capacity

13 Mauser box magazine, 5 round capacity

14 Mannlicher box magazine, 3, 5 & 6 round capacity

15 Lebel tubular magazine, 8 round capacity

FEED DEVICES

8-mm Mannlicher M88/90 Austria — 1 4 14

8-mm Mannlicher Carbine M90 Austria — 1 6 14

8-mm Mannlicher M95 Austria — 1 6 14

8-mm Mannlicher–Berthier fusil 07/15 France — 1 10 14

8-mm Mannlicher–Berthier fusil 1916 France — 1 10 14

6·5-mm Mannlicher M1893 Rumania — 1 7 14

·303-in Short Magazine Lee-Enfield No.1 Mk.III Britain — 1 8 11

8-mm Lebel M1886/M1893 France — 1 10 15

7·62-mm Moisin–Nagant M1891 Russia — 1 9 12

Chris Barker

Top, centre and above: The Lewis gun. An air-cooled, American designed .303-inch light machine gun. The ammunition was drum fed, each drum containing 47 rounds. The Lewis gun was a useful infantry weapon, but it was prone to jamming, especially in wet or muddy conditions. *Above right:* Hand and rifle grenades of 1914/15. Column one, a British No 2 Mark I hand grenade. Column two, a German ball grenade *(top)*, a German oyster grenade *(centre)*, a French pear-shaped grenade *(bottom)*. Column three, a British No. 3 Mark I rifle grenade. Column four, a British Malta grenade *(top)* — this was made exclusively in Malta for the Gallipoli Campaign, a British No 12 hand grenade *(bottom)*. Column five, a French Bessozi hand grenade *(top)*, a British No 5 Mark I Mills grenade *(centre)*, a British No 1 Mark II hand grenade *(bottom)*. Last column, a German 1914 rifle grenade

The first sub-machine gun to be used in military service

Top left: **1** The Vetterli Vitali M1871/87 10.4-mm. **2** The Vetterli Vitali M1871/87 10.4-mm converted to 6.5-mm. These two rifles were still in fairly extensive use at the beginning of the Italian campaign. **3** The Mannlicher Carcano M1891 6.5-mm. **4** The Mannlicher Carcano 91TS Carbine 6.5-mm. **5** The Mannlicher Carcano M1891 Carbine 6.5-mm with folding bayonet. The Mannlicher Carcano has a Mauser-type bolt action with a Mannlicher six-round magazine
Top right: **6** The 10.35-mm Glisenti M1891 revolver with folding trigger. **7** The 10.35-mm Glisenti revolver. **8** The 7.65-mm Beretta M1915 pistol. **9** The 9-mm Glisenti M1910 automatic pistol. **10** Flare pistol. **11** The 9-mm Beretta M1915 Glisenti pistol
Left, below left and below right: The Villar Perosa 9-mm sub-machine gun, the first actual sub-machine gun used in military service. Originally designed for aircraft, its light weight (14 lb 4 oz) made it useful for infantry fighting in mountainous regions. Each magazine held 25 rounds, and its two barrels could be fired individually. Here it is shown in a back pack with a container for cartridges (left), modified for infantry use with a bipod (below left), and with a mounting for aircraft or bicycle use (below right)

Photographs by Jack Pia

◁ The Italian 65-mm mountain gun with shield. This piece broke down into six mule-pack loads. *Range:* 7,100 yards. *Rate of fire:* 10-20 rounds-per-minute. *Muzzle velocity;* 1,100 feet-per-second. *Weight in firing position:* 1,200 lb

John Batchelor

VERD

UN THE STORM BREAKS

At dawn on February 21 the German bombardment of Verdun and its defences began, a bombardment so massive that it was heard as a steady rumbling 100 miles away. The Germans, superior in the air, in artillery and in numbers of fighting men, seemed poised for a stunning victory, and the fall of Fort Douaumont, the largest of the forts guarding Verdun, was seen as the beginning of a major French catastrophe. Yet the Germans let their opportunity slip, largely owing to caution from above. Fighting desperately under the inspiring leadership of Pétain, the French began to slow the German advance.   *Below:* The effect of the German bombardment—the devastated entrance of Fort Souville, one of the forts guarding Verdun *Alistair Horne.*

It was chance—even bad luck—that in the early morning of February 12, 1916, the day fixed for the German assault on Verdun, there was a ferocious blizzard. At dawn deep snow lay everywhere, the storm still raged and mist lay across the whole countryside, concealing all the meticulously pin-pointed targets for the German artillery, on whose accuracy success depended absolutely. So their opening bombardment had to be postponed.

This initial postponement did in fact prevent immediate disaster for the French. On that morning, two newly-arrived French divisions, the 51st and the 14th, were not yet in position. If the Germans had attacked then, with their blanketing artillery and their battalions of chosen assault troops, they would have found the French in half-completed positions—the French 72nd Division alone facing the six German attacking divisions, and the other four French divisions, including the two newly-arrived, spread about through the citadel and the rest of the Verdun salient. Some of the French troops holding the front line were elderly Territorials.

While the Germans waited for the stormy weather to abate, the French settled into their new dispositions. There were now three French divisions—making up General Chrétien's XXX Corps—facing the Germans between the Meuse and the railway to Etain. Of these, the 72nd and 51st Divisions, with 20 battalions, manned the north-eastern curve of the salient, which was to be the sector of the main German attack; and there were 14 further battalions on the French flanks or in close reserve. An elderly gunnery officer, General Herr, was in immediate command of the French troops in Verdun and the salient; but having lost a large part of his fortress artillery to Joffre's recent purges of fixed emplacements, Herr felt himself at a loss in a world of trenches, infantry, wire and chronic lethargy. As a fortress commander, Herr was directly responsible, not to a field army headquarters, but to General de Langle de Cary, commanding the Central Group of Armies.

Opposite these 20 French battalions, the main German attacking force was made up of 72 battalions, or six divisions. On the German right, from the Meuse at Consenvoye eastwards to Flabas, was *VII Reserve Corps* under General von Zwehl—Westphalians. Next, on a short sector opposite the Bois des Caures, was *XVIII Corps* under General von Schenck—mostly Hessians. On the left, from Ville to Azannes, was *III Corps*: these were the famous Brandenburgers, and their commander, General von Lochow, had already gained a reputation for aggressive action—in particular, against Pétain's thrust towards Vimy Ridge in the previous spring. Supporting troops of *V Reserve Corps* and *XV Corps* were on the German left.

But the principal feature of the German line-up was the concentration of guns—over 1,200 for an assault frontage of barely eight miles. There were 654 'heavies', including 13 of the 42-cm mortars, the 'secret weapon' of 1914 that had shattered the Belgian forts, and two 38-cm long-range naval guns earmarked to interrupt communications behind Verdun. There were 21-cm howitzers to pulverise the French front lines, and 15's to seek out and destroy the French batteries. Two and a half million shells had been

Südd Verlag

Left: A German 21-cm short howitzer. A sudden thaw on February 28, following the long spell of cold weather, turned the surface into a sea of mud and made it difficult for the German artillery to advance

Above: A French soldier is hurled violently back by the impact of a German bullet. By the end of March, 81,607 Germans and 89,000 French had been killed—not only France, but Germany too, was being bled white

brought up to supply this greatest concentration of artillery yet seen on any battlefield.

To preserve secrecy, the Germans had deliberately restricted their front and not included the eastern side of the salient for their attack; for the Woëvres Plain on that side was overlooked by the French-held Meuse Heights. Of much greater significance, however, was the German decision not to attack at the same time on the left, or western, bank of the Meuse. This limitation, and the later German efforts to rectify it, were to be among the terrible hall-marks of the Battle of Verdun.

For nine days bad weather held up the opening of the German bombardment which was to precede the attack of their assault troops. There was snow again; a thaw with fog, rain and gales; more rain and gales; wind and snow squalls; mist and cold. The French troops at least were accustomed to a rough life in poorly finished trenches and improvised dug-outs, with shelter for some in the forts, now largely deprived of their guns, which ringed the inner fortress of Verdun. The Germans probably suffered more in these harsh days of waiting, keyed up as they were for the attack. The concrete *Stollen* in which they assembled expectantly each day were not meant as a permanent shelter for these large bodies of troops; so most of them had a seven-mile march each night and morning to and from their billets through freezing sleet or snow.

On February 19 and 20 the weather improved. So at dawn on the 21st, the massive German bombardment started—heralded by a poor shot from one of the two long-range, long-barrelled 38-cm (15-inch) naval guns which, instead of destroying the Meuse Bridge in Verdun, exploded in the courtyard of the Archbishop's Palace, knocking off a corner of the cathedral. The other naval gun, aiming at Verdun Station, had more success. The ordeal of the salient had begun.

The bombardment of the French lines and rear quickly rose to a shattering peak of intensity, and continued without abatement for nine hours. In all the great artillery barrages of 1915, nothing compared with this concentration of high-explosive shells, with this appalling weight of flying, disintegrating metal. From left to right, from front to rear and back again in the narrow sector of the impending German infantry attack, everything was methodically bombarded. Gas and tear-gas shells were included too, with the aim of incapacitating the French artillery. The French trenches, poorly prepared, were quickly obliterated and many of the troops manning them were buried.

Lieutenant-Colonel Driant, whose warning voice had first drawn attention to the deplorable state of the Verdun defences, was now in the front line in the Bois des Caures, with his *Chasseurs,* as a detachment of 72nd Division—in the very centre of the German attack sector, opposite *XVIII Corps.* They experienced the full intensity and horror of the shelling. It seemed to them as if the wood was being swept by 'a storm, a hurricane, a tempest growing ever stronger, where it was raining nothing but paving stones'. Through the din of the explosions came the splintering crash as the great oaks and beeches of the forest were split or uprooted by the shells. The bombardment was heard nearly 100 miles away on the Vosges front as a steady rumbling.

Unpreparedness played as much a part as the German gas-shells in upsetting the French artillery. Their counterbattery work was generally ineffective from the start: their fire was spread rather aimlessly, and ceased to count as visibility decreased and contact with the infantry broke down. All telephone communication with the French front line had been cut by the shelling within the first hour, and runners often found it impossible to get through the avalanche of shells. As a result, effective command rapidly broke down. There was no question of sending up reinforcements; and in Verdun itself the shelling from the 38-cm naval guns had already dislocated the unloading of trains.

About mid-day there was a sudden pause: the shelling stopped and the French troops emerged from the debris of their line, ready to face the expected onslaught of the German infantry. But it was a trick. The Germans quickly took note of those parts of the French line which were still manned, and then at once took up the bombardment again, concentrating their short-range heavy mortars on the sections where the French had shown themselves, and shelling every part with the same unrelenting fury. To the German infantry, after long days in and out of the flooded *Stollen,* the sight of the French trenches disintegrating was intoxicating.

Even so, the Germans were taking no risks. When the bombardment at last finished at 1600 hours, they cautiously sent forward powerful fighting patrols who, making skilful use of the ground, probed for the sectors of least resistance. True to Falkenhayn's directive for a controlled but insistent advance, the Germans were here evolving a new method of approach and attack, which was quickly to become characteristic of the fighting at Verdun on both sides; and, paradoxically, by prolonging individual survival, these tactics also prolonged the duration and suffering of this inhuman battle.

On this first day at Verdun, however, German caution from above, and their unreadiness to follow up the probing, infiltrating patrols at once with assault troops, lost them their opportunity. For once, the massed waves of attacking infantry, which until now had been the ultimate weapon all along the Western Front, incurring always suicidal losses—for once, these disciplined lines of infantry, coming over immediately while the French were still stunned and shattered from the immensity of the bombardment, could have given the Germans a quick breakthrough and a clear road to Verdun. As it was, two of the corps' commanders stuck rigidly to orders and held back their main bodies of infantry until the next morning, leaving their patrols to do no more than explore French weaknesses. Only Zwehl, commanding *VII Reserve Corps* on the German right, obstinately improved on his orders and sent in his first wave of storm-troops hard on the heels of the patrols, and at once achieved an important success. They man-aged to occupy the whole of the Bois d'Haumont before dusk and so effect the first breach of the main French defences.

Elsewhere on the French 72nd Division front, and to the east on the 51st Division front, the German patrols, even without support, did damage enough to the French line, exploiting the gaps made by the shell-fire and using their new weapon of horror, the flame-thrower, with terrifying effect, causing panic through the French ranks. There still remained stubborn and heroic pockets of French resistance, flaring out even into disconcerting counterattacks.

None of this, however, was the easy success the Germans had expected. The concentration of shell-fire from the unprecedented opening bombardment had been planned to destroy all life in the French front-line trenches and block-houses. But somehow men had survived. Driant's sector, for example, in the Bois des Caures had consisted of a complex network of redoubts and small strongholds, quite unlike the usual continuous trench lines. Here and elsewhere the German troops were therefore disconcerted to meet intense machine gun and rifle fire from defenders who ought to have been buried in the wreckage of the uprooted forest.

Full-scale attack
By nightfall, Knobelsdorf, Prince Wilhelm's Chief-of-Staff, had become impatient of this cautious progress, and ordered a full-scale attack for the morning after another softening-up bombardment. It was the French, however, who surprisingly took the initiative at dawn on the 22nd, attempting several counterattacks with

△ One of the *Stollen* (concrete bunkers) which the Germans built near the French line to permit first-wave troops to concentrate safely
▽ Douaumont after the German bombardment

Musée de la Guerre

Bibliothek für Zeitgeschichte

A German shell explodes and the 'mincing machine' grinds on. Making skilful use of the ground, the Germans sent out powerful fighting patrols probing for the sectors of least resistance

the spirit and dash typical of their army's tradition. But the means were not there, nor the organisation and communications: many attacks failed to get going, others were soon swamped.

Even though Knobelsdorf now placed no limits on corps' objectives the *XVIII Corps*, opposite the Bois des Caures, was still a model of caution, faced as it was with the verve and flexibility of Driant's *Chasseurs*, which masked the absurdly small size of the French opposition; and it took the Germans all day, with the help of their comrades on either flank, to silence Driant's valiant resistance. Zwehl's *VII Reserve Corps* had captured the village of Haumont on Driant's left, after a hard fight lasting into the afternoon, and now the Brandenburgers of *III Corps* came round on Driant's right through the Bois de Ville, split up by the cross-fire from the surviving French machine guns, but relentless with their flame-throwers and overwhelming in their numbers. They surrounded the French positions and picked off their strong-points one by one. Driant himself and a handful of men tried to hold out in the last strong-point, in vain; and as they broke out to the rear, they were mown down by enfilading fire.

The German losses in silencing the Bois des Caures had been unexpectedly heavy, and the confidence of their assault troops was shaken. Above all, their offensive had been held up during one whole day by Driant's resistance in the very centre of the German attack. Nor was Driant alone in this. The anchor position on the left of the French line at Brabant on the Meuse was still held by other elements of 72nd Division; and on the right, 51st Division continued to fight bitterly in Herbebois, holding up the advance of the Branden-

burgers. These delays, though seeming small in the overall picture, robbed the German assault of its required momentum.

Earlier on this day, the French artillery had improved their shooting, and had been reinforced. Fire from French batteries on the left (western) bank of the Meuse onto the Germans' flank was starting to cause trouble. Falkenhayn's parsimony in keeping back reserves for Verdun had deprived the German *VI Reserve Corps,* holding the line on the left bank, of adequate artillery, and this weakness prevented them from silencing the French guns on this side. But on the right bank, behind the battlefield itself, the French field guns were being knocked out one by one by the fire of the long-barrelled 15's.

Once more on the next day, February 23, the Germans made surprisingly little progress, even though they were still held only by the remnants of 72nd and 51st Divisions, whose losses continued at a terrible rate. Brabant had been evacuated, but mixed elements managed to hold out all day in Beaumont, on a rise behind the Bois des Caures. Infantry of the German *XVIII Corps* pressed forward against this position in dense formations, one wave pushing in closely behind another, in the established style of the Western Front, to be scythed down in turn by the French machine guns. At the same time, the French heavy guns under XXX Corps' command had found the range of the advancing Germans, who were suffering too from their own shells falling short. Official German records speak of this as a 'day of horror'.

The French infantry were also starting to get the measure of the dreaded flame-throwers. They were learning to pick off the German pioneers who wielded them, as they moved clumsily under the heavy bur-

den of their equipment, before they came within flame-throwing range. So 51st Division on the right were still able to cling tenaciously to Herbebois. On the other side of the sector, 72nd Division managed to hold up Zwehl's corps at last in front of Samogneux on an 'intermediate line', which de Castelnau had ordered to be constructed in January. When this line was broken, a battalion still held out in Samogneux itself till late into the night, when it was suddenly wiped out by a barrage of French 155's, firing across from the left bank in the belief that the village had already fallen to the Germans.

With this final tragedy, 72nd Division virtually ceased to exist. The two first-line French divisions, 72nd and 51st, with an original combined establishment of 26,523, had together lost 16,224 officers and men.

The Germans, despite their rebuffs, felt that Verdun was now theirs for the taking. So it was. They overran the whole French second position, inadequately prepared to start with, and now pounded out of existence, in three hours on February 24. But following the unexpected and savage opposition which they had experienced in the previous two days and the serious losses they had suffered, the Germans were no longer poised to exploit the situation fully, and their cautiousness had increased. Once more, they missed the opportunity of breaking right through.

The gap in the French lines left by the decimation of 72nd Division was now filled by 37th African Division—the Zouaves and Moroccan *Tirailleurs*. But the bitter, freezing weather, which had returned once the German offensive was launched, and was causing suffering enough to European troops, had cowed the temperamental North Africans. Furthermore, in an attempt to plug the disastrous holes in the French defences, they were being split up into small units under strange officers—survivors of the 72nd and 51st. The incessant bombardment, the horror of which was beyond their comprehension, was the last straw. When the North Africans saw the great grey carpet of German infantry rolling out towards them, some of them lost their nerve and fled.

Crumbling morale

By the night of February 24, French morale was crumbling seriously. Their guns were silent, their clearing stations overflowing with casualties, untended, their wounds often frozen by the intense cold. Only a fraction could be got out: the German 38's, firing with 'diabolical precision', had cut the one full-gauge railway out of the Verdun salient. Chrétien's XXX Corps was finished. Balfourier's XX Corps from the Lorraine front was to relieve them, but only the vanguard had reached Verdun, cold, hungry, and exhausted. Despite every protest, Chrétien insisted on throwing them into the battle at once; but it seemed doubtful if they would hold till the corps' main body, en route in a desperate forced march, could arrive.

It was on the following day that the French Command took decisions which committed them finally to the defence of Verdun, whatever the cost.

On the evening of February 24, de Langle de Cary obtained permission from Joffre to shorten the line in front of Verdun drastically on the still unthreatened Woëvres Plain side of the salient, and to withdraw

The guns were the masters of the battlefield, their thunder was 'like a gigantic forge that never stopped, day or night'

Below: The German 17-cm naval rail gun.
Maximum range: 25,700 yards. *Barrel:* 22' 6". *Traverse:* 13° left to 13° right. *Weight of gun and carriage:* 25 tons. *Weight of shell:* 141 lbs. *Rate of fire:* 1 round-per-minute. *Crew:* 12 men.
Bottom right: The French 370-mm mortar, one of the big guns that helped to press the French advantage at Verdun. It had a range of over five miles, using a 250-pound shell. It weighed 30 tons, complete with platform, could fire one round every two minutes and required a crew of 16 men

Above: A French field ambulance. The drivers of these vehicles took enormous risks to get the wounded away from the front line

Right: Rain-filled craters surround the ruined outer walls of Fort Douaumont

E.C.P.-Armées

John Batchelor

from the Woëvres Plain to the Meuse Heights east and south-east of the city. Later that night, with the news desperate, Joffre, against all orders and precedent, was rudely wakened from his routine allocation of sleep. One authority says that it was de Castelnau who insisted on waking him; another that it was the Prime Minister himself, Briand, who had driven over from Paris to General Headquarters at Chantilly; a third merely states that Joffre rose to the occasion. The consequence, in any case, was of supreme importance. Joffre sent de Castelnau off to Verdun that night with full powers to do whatever was needed. De Castelnau, as the recently-appointed Chief-of-Staff at French General Headquarters and Joffre's closest colleague (and rival), was the obvious choice for such a critical mission. But the very choice of de Castelnau made certain that the decision over Verdun would be a firm one. He was still very much a 'fighting general', as well as being outstandingly intelligent, quick-witted and flexible; and he had a way of inspiring staff officers and front-line soldiers alike.

De Castelnau reached Verdun at breakfast-time on February 25. He found Herr, who was still in command of Verdun and its salient, 'depressed' and 'a little tired'. He then went straight to the battle-torn right bank, made rapid and accurate appreciations, and effected miracles in reanimating the defence, with his experience and insight and his boundless energy: 'wherever he went, decision and order followed him'. He saw that Verdun could be saved, that an effective defence could be maintained on the remaining cross ridges of the right bank. He telephoned his conclusions to Joffre's headquarters that afternoon, and without waiting for agreement gave orders that the right bank of the Meuse should be held at all costs, and that there must be no retreat to the left bank.

On the previous evening, Joffre had already agreed that General Pétain, the tenacious commander of the French Second Army, should be brought over to defend the left bank at Verdun. Now de Castelnau recommended that Pétain should be put immediately in total command at Verdun, of both sides of the river, and despatched the necessary order without waiting for Joffre's approval. Pétain enjoyed a considerable reputation as a master of the defensive: he had been one of the first to recognise the full implications of firepower. He was also a very able commander, meticulous in his preparations for action, with a real concern for his troops, who therefore trusted him. He had shown his mettle in attack at Vimy Ridge and, less successfully, in the Champagne. Austere, aloof, distrustful of politicians, he was a dedicated soldier.

De Castelnau, by insisting on the defence of the right bank, had accepted the challenge of the German assault on Verdun: without knowing it, he was acting as Falkenhayn wished and expected, allowing the French army to be drawn inexorably into the Verdun salient, to be bled there by the remorseless German pressure. And in appointing Pétain, de Castelnau was ensuring that his decision to defend Verdun would be carried out.

The French, in theory, need not have taken up the challenge. They could have withdrawn to the left bank, eliminating the dangerous salient and shortening their line

considerably. Verdun and its ring of forts were no longer of practical defensive value: their guns had by now mostly been withdrawn to augment the French artillery barrages for Joffre's hopeful offensives, and the forts stood there imposing and toothless. In the hilly country behind the Meuse, the French could have conducted a fighting withdrawal with advantage, exhausting the attacking Germans and overstraining their lines of supply. As Winston Churchill wrote at the time: 'Meeting an artillery attack is like catching a cricket ball. Shock is dissipated by drawing back the hands. A little "give", a little suppleness and the violence of the impact is vastly reduced.' Yet de Castelnau's decision to hold was based not only on his own aggressive spirit, but on an intuition of a greater truth: that perhaps, after 18 months without success, the French army was not capable of a controlled, fighting retreat in the face of superior forces. Nor, as Briand was aware, would the French nation or his government have easily survived the shock of abandoning a fortress with the immense symbolic value which Verdun held for the French, a factor of which Falkenhayn in laying his plans was conscious.

Brutal shell-fire

On the ridges before Verdun, whose great forests were being rapidly torn down by the brutal weight of shell-fire, there was still some French resistance on the left, facing *VII Reserve Corps*. But elsewhere in the salient on the morning of February 25 —while de Castelnau was appraising the terrain with his quick, experienced eye— the Germans had before them only the forts which ringed Verdun, sinister guardian monsters which the Germans thought were still fully manned and armed. Fort Douaumont was the first that lay in their path, and the strongest. From every angle its great tortoise hump stood out, stark, menacing, fascinating. It was, in fact, occupied by only a small detachment of territorial gunners, manning the 155-mm turret gun which had survived Joffre's purge; its approaches were inadequately covered by the French infantry. Small bodies of Brandenburgers, heroically defying a powerful garrison existing only in their imagination, managed to edge into the fort unobserved during the afternoon of the 25th and to capture its elderly occupants.

The reaction to the fall of Fort Douaumont was electric. In Germany church bells rang; a newspaper declared, 'Victory of Verdun. The Collapse of France'. In Verdun itself morale went to pieces. An officer ran through the streets crying *'Sauve qui peut'*, and civilians poured out of the city, jamming the vital roads. Worse still, the commander of the 37th African Division, on hearing the news, blew up the unthreatened Meuse bridge at Bras and withdrew his battered troops, quite needlessly, back to the last ridge before the city itself.

Pétain took over command at midnight and set up his headquarters in the village of Souilly, on the main road into Verdun from the south-west. His journey in the rigours of winter weather had been long and tiring, and the last stage, through the distracted rear of the French army in defeat, harrowing. He received his instructions briefly from de Castelnau, who then left. Pétain contacted his corps' commanders by telephone, and spent the night huddled

Risking the shell-fire, French stretcher bearers attempt to reach a fallen comrade

in an armchair in an unheated room. Next morning he had contracted double pneumonia; but the secret was strictly guarded —with reason, for the mere knowledge of his arrival, that he was now in command at Verdun, had stiffened the French resistance and given new heart to every man, from General Balfourier down to the exhausted troops holding out in the front line, so high was Pétain's reputation in the army.

In the defence lines themselves the turning-point came at the same time with the arrival of the main body of Balfourier's seasoned XX Corps, the 'Iron Corps'. All troops in the salient were now regrouped under four corps' commanders, responsible to Pétain and his Second Army staff. I Corps was coming in from reserve, and others were on their way. Haig too had at last agreed to relieve the French Tenth Army, which was sandwiched between the British First and Third in the area of Arras.

Pétain, on his sick-bed, took up the threads of command with remarkable vigour. He realised that the loss of Fort Douaumont did not mean final disaster, that the other forts remained, and could be manned and linked into a formidable defence perimeter. He issued orders accordingly: from this line there must be no withdrawal. With his profound understanding of the defensive power which guns could provide, he now had the artillery round Verdun reorganised into one concentrated and effective weapon. From this moment, says the German official history, 'began the flanking fire on the ravines and roads north of Douaumont that was to cause us such severe casualties'.

It was the precarious supply route into Verdun which was Pétain's next concern. The full-gauge railway had been rendered useless by the German long-range shelling. The only substitute was motor transport on the one road in, the narrow second-class road from Bar-le-Duc, just 21 feet wide. Pétain and his able transport officer, Major Richard, threw all their energies and organising ability into making this road a life-line for Verdun. Richard went out requisitioning lorries throughout France, and gangs of Territorials were detailed to devote themselves entirely to the upkeep of the road. It was their tireless labour which kept the road intact and the lorries moving when a sudden thaw on February 28, following the long spell of hard weather, turned the surface to a sea of mud. The road was reserved strictly for the ceaseless flow of motor traffic in both directions. Any lorry that broke down was heaved aside into the ditch. With their solid tyres and top-heavy weight, many skidded on the bad surface; others caught fire. Drivers were inexperienced, and always fatigued.

At night, the procession of dimly lit vehicles resembled 'the folds of some gigantic and luminous serpent which never stopped and never ended'. It is astonishing that the Germans never thought of bombing the road, which would so easily have been blocked: they had the aeroplanes to do it—C-class aircraft—and Zeppelins. Eventually vehicles were passing along the road at a daily average of one every 14 seconds, and for hours on end at a rate of one every five seconds; and the equivalent of more than a division of soldiers was kept mending it. The road was the artery through which the life-blood of France was pumped into Verdun. Maurice Barrès gave it the immortal name of the *Voie Sacrée*.

The tide, for the moment, had turned. By February 28, as the German official history says, 'the German attack on Verdun was virtually brought to a standstill'. The French now were fresher and more determined. Their original divisions had been replaced and the numbers greatly reinforced. The German formations, on the other hand, had not been relieved at all and their troops were feeling the strain of a week's intensive fighting: promised reserves were not forthcoming.

Behind this shifting balance between attacker and defender can be seen a change in the balance of artillery; and it was the artillery's positioning and fire-power which were to rule the battlefield—no longer as a prelude, an opening barrage to clear the path, but as the constant and most demanding element of the battle. Now the German guns were flagging: they were having extreme difficulty in moving forward over the ground which they themselves had so violently cratered; and the sudden thaw turned the clay to deep mud. Worse still, the French had increased their heavy guns in the salient from 164 to more than 500, and they were shelling the German infantry with continuous and effective flanking fire from the left bank of the Meuse, in particular from the Bois Bourrus ridge.

The left bank had therefore become an immediate problem to the Germans, and pressure to open an attack on it intensified in the Crown Prince's *Fifth Army*. The commanding height in this western sector, le Mort Homme, was the obvious objective; for its capture would also neutralise the Bois Bourrus ridge, behind which much of Pétain's artillery was dug in. As late as February 26, with the right bank apparently within the Germans' grasp, Falkenhayn had again refused permission for an attack

on the left bank; but the next few days changed his mind, and he let Knobelsdorf have his agreement on February 29, at the same time sending up reinforcements behind *VI Reserve Corps* holding the left bank trenches—*X Reserve Corps*, two further divisions and 21 batteries of heavies.

Prince Rupprecht of Bavaria, one of the most responsible of German commanders, noted at his headquarters in northern France: 'I hear that at Verdun the Left Bank of the Meuse is to be attacked now, too. It should have been done at once; now the moment of surprise is lost.' These German reserves—quite apart from those held immobilised opposite the currently inactive British front in the north—would have ensured a German breakthrough on the right bank to Verdun itself.

Before the new German offensive could be launched, the increasing weight of French guns on the left bank was already taking a terrible toll. Many of these guns were old 155's, firing visually into the German ranks; and *VII Reserve Corps*, which had done so well initially on the Meuse flank, suffered prohibitive losses. The German wounded streaming back were 'like a vision in hell'. Franz Marc, the painter, wrote in a letter from the Verdun front on March 3: 'For days I have seen nothing but the most terrible things a human mind can depict.' He was killed next day by a French shell.

The French at this time were slowly wresting back air superiority over the battlefield. The dramatic step had been taken of assembling some 60 of the French air aces, including Brocard, Nungesser, Navarre and Guynemer, and banding them together into the famous *Groupe des Cigognes* (the Storks). Altogether the French brought in 120 aeroplanes over

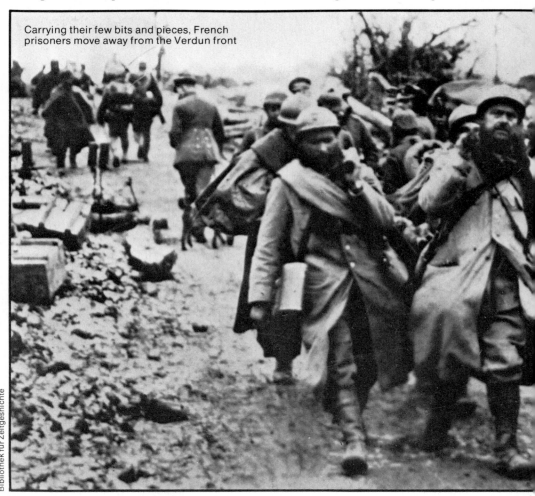

Carrying their few bits and pieces, French prisoners move away from the Verdun front

Verdun, to set against the Germans' 168 planes, 14 observation balloons and four Zeppelins. Poor German tactics and French verve tipped the scales, and in the next two months, while the German balloons were shot down in flames, French observation planes were to contribute greatly to the success of their artillery, who once more had eyes. The German aces, Boelcke and Immelmann, failed to upset the French supremacy, which the new Nieuport plane later helped to consolidate.

It was clear to the French that the Germans would attack on the left bank now; but the first days of March slipped by, and the French were given time to assemble four divisions on that side and one in reserve, under General Bazelaire, the French VII Corps commander. As the German attack still failed to materialise, Pétain was heard to remark, 'They don't know their business.' All the same, when it came, on March 6, starting with a bombardment comparable to that of February 21, the Germans at first had considerable success. They took the Meuse villages of Forges and Regnéville and advanced towards the ridge of the Mort Homme on its north-eastern slope; but their attack on the northern side was held by a wall of fire from the French guns.

The French 67th Division, defending the north-eastern approach to the Mort Homme had given ground too readily following the terror of the German bombardment, and over 3,000 of its men had surrendered by the end of the second day. It took a brilliant bayonet charge by a superbly disciplined regiment at dawn on March 8 to hold the Germans on this flank of the hill and force them to delay the final assault. In fact, the front now established on this north-eastern approach barely

shifted for the next month.

The Germans had planned a simultaneous attack on the right bank of the river, with Fort Vaux as their objective. The difficulties of bringing up ammunition to the guns over the bogged and cratered ground delayed them for two days. They then blundered in thinking the fort had been taken and marched up in column of fours straight into the French machine gun fire.

The 'mincing machine'

The terrible frontal assault on the Mort Homme from the north began on March 14. With German reserves flowing in more freely, there seemed no limit to the men and shells they were willing to expend to gain possession of this desolate hill. Attack and defence were evenly matched and the fighting swayed forward and back, until a deadly pattern of combat was established. It continued in this sector for the next two months. There would first be several hours of German bombardment; then their assault troops would surge forward to carry what remained of the French front line, which was no longer trenches but clusters of shell-holes. When the German attack had exhausted itself, ground down by the barrages from the French guns on the Bois Bourrus ridge to the south-east, the French would counterattack within 24 hours and drive the surviving Germans back again. But each flow and ebb of the tide brought the German high water mark a little further forward. The cost was terrible: by the end of March, 81,607 Germans had been killed and 89,000 French; and in this compressed and shelterless battle area a high proportion of the casualties were senior commanding officers.

Here, on the bare slopes of the Mort Homme, there were no woods or ravines to

favour infiltration, so that the Germans had lost the advantage they had gained elsewhere by their expert use of these tactics. Their flame-throwers had become suicide weapons, for the pioneers were easy targets in open country; and the French flanking fire was even more crippling on these naked hill-sides.

The Germans, in attacking the Mort Homme with the object of eliminating the threat to their exposed Meuse flank, now found their new right flank on the Mort Homme itself a target for crippling French shell-fire—this time from the neighbouring hill on the west side, Côte 304. So this too would have to be attacked and taken. The German army, even more reluctantly than the French, was being sucked into this ever expanding battle in the Verdun salient. The German Command was still not facing the full implications of its extended attack. Replacements were not being provided: the divisions were being kept too long in the line, and the gaps in the ranks merely filled with unseasoned youths. The French, in contrast, accepting the German challenge in its entirety, were committed to a scheme of rapid rotation of units at Verdun. Pétain, facing this same problem of exhaustion, was insisting, through his *Noria* system of reliefs, that no division remained more than a few days under fire. As a result, two-thirds of the French army was to be fed through the 'mincing machine' of Verdun, and its reserves drained. This was what Falkenhayn had hoped and expected—but he had not anticipated that the German army would also be 'bled white'.

A key position at the base of Côte 304 fell to the Germans on March 20, after French deserters had given them information on the defences. But this success brought no further advantage, only staggering losses under the French machine gun fire. Signs of exhaustion and unwillingness to attack were increasing in the German ranks.

The German *Fifth Army* command structure was now simplified in preparation for a final assault. Mudra, a corps commander from the Argonne front, was put in command of the right bank, and Gallwitz, a gunner, fresh from successes in the Balkans, in command of the left bank. On April 9 a massive simultaneous attack was mounted on Côte 304 and the Mort Homme. The Germans reached only a secondary crest of the Mort Homme; and on Côte 304 the French guns kept up their relentless, devastating fire on the exposed German flank. Pétain, recognising that an extremely dangerous attack had been held, issued next day his famous Order No 94, which he ended with the exhortation: *'Courage! On les aura!'* ('We'll get them!').

Further Reading
Falkenhayn, E. von, *General Headquarters, 1914-1916* (London 1960)
Horne, A., *The Price of Glory, Verdun 1916* (London 1962)
Joffre, Marshal, *The Memoirs of Marshal Joffre* (London 1932)
Palat, Gen. B. E., *La Grande Guerre sur le Front Occidental*, Vols. X-XII (Paris 1925)
Romains, Jules, *Men of Good Will*, Vols. 15-16 (London 1926)

The big guns—rivals at Verdun

Above: One of the two 38-cm long-range (29 miles) naval guns earmarked by the Germans to interrupt communications behind Verdun.
Below: A French 370-mm howitzer, part of France's inadequate defences

THE SOMME BARRAGE

British and French tactics for the Somme offensive hinged upon a massive and prolonged artillery barrage. Despite recent examples to the contrary, it was hoped that an intense seven-day bombardment would destroy all German resistance and leave the way open for easy infantry penetration. Accordingly, the British and French marshalled over 1,300 heavy guns and more than 2,000,000 shells, and began to pound the German line. By the seventh day most of the shells had been fired with an effect so stunning that nearly all present were convinced that there could be nobody left alive in the German trenches. *Major-General Anthony Farrar-Hockley.*

The Somme barrage gets under way—British howitzers in action

So much tragedy, so much emotion now pervades our view of the First World War that we tend to overlook the perspective of the men involved, not least of those engaged in the direction of the war. For example, at the end of 1915 the British cabinet was appalled that they were not a whit nearer victory despite a year of hard fighting and a casualty list exceeding 500,000. But whenever they talked of an armistice, their debate was frustrated by an intolerable fact: Germany, the aggressor, the invader, occupied almost all Belgium and a rich tract of France. So, on December 28, the cabinet approved a paper of intention prepared by its war committee, which included this paragraph:

Every effort is to be made for carrying out the offensive operations next spring in the main theatre of war (France and Flanders) in close co-operation with the Allies, and in the greatest possible strength.

Yet within a week their apprehensions of mass slaughter persuaded them to hesitate. At the end of this paragraph, the following was added:

although it must not be assumed that such operations are finally decided on.

Imperial War Museum

Weekly—sometimes daily—until April 1916, Mr Asquith and his cabinet colleagues, severally and collectively, discussed ways and means of defeating the Germans without heavy loss; all the while agreeing jointly with the French that 'we have to destroy the morale of the German Army and nation'. At length, with the crocuses bursting through the grass in St James's Park, with all prospect of a spring offensive past, the decision had to be taken. On April 7, the Chief of the Imperial General Staff, Sir William Robertson, was able to telegraph to General Haig in France that the government approved a combined offensive with the French in the summer.

The planning staffs of the Allied commanders-in-chief in France had not of course been waiting on this authority. Since February, Joffre and Haig had struck a form of bargain: they would

△ A British shell explodes in the German trenches prior to the attack on La Boiselle, half way along Fourth Army's front
◁ The lanyard is pulled, and one of the 1,732,873 shells expended by the Allies in the preliminary bombardment is fired from a British 8-inch Mk V howitzer

jointly undertake a major assault on the German defences on either side of the River Somme. They do not appear to have been attracted to this sector by any special strategic prize. It was more a matter of convenience: along the river the British and French armies joined together. When the bargain was made, Joffre believed that a common action round this junction point would make it easier for him to retain control of the timing and direction of the offensive. Haig's agreement was qualified by private reservations. While General Rawlinson and the headquarters of the newly created Fourth Army studied the Somme lines, preparations for offensive operations in other British sectors continued. Haig's preference was for a summer campaign in Flanders; but he was not anxious to be drawn into the battles of attrition which Joffre believed to be necessary. But while the planners of both nations were still busy at their maps and sums, their chiefs were reminded that the initiative did not lie with them alone. At 0430 hours in the morning of February 21, 1916, the Germans fired the first shot of their opening barrage at Verdun. After drenching the

French defences with high explosive for eight hours, the German and French infantry locked in a dreadful struggle.

The events at Verdun soon put the British and French at variance in the matter of timing for their summer offensive. As more and more French divisions were drawn in to bolster the crumbling French line across the Meuse—from which they emerged exhausted and depleted after a period of days—it was only reasonable from the French point of view that the British should be asked to hasten the date of the Allied offensive. A little after 11 o'clock on the morning of Friday, May 26, Joffre came to Haig's headquarters to ask directly for an opening date. 'The moment I mentioned August 15,' Haig wrote in his diary, 'Joffre at once got very excited and shouted that "The French Army would cease to exist if we did nothing till then". The rest of us looked on at this outburst of excitement, and then I pointed out that, in spite of August 15 being the most favourable date for the British Army to take action, yet in view of what he had said regarding the unfortunate condition of the French Army, I was prepared to commence operations on July 1 or thereabouts. This calmed the old man, but I saw he had come to the meeting prepared to combat a refusal on my part, and was prepared to be very nasty.'

In the previous winter, the French offensive had been conceived as a massive venture employing 40 divisions from the Somme southward to Lassigny. It was hoped that the British would employ 25 divisions to the north of the river. Now on the last day of May, the French President, Prime Minister and Minister for War came from Paris to see Haig with the brief that 'one can and one must foresee the eventuality of the British army conducting the offensive'. The change of view had already been recognised by Haig. Recounting the events of the meeting in his diary, he remarked: 'The slow output of French heavy guns was pointed out and the need for supplying Verdun with everything necessary was recognised, and I said that *in view of the possibility of the British having to attack alone,* it was most desirable to bring to France the Divisions which the Allies held at Salonika. Beat the Germans here and we can make what terms we like!'

Haig was now in difficulty. Having agreed to attack on the Somme so as to combine directly with the French it was now clear that France might not participate. There was a British plan for an independent attack in the sector but it showed little promise. Flanders beckoned Haig strongly still.

'D' day agreed

Joffre was aware from the reports of his liaison staff at the British headquarters that Haig was not enthusiastic for the Somme project. He feared that, lacking a French presence, the British might withdraw altogether from offensive action in 1916. The Russians had achieved nothing in their assaults round Lake Narotch and were asking urgently for heavy ordnance to help them in a new operation. The Italians were calling similarly for help after their defeat in the Trentino. The needs of these allies might offer a ready excuse for British inactivity in France. But Joffre misconstrued Haig's reluctance; the question in the latter's mind was not 'whether?' but 'where?' When Joffre wrote blandly on June 3 to ask what notice Haig required to open the offensive on July 1, he obtained a straight answer—'12 days' notice for an attack on July 1 or later,' and a direct question, 'how many French divisions will be taking part?' Since Joffre's staff had been quite unable to find 20 divisions, the reply was vague: General Fayolle's Sixth Army would attack astride the Somme 'to support the British'. Now they had it. Fayolle had but 12 divisions and his assault frontage was limited to about eight miles. This contribution, necessarily diminished by the demands of Verdun, was but a fragment of the original scheme; but it was enough to ensure that the British would fight also on the Somme that summer.

The trenches of the British Fourth Army ran for 20 miles from the village of Hébuterne south across the Ancre to the Willow Stream by Fricourt, then east to the Bois de Maricourt. The wood was held by the French, Maricourt village just behind was shared by British and French companies. Two miles to the south lay the left bank of the Somme. The country here, both north and south of the river, is downland, open

grazing above rolling chalk hills with a scattering of woods. It had been a quiet sector. The woods and villages were mostly unbroken, the trees in full leaf; patches of the grassland were bright with larkspur.

Opposite both Rawlinson's and Fayolle's armies lay the *Second Army* of General Fritz von Below, comprised of three corps and, depleted by the removal of forces for the attack on Verdun, lacking any appreciable army reserve. In May, Below and his Chief-of-Staff, Grünert, became convinced that they were about to be attacked. From about Hébuterne to the Ancre, Below's regiments were on ground generally overlooked by the British though often hidden by woods and re-entrants. The Serre knoll was an important exception, offering an excellent view north-west to Hébuterne, west to the copses amongst the British trenches and south along the road to Beaucourt. Below the Ancre, the Germans held all the high ground to the valley of the Somme and south again across the Flaucourt plateau. Most importantly, the first line of German trenches had been cunningly dug amongst the many outcrops of the main ridge line, so as to command every approach from the west.

Aware of their enemy's advantages in observation, the British and French took care during their preparations, confining much of their movement and construction work to the night. They used wire netting, hessian and paint in camouflage successfully by day but had not the means or as yet the skill to deny all their activity to the air observers in aircraft or balloons. The very fact that the allied flying corps concentrated progressively to deny access to German aircraft and intensified their attacks on balloons confirmed that something of importance was happening to the west. The sightings of new roads, railways and hutments in rear, the glimpses of new battery positions, were more than enough to suggest what all this presaged.

While preparing to open the onslaught at Verdun, Falkenhayn had warned all army commanders that they must expect Allied relief attacks elsewhere. Since he would be unable to send reinforcements to any other point along the German line, he advised—and they would have needed very good reasons for ignoring his 'advice'—that each regimental front should be held in strength as far forward as possible. They should not surrender a metre of ground. If a section of trench should be lost it must be retaken immediately. The officers and men forward must understand that the order was to defend their position to the last man, to the last round; orders which would surely persuade them to fight tenaciously from the outset since they would realise that there was no hope of being told to fall back if pressure became intense. The consequences of this policy were twofold. First, as the majority of each division was within the range of the Allied field artillery, it was necessary to provide them with adequate shelter. Deep shafts were sunk into the chalk below the trenches and galleries were run out on either side, providing safe living quarters in dormitories for the soldiers and separate rooms for the officers. Fresh air was pumped in; stocks of bottled water, biscuits and tinned food were cached against emergencies when fresh rations could not be brought up daily. Secondly, surface strong points were provided a little in rear of each front trench to house

medium machine guns and many of these positions were constructed in reinforced concrete by the end of June. In certain areas, the strong points were connected by tunnels to form enclosed fortresses. Throughout the second line of defence—on average 4,000 yards behind the first—there were deep dugouts and a number of deep shafts and galleries. When Below warned Falkenhayn of his expectations, he was sent an additional detachment of 8-inch howitzers, captured from the Russians, and a reinforcement of labour units to speed the development of the third line, five miles behind the first. Between mid-March and the beginning of June, the German wire was consistently thickened in front of the forward defences.

Despite the progress made in preparations against enemy attack, Below and Grünert remained anxious. In each divisional area, almost all the infantry were committed to the first line; even the corps reserves had been tapped to man trenches at critical points between divisions. On May 25, Grünert proposed to Supreme Headquarters that they should make a preventive attack on the British front. He asked tentatively for more infantry. With the battle at Verdun at its height, there were none, though Falkenhayn made no objection to a local venture within their own resources. As encouragement, he sent two more batteries of artillery. By June 6, Below was more sanguine about the British threat but still very anxious about the French below the Somme. He reported that: *The preparations of the British in the area Serre-Gommecourt, as well as the increase of 29 emplacements of artillery in the past few days, detected by air photographs, lead to the conclusion that the enemy thinks first and foremost of attacking the projecting angles of Fricourt and Gommecourt. In view of the ground and the lie of the trenches, it is quite conceivable that he will attempt only to pin the front of* 26th Reserve Division *by artillery fire (that is, the ground immediately north and south of the Ancre valley), but he will not make a serious attack. To oppose (the French south of the Somme),* XVII Corps *is too weak, both in infantry and guns. Even against an enemy attack on a narrow front made only as a diversion the* Guard Corps *(on the extreme left of his line) is also too thin; it is holding 36 kilometres with 12 regiments, and behind it there are no reserves of any kind.*

It was on this day, June 6, that Haig accepted that he was committed to the Somme offensive. Perhaps due to the uncertainty, he had not given Rawlinson precise orders during the long preliminaries of reconnaissance and preparation, an omission which had inhibited Fourth Army commander. Yet, whatever his task was to be, Rawlinson was very clear by June that the enemy defences were formidable; any attempt to breach the two main lines would be costly. Imaginative and shrewd, he was also an ambitious man. In April, it is probable that he hoped to cover himself against failure by suggesting that: *It does not appear to me that the gain of 2 or 3 more kilometres of ground is of much consequence, or that the existing situation is so urgent to demand that we should incur very heavy losses in order to draw a large number of German reserves against this portion of our front. Our object rather seems to be to kill as many Germans as possible with the least loss to ourselves, and the best way to do*

The date is agreed. Early on Sunday morning the clouds cleared. It was Z day, Zero hour

Top: The British 8-inch Mk VI howitzer, the power behind the Somme barrage. *Range:* 10,000 yards. *Weight in action:* 9 tons 9 cwt

Centre: The British 6-inch 26 cwt howitzer. Designed in January 1915 to replace the 6-inch 30 cwt howitzer, this piece was coming into use by the time of the Somme. *Range:* 10,000 yards. *Weight in action:* 4 tons 6 cwt

Below: The guns at work—a painting by Hamlyn Reid entitled *Barrage on the Somme*

this appears to me to be to seize points of tactical importance which will provide us with good observation and which we may feel certain the Germans will counter-attack under disadvantages likely to conduce heavy losses.

Haig rebuked him for this limited view but it was June 16 before the strategic concept was finally made clear, when the principal objectives were issued to Fourth Army and subsidiaries to First, Second and Third, acting in support. In brief, Rawlinson was to seize the main feature in front of him between the Ancre and Montauban. If all went well, the cavalry under Gough should exploit any full breach of the enemy defence lines by passing through into the open country in the enemy rear while the infantry attack swung north towards Arras up the line of the enemy trenches. Alternatively, Haig's orders continued, 'after gaining our first objective as described we may find that a further advance eastwards is not advisable. In that case, the most profitable course will probably be to transfer our main efforts rapidly to another portion of the British front but leaving a sufficient force on the Fourth Army front to secure the ground gained, to compel the enemy to use up all his reserves and to prevent him from withdrawing them elsewhere.'

Between January and June, 19 divisions were sent to France to join the British Expeditionary Force. Eleven had seen active service before—some were Gallipoli veterans—the remainder were from the New Armies formed by Kitchener. By May, Rawlinson had 16 divisions in his army, including a share of those recently arrived, and had allocated three to each of his five corps headquarters. His plan envisaged an assault by two divisions in each corps with the third ready to exploit or reinforce. In retrospect, there is an ominous similarity in the orders issued within each formation for the first assault, even though the ground and the enemy in front of each division was markedly different. But it is easy to criticise, to forget that an operation was developing on a scale never attempted before by the British army. Its professional commanders still had much to learn in the handling of vast numbers of men; their communications were inadequate for the type of operation envisaged; many of the subordinate commanders and staffs were amateurs, the majority of the regimental officers and men raw. None knew this better than Haig. It may sometimes be said of him that he was overconfident in himself but he was seriously concerned to keep matters simple for the assault forces, without inhibiting the enterprise of the junior commanders. Stage by stage he discussed the tactics to be employed with Rawlinson, and with Allenby whose right flank corps was to attack Gommecourt as Rawlinson's men went forward.

Along the whole front from mid-June onwards there were to be local attacks and raids: no hint was to be given that one sector was more important than another. A barrage of some days' duration was to be fired by the Royal Artillery with the aim of breaking the enemy wire and destroying the other defences; eroding the strength of the German troops in the first line; reducing to as great an extent as possible their guns, howitzers and mortars by a great weight of counter battery fire; and striking the enemy's routes forward into the battle area. Because telephone lines were so often

Loading one of the 305-mm guns

cut, all British artillery fire for the assault was to be controlled by time. At a given time, zero hour, the guns would lift to let the infantry cross No-Man's Land into the first of the enemy trenches. After a time judged to be adequate to complete the subjection of these, the fire would lift again to permit a second advance. Provided the Germans knew and obeyed the rules of this theory, the general plan must succeed.

In the French sector, General Fayolle had borne with good humour the many visits paid to him. The British called periodically and a valuable friendship developed with Rawlinson and his headquarters. Amongst the French, Foch appeared often. As Commander of the northern group of armies it was his task to distil practical directions from the high sounding but vague orders issued by Joffre's staff for the offensive. Foch wished to delay the attack of Fayolle's army for at least several days after the British attack, believing that the French divisions would gain the advantage of surprise. Understandably, Rawlinson did not agree; one of Fayolle's corps, XX, was directly on his right on the north bank of the river. Any delay by the French here would uncover his flank. Foch continued to argue doggedly for his proposal and won eventually the concession that the I Colonial and XXXV Corps south of the river might attack a little after zero but on the same morning. The objective of XX Corps was Hem, where they expected to breach the enemy first line. The other two were directed to pass through both the first and second lines to capture the Flaucourt plateau. To support this attack, the French artillery was to fire for eight days beforehand, 117 heavy batteries supplementing the many field and medium guns.

The British artillery support for the offensive was unique. The preliminary bombardment was to be fired over five days, U, V, W, X and Y. On U and V days the gunners were to register and cut enemy barbed wire; on W, X and Y the shells were to rain on enemy defences while wire-cutting continued. Counter-battery fire would feature on every day. There would be checks and pauses to deceive the enemy, to persuade them that an assault had begun so that they would hasten up the steep ladders from their shelters to man the fire

strips only to be raked with shellfire. When these stratagems no longer tricked the foe, gas would be fired to persuade them that an assault had begun at last. The programme for Z day, the day of assault, was so arranged that the usual 80-minute bombardment at that time should be fired for only 65 minutes. It was hoped that the enemy would be sufficiently used to the former to stay below while the British infantry crossed.

This mass of shells and mortar bombs, high explosive, shrapnel and phosphorus gas was to fall upon a frontage of attack of 25,000 yards. 1,010 British field guns and howitzers, 427 heavies and 100 French pieces fired for Rawlinson's army. 2,000,000 shells and bombs lay stacked ready for their use.

Vague orders

As all the preparations went forward, there were a series of final crises among the Allied chiefs as to Z day. On June 12 the Germans renewed the assault at Verdun and Clemenceau sought to bring down Briand's government in Paris. Joffre urged Haig to bring forward the opening date to June 25. Haig agreed. On the evening of the 16th came a telephone call to say that Verdun was secure and Briand's government had won a vote of confidence. June 29, even July 1, would now be preferable, Joffre suggested, for Z day. After some demur, the 29th was accepted at GHQ. At 0700 hours on June 24, therefore, the first of the heavy guns was loaded and the gun position officer cried 'Fire'. The bombardment had begun.

Sunday the 25th was a fine warm day in contrast to two preceding days of summer storms. The Royal Flying Corps scouted or spotted for the guns. They found 102 enemy batteries and began early the counter-bombardment. But this was the last day of good weather for some time. Morning mist, low cloud and bursts of heavy rainfall hampered observation on the ground and in the air. Numbers of dud shells or fuses delayed still more the gunners' work. The high rate of fire wore seriously the buffer springs and smoothed those gun barrels which had already once been relined. On Wednesday, it was decided to go on firing until the 1st and assault on that day. Forward, the infantry trenches were manned by skeleton forces while the bulk of each battalion rested in such billets as could be found immediately in rear. On the Friday night, June 30, commanding officers consulted with their brigade commanders and there were some disquieting reports that long stretches of enemy wire remained uncut. Still the boom and bang of the bombardment, faithfully maintained by the weary gunners after a week, raised many hopes.

Early on the Saturday morning, July 1, the clouds cleared. Breakfast was eaten in the dark, kit was packed and dumped. Company guides began to lead their fellows forward across the dark wet ground. The German lines were quiet as the soldiers marched heavily into the foremost trenches, weighed down with full marching order: rifle and ammunition, grenades or bombs, a digging tool and perhaps some other special load. Below ground, the miners waited, sweating in the heat of the narrow tunnels leading to the mine chambers they had cut under the enemy positions.

The warm sun rose dispelling the mist. It was Z day. Zero hour approached.

For a third week, the gunners laboured . . .

Bayer Armee Museum Ingelstadt

Left: The British 60-pounder gun, Mark 1, breech loading
Range: 10,300 yards. *Height:* 6 feet. *Maximum width:* 6½ feet. *Length:* 21 feet 7 inches. *Weight of carriage with gun:* 58 cwt 1 lb. *Weight of shell:* 60 lbs. *Traverse:* 4° right to 4° left. *Rate of fire:* 2 rounds per minute

Top: A contemporary French painting shows horses killed by Allied counterbattery fire. The toll of animals that died during the Somme fighting was considerable. *Below:* The German 105-mm howitzer, used extensively on the Western Front. *Maximum range:* 6,300 yards. *Length of barrel:* 1.825 metres. *Elevation:* − 10° to 40°. *Traverse:* 2° left to 2° right. *Weight in firing position:* 2,449 lbs. *Weight of shell:* 30 lbs (approx)

John Batchelor

The weapons—large and small— of the attack 'organised for amateurs by amateurs'

1 *Top to bottom:* Canadian Ross rifle Mark III .303 calibre; Canadian Ross rifle Mark II .303; .303 long Lee Enfield rifle Mark I; .303 rifle No 1 with short magazine; .303 pattern 14 (P14) rifle. The Ross rifles have been the cause of considerable controversy. Issued by the Canadian government to their troops, they often proved troublesome in muddy conditions and were frequently discarded in favour of the SMLE. However, this rifle had a large following and was used extensively for sniping purposes. **2** *Top:* .303 P14 rifle fitted with telescopic sight. Rifle .303–inch, No 1 Mark III, Short Magazine Lee Enfield with telescopic sight. **3** .303 Vickers machine gun Mark 1. Originally called the Vickers Maxim, this gun was adopted by the British in 1912 and has an extremely sound reputation.

Opposite page, top: The German 5·9-inch howitzer. *Elevation:* 0° to 45°. *Traverse:* 4° left to 4° right. *Maximum range:* 9,296 yards. *Weight:* 92 lbs. *Opposite page, left:* The French 120-mm short gun, made in about 1890 but nonetheless in service throughout the war. *Opposite page, bottom:* The British Mark 7 naval gun on an artificial mounting which adapted it for use on the battlefield. *Bottom:* The British Mark 1 9.2-inch howitzer. *Maximum range:* 10,000 yards. *Rate of fire:* 2 rounds per minute. *Below:* The latest toll of deaths on the Somme

British 158 786   103 000 German

French 49 859

July 2-14

John Batchelor

4 *Top left:* Oval grenade — 'Egg'. *Top right:* Hand grenade, the Mills Bomb. *Centre:* An unidentified percussion grenade. *Bottom:* Grenade No 2, or Tonite Grenade. **5** *Top:* Two flare pistols by Scott and Co of Birmingham. *Left:* Wire cutters to be attached to a rifle muzzle. *Bottom:* One of the more bloodthirsty 'specials' improvised at trench level. **6** *Top to bottom:* Newton rifle grenade; a cheap form of Hales rifle grenade; Hales grenade; hand grenade. **7** The Webley .455 Automatic pistol Mark 1 No 2, with detachable stock and holster — again made by Scott and Co. **8** *Top left:* Webley .455 pistol Mark V. *Centre left:* Webley-Fosbery automatic revolver .455. *Bottom left:* Webley automatic .455 Mark 1 No 2. *Centre:* Webley-Green .455 revolver. *Right:* Webley .455 pistol Mark VI No 1

Jack Pia

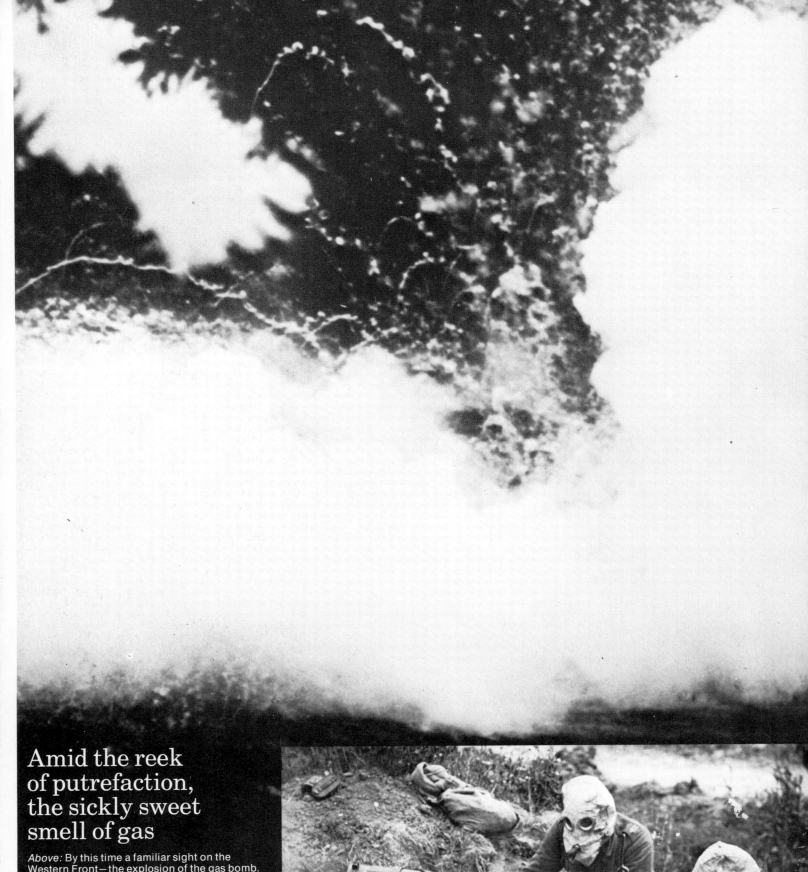

Amid the reek of putrefaction, the sickly sweet smell of gas

Above: By this time a familiar sight on the Western Front—the explosion of the gas bomb. *Near right:* British machine gunners wearing their gas masks. They worked with the masks pinned to their shirts, ready to be pulled on when the gas bells clanged. *Centre:* Though only partially effective, the gas mask was an essential part of life at the front; here, men of the RGA operate a Fullerphone. *Far right:* A gas sentry ringing a make-shift alarm

The front now had the aura of a decaying suburb . . .

Fortified ruins

German front line

No-Mans Land

British front line

**Forward Observation
Officers Post**
with telephone line
(partly buried
to battery), containing
FOO and signallers
to observe enemy
movements

Average range
2000-5000 yards
depending on
ground

Gunlayer to put
on range and angles
and sight aiming
post.

Man to open and
close breech after
shell and charge
are loaded and
fired

Three men to set
fuses and handle
shells and charges
as required

Guns camouflaged
in dip in ground

NCO in charge of
gun. He received and
acknowledged orders
by holding out his
right arm.

Signallers and Officer
in charge of guns.
Orders given vocally
as to range, angles,
and rate of fire

Telephone line
to wagon and horse
lines, store,
ammunition, limbers etc.
Average distance from
guns 1000 to 2500
yards according to
roads available.

Line to Brigade HQ

Top: Resourcefulness in adversity. Royal Engineers build a makeshift bridge over the Ancre swamps near Aveluy. Rain had been falling for several weeks, breaking up the ground, and the infantrymen were often wet to the skin even before they went into battle. *Left:* The chart shows the layout and establishment of an 18-pounder battery. *Above:* Exhaustion sets in: British troops sleep in their trenches near Thiepval Ridge. This area was not as badly damaged as that south of the Somme, but rain and cold had seriously debilitated the troops

On July 29, Sir William Robertson, the Chief of the Imperial General Staff in London, wrote to Haig:

'The Powers that be are beginning to get a little uneasy in regard to the situation. The casualties are mounting up and they were wondering whether we are likely to get a proper return for them . . . In general, what is bothering them is the probability that we may soon have to face a bill of 2-300,000 casualties with no very great gains additional to the present. It is thought that the primary object—relief of pressure on Verdun—has to some extent been achieved.'

The relief of pressure on Verdun had never been the primary object of the summer campaign; it had simply been the reason for hastening its opening. On this document, Haig wrote in his own hand, 'Not exactly the letter of a CIGS.'

Next day, August 1, he replied to Robertson in London, setting out the strategic advantages won during the preceding month by the British Expeditionary Force. In his diary on August 3, he summarised these views and his own intentions:

Principle on which we should act. Maintain our offensive. . . . *It is my intention:*

(a) To maintain a steady pressure on Somme battle.

(b) To push my attack strongly whenever and wherever the state of my preparations and the general situation make success sufficiently probable to justify me in doing so, but not otherwise.

(c) To secure against counterattack each advantage gained and prepare thoroughly for each advance.

Proceeding thus, I expect to be able to maintain the offensive well into the autumn.

It would not be justifiable to calculate on the enemy's resistance being completely broken without another campaign next year.

Some of Haig's critics have seized on this

THE SOMME
Debut of the Tank

Flers-Courcelette was Haig's third effort to break through on the Somme. This time he had a new weapon—the tank. Though slow and unreliable, the few tanks available gave the infantry worthwhile support, but all to no avail—the Germans were able to plug the breaches in their line. *Anthony Farrar-Hockley. Above:* D17, which helped to take Flers, on September 21, 1916

last sentence as a true indication of his state of mind: a growing pessimism as a result of the inability of his armies to make a breach in the German line. There is little evidence to suggest that he had lost confidence in the campaign. Just over four weeks had passed since Z-day. He had planned and stocked for a seven-week battle. There was evidence that Falkenhayn was weakening other sectors of the Western Front to reinforce the Somme; if he could judge the time nicely, it might yet prove possible to break through north or Arras in conjunction with a blow above the Somme.

The plans drafted at this time, the attempts to sound out the line to the north—however abortive—do not reflect a picture of a desperate commander but of one pressing forward hopefully in a great endeavour, his chief anxiety being to discern and exploit the opportunities of the battlefield. Certainly he was misled by the erroneous reports of his Chief of Intelligence, Brigadier-General Charteris, and by such subordinate commanders as General Monro, who directed an Australian and a British division in a 'sounding out' attack opposite Lille in July with chilling ineptitude. But there were indisputably masses of prisoners and an abundance of German dead still lay above and below ground between the Ancre and the Somme. The prisoners told of being drawn in from north and south to the Somme sector. Their stories of terror and disaster were corroborated by the quantities of German weapons and equipment captured or seen to be smashed in the portions of the German line now in Allied hands or under view.

Such fears as Haig had were more precise than those of the Cabinet. He was worried—and with reason—by the low standard of staff work: the British army had expanded a hundredfold, and while it had taken in many able and highly intelligent civilians as staff officers, the majority lacked the basic and essential knowledge which could only be gained in a fighting unit. In the fighting units, many of the best and most experienced leaders had been lost by death or wounds during the terrible actions since 1914. How could he ensure that the staffs directed, and the regimental officers and men fought, the battle ahead to gain a positive and advantageous end? The Commander-in-Chief's remedy was a keener scrutiny of his army commanders' plans, a readiness now to intervene at once if they did not conform to his requirements and the continual reminder to every headquarters he visited that they must make 'thorough preparation' for every operation.

One aspect of this preparation was the capture of certain German positions which remained as outworks of defence along the ridge: Thiepval, Mouquet Farm and the high point between Pozières and Martinpuich; High Wood; the cramped front of Delville Wood; Ginchy; Guillemont; Falfemont Farm and Leuze Wood on the long spur above the Combles ravine. A series of local operations was begun to take these positions during August. These operations, limited in scope and success, rarely excite interest or comment now, yet were among the bitterest actions of the war. Deter-

mined not to repeat a frontal attack on Thiepval, Gough attempted a pincer movement by V and II Corps while the ANZAC inched forward from Pozières, clawing into the German defences. High Wood remained impenetrable. The gains in Delville Wood were partially lost to a counterattack and so it became necessary to begin a recovery operation just when it was hoped the men there might be rested. After breathless, bloody scrambles along 'the terrible road into Guillemont, straight, desolate, swept by fire', the ruined village fell at last to the devoted 20th (Light) Division. Ginchy succumbed to an ardent assault by the depleted battalions of the 16th (Irish) Division. Slowly the line swung forward to the edge of Leuze Wood.

Spectacular advance

These engagements occupied August and the first part of September. Meanwhile, the French Sixth Army had made a spectacular advance along the north bank of the Somme, following the capture of Falfemont Farm by the 1st Norfolks on September 5. No longer hampered by the enfilade fire poured out from the site of the farm and the posts dug into the edge of the Combles ravine, no longer under the eyes of the German artillery observers in the cornfield above, the French left flank moved on with a rush to catch up the divisions advancing through Cléry and Ommiècourt. An attempt by the Colonial Corps to take the southern outskirts of Combles as it passed failed; here the Germans were protected by masonry and steel above ground and found absolute safety from artillery in the ancient caves and galleries below. It was agreed between Foch and Haig that they should envelop the town and cut it off. But as Fayolle began to swing his line of assault to the north-east the weather changed, a series of heavy showers turning the tracks once more into mud. The process of reliefs was delayed, the forward movement of the guns hampered. It was the 12th before the French began to attack again. For a few hours, the assault was indecisive, as scores of small groups of infantry disappeared into the German front trenches where a ferocious struggle seemed to be taking place. Then, before noon, the brigade on the right of the Colonial Corps was seen to be in pursuit south-east of Le Forest, pushing swiftly on to capture the spurs above the Bois Marrières. The local trench lines were now broken open: the remainder of the Colonial Corps advanced north-east round Combles to capture the road to Rancourt. For a little while Foch urged Fayolle to push on to Sailly-Saillisel but the infantry was ex-

hausted by its struggles through the mud and the intense German shell fire. Fayolle had to tell Rawlinson that he would be unable to assault again with the British when the main offensive began on September 15, but promised, as before, the fullest support of his guns. Not that the French had need to make apologies; they had carried the whole Allied line round in a spectacular turning movement. Small wonder that Haig agreed with the ever optimistic Joffre that they might now be on the eve of a great triumph.

Haig's plan for the third major offensive above the Somme envisaged three stages. In the first, the infantry of the Reserve Army and Fourth Army should capture what remained of the original German line along the ridge, their movement forward being helped perhaps by the 'tanks', the new armoured caterpillars of the Heavy Section, Machine Gun Corps. In the second stage, the Reserve Army would hold the left flank of the captured ground, while Rawlinson would dispose a force to defend his own right. The remainder of Fourth Army would complete the breach of the German line somewhere between the Albert-Bapaume road and the village of Flers, and once this was completed a cavalry corps of five divisions would pass through into the country behind, the third stage.

Above: The ruins of the main street of Flers, reduced to rubble but not, as yet, obliterated by the British and German guns. *Below:* Over the top: an officer leads his party out of the comparative safety of a sap into the bullet-swept waste of No-Man's Land and the German lines

In concept, it was the strategic plan of July 1, though now on a narrower front of about 12,000 yards. Of the 14 fresh divisions, eight went to Rawlinson, and six to Gough, with a provisional allotment of 36-42 and 18-24 tanks respectively.

Gough continued his attempts to envelop the rubble of Thiepval through the second half of August into early September. He was very much aware of the formidable defences which he ordered II Corps and I ANZAC to overcome, but kept them at it so as to be able 'to shoulder the enemy off the western end of the ridge when the offensive begins', as he told Birdwood, commander of the ANZAC. As a secondary benefit of his preliminary operations, he hoped to gain space on either side of the Albert-Bapaume road. Shortly, the Canadian Corps would arrive to relieve the Australians and from their narrow territory, perhaps 2,500 yards across to the east of Pozières, he had to launch forces which would prove irresistible. Thus, to their very last day in the line, the Australians were kept at the deadly task of securing Mouquet Farm and the *Fabeck Graben*. The rain which checked Fayolle added similarly to their burdens and, in the end, denied them success. They were not sorry to see the Canadians coming in to take over.

Reliefs were taking place similarly along most of the Fourth Army front. High Wood remained in German hands. The south-east corner of Delville Wood contained three German machine gun posts, a tiny salient connected to the switch trench of Armin's defences by Hop and Ale Alleys, Pint Trench and Lager Lane. Elsewhere, the preliminary operations had cleared the start lines on which Haig had insisted. All formation plans were complete by September 11 and the guns began the bombardment at 0600 hours on the 12th.

A repeated error

Rawlinson's first plan, a deliberate and limited advance on each of three successive nights, had been rejected by Haig. He foresaw the same loss of initiative which, as he now knew, had held back Congreve on July 1. Rawlinson's attempts to justify his proposal on the grounds that night operations would preserve the secret of the tanks were not accepted. GHQ orders on August 31 reminded both Gough and Rawlinson that: *The exploitation of success to the full during the first few hours is essential to a decision and it must be impressed on all Corps and Divisional Commanders that the situation calls for great boldness and determination on their part. It lies with them to feel the pulse of the battle and to turn favourable opportunities at once to the fullest account ... The necessity for great vigour and determination in this attack, and the great results that may be achieved by it, must be impressed on all ranks as soon as considerations of secrecy will permit of their being informed of what is required of them ... The remarks ... apply more particularly to the Fourth Army as regards the earlier operations, during which the Reserve Army, acting as a pivot, will have a more limited scope ...*

Rawlinson's revised plan subscribed to these requirements. While assaulting along his entire front early on Z-day, aided by the tanks, his main effort would be directed towards the capture of Geudecourt, Lesboeufs and Morval before nightfall. These three villages lay beyond the

German trench system – a few shallow unwired and unconnected defences apart – and their possession should certainly mean a breach had been opened. We do not know whether Rawlinson believed this operation to be practicable or whether he simply offered it in the belief that it would be more acceptable to his Commander-in-Chief. Some of Rawlinson's comments to friends and subordinates, some of his documents may make us suspect the latter. Why else should he be wondering whether '... we can maintain ourselves on this high(!) waterless(!) and roadless plateau after we have captured it'?

On August 27, Rumania entered the war on the Allied side and almost at once began operations against Austria-Hungary. The event persuaded the Kaiser finally to call Hindenburg and Ludendorff from the Eastern Front to give alternative advice on the future conduct of the war. In the aloof style of the third person which he used for his war memoirs, Falkenhayn tells us that he '... had to reply [to the Kaiser] that he could only regard this summoning of a subordinate commander, without previous reference to him, for a consultation on a question the solution of which lay in his province alone, as a breach of his authority that he could not accept and as a sign that he no longer possessed the absolute confidence of the Supreme War Lord which was necessary for the continuance of his duties. He, therefore, begged to be relieved of his appointment.' The Kaiser acceded – had perhaps counted on the request for relief – and by a happy arrangement sent his former Chief of the General Staff to command the forces of the Central Powers against Rumania.

The new brooms arrived to see the Kaiser at Pless on the morning of August 29, where General von Lyncker, senior imperial aide-de-campe, informed them that '... *Feldmarschall* von Hindenburg had been appointed Chief of the General Staff of the Field Army and that I [Ludendorff] was to be Second Chief. The title "First Quartermaster-General" seemed to me more appropriate ... but in any case, I had been expressly assured that I should have joint responsibility in all decisions and in all measures that might be taken.'

On September 5, the two victors from the Eastern Front visited the front against the West. Due to the continuing onslaught on the Somme, they made for Cambrai, where Crown Prince Rupprecht of Bavaria had recently established an army group headquarters to control all forces engaged in the battle. All army commanders and chiefs-of-staff in the West were present. From the Somme, *Colonel von Lossberg in his serious way, and Colonel Bronsart von Schellendorf with his usual vivacity, supplemented General von Kuhl's report of the battle ... The loss of ground up to date appeared to me of little importance in itself. We could stand that; but the question how this, and the progressive falling off of our fighting power of which it was symptomatic, was to be prevented, was of immense importance.*

I attached great significance to what I learned at Cambrai about our infantry, about its tactics and preparation. Without doubt it fought too doggedly, clinging too resolutely to the mere holding of ground, with the results that the losses were heavy. The deep dugouts and cellars often became fatal mantraps. The use of the rifle was be-

ing forgotten, hand-grenades had become the chief weapon, and the equipment of the infantry with machine guns and similar weapons had fallen far behind the enemy. The Feldmarschall *and I could for the moment only ask that the front line should be held more lightly, the deep underground works be destroyed, and all trenches and posts be given up if the retention of them were unnecessary to the maintenance of the position as a whole, and likely to be the cause of heavy losses.*

A policy reversal.

So the policy for defence was to be profoundly changed – almost reversed. It is arguable that Falkenhayn's rule of holding everything had sapped the strength from the assaults of the Allies; but if it had done that it had sapped even more the long-term power of the Germans to resist. In the counterattacks on the Australians at Pozières and during the defence of the line, for example, the *18th Reserve Division* had lost 178 officers and 8,110 soldiers between July 24 and August 9. In every purely defensive action from Mid-August to September 10 from Thiepval to Courcelette, the average loss in each battalion was just over 40% of its strength, this proportion being that of those men killed, mortally wounded or sufficiently seriously incapacitated to be evacuated behind the corps casualty stations. Within 72 hours of Hindenburg and Ludendorff leaving Cambrai, new orders had been received in all regiments along the Western Front concerning the policy for defence. Just prior to the third British offensive, therefore, a high measure of tactical initiative was restored to corps and divisional commanders in the German line.

Five German divisions now awaited the assault between the Ancre and Combles, the latter area being occupied by the *185th*, which had been in the line on July 1 and had now returned, reinforced, for a second tour. All formation commanders expected an offensive. Though the Allied air forces still held their superiority, a few German scouts had penetrated their patrols and the reports of pilots and observers confirmed those of the kite balloon crews that roads and dumps were everywhere expanding. The latter had spotted some 'large armoured cars' moving behind the British front – probably tanks – but the observation does not appear to have excited German Intelligence. British and Australian prisoners captured in the preceding fortnight had little to tell; and the French falling into German hands by Combles thought that their allies wanted only to capture the ground immediately on the left. But when the Allied bombardment began at 0600 hours on the 12th and when the extensive night-firing programme took up the work at 0630 hours that evening and the reports of wire-cutting came back from every sector, the expectation of assault became conviction.

A common mood appears to have entered the Canadian, New Zealand and British troops waiting for Z-hour; a mood which overtook them when it became confirmed that the 15th was to be Z-day. Between those small numbers who, for one reason or another, were absolutely fearless and those who were haunted sleeping and waking by terror, the majority seem to have been possessed by a form of exhilaration tempered by anxiety. The veterans admitted that

Above: Success! As the French attackers sweep into a trench, its late German defenders flee.
Below: Albert Cathedral, and its famous 'leaning Virgin'. Legend had it that the war would end shortly after she finally toppled. The prediction did come true—though the British helped . . .

they were impressed by the extent and weight of preparation. Novices were eager to be engaged in the fighting.

In the last hour of daylight on the 14th, the assault battalions finished their meals, put on their webbing, heavy with ammunition and marched quietly forward into their assembly trenches. A proportion of the support battalions who followed them later were tired after carrying loads of ammunition and supplies forward during the

day. It was cool enough for those men at rest in the trenches to wear greatcoats that night. But while some slept, the roads and tracks around Pozières, Bazentin le Petit, Longueval, Ginchy and Guillemont were busy as guides, porters and messengers passed to and fro in the moonlight.

The roaring engines of the tanks were scarcely noticed against the rumbling night bombardment. Guides with torches led forward the ungainly caterpillars, but not all succeeded in reaching their starting points. The most successful were the six supporting the Canadians. As planned, three arrived at the rendezvous 500 yards north of Pozières and three by the mill site on the road to Bapaume. Other than these, two took up their station behind the 15th (Scottish) Division for the assault on Martinpuich, two came into position between the two assault brigades of the 50th (Northumbrian), below High Wood were three (instead of four), four reached the 2nd New Zealand Brigade, seven of ten took up station for the 41st Division between the northern end of Longueval and the track leading north from Delville Wood, one of three reached the north-east of Delville Wood, one the road running away from the wood to Ginchy and from Ginchy to Leuze Wood, only nine of the 16 allotted to XIV Corps arrived.

The single tank which had stationed itself correctly on the road leading from Delville Wood to Ginchy was under the command of Lieutenant H. W. Mortimore. It was numbered D1—tank number 1 of D Company. At 0520 hours it lumbered into action, firing towards the Germans as it moved. Behind it were two rifle companies of 6th King's Own Yorkshire Light Infantry. The few Germans in Hop Alley were astounded by its appearance and quickly surrendered. Covered by the tank, the remainder of the KOYLI hurried on towards Ale Alley to complete the capture of this longer trench, prior to the main assault. Before they could reach it, they were caught in enfilade by machine gun posts in several nearby craters. All the officers were killed or wounded but the surviving sergeants took command, saw to the bombing of the crater posts, cleared Ale Alley and had their men ready for zero. Lieutenant Mortimore and his crew, the first ever to take a tank into action, were following them when, by chance, they received two direct hits by shells. Two of the men inside were killed but the remainder of the crew jumped clear.

The creeping barrage

The sun rose at 0540 hours on the morning of the 15th. Behind, the guns and howitzers and mortars boomed and banged as the British and French batteries main-tained their fire; overhead the shells and bombs swished: beyond, they burst in flashes of flame and splashes of smoke. There was no abatement as Z-hour approached at 0620 hours. To the minute, the infantry began to leave their trenches to draw up to the edge of their own field artillery fire which at zero plus six minutes was due to start creeping ahead of them at the rate of 50 yards a minute until halting just beyond the trenches of the first objective.

The six tanks allotted to the Canadian assault had been ordered to advance in two groups of three on either side of the road to Bapaume. When they began the final run up in darkness a number of the infantry ahead were already fighting—ejecting the last of a series of bombing raids into their trenches begun at 0300 hours that morning, apparently seeking Allied prisoners. At Z-hour, six assault battalions followed the creeping barrage north-east towards Courcelette, keeping pace with their barrage, searching out swiftly and vigorously each German trench until, by 0700 hours, they had captured the Sugar Factory 1,200 yards beyond their start line. Indeed, they had made such excellent progress that they had outstripped the tanks, one of which had broken down behind the line, while three others had become stuck or bogged among the German trenches captured. The two survivors came on faithfully and caused a number of Germans in positions on either flank of the Sugar Factory to surrender as they came forward. Embarked on a tide of success, the Canadians pushed on steadily through the day to capture Courcelette, despite increasing shellfire from the German medium guns and howitzers. Northwest of Pozières they secured two extensive stretches of *Fabeck Graben* by dusk and brought their line within grenade range of Mouquet Farm.

Next to the Canadians, the 15th (Scottish) Division hastened forward at zero hour, passing into its own creeping barrage at several points in its eagerness. Behind it came one tank—the other had been hit by shellfire just after zero—which gave much help in the clearing out of captured trenches. At 1500 hours that afternoon, the 6th Cameron Highlanders advanced to clear the last of the Germans from Martinpuich. Beside a huge bag of prisoners, the division had taken during the day a field battery and a howitzer in an action lasting 11 hours.

To the right of the Scottish division was the 50th, and right again the 47th. Before the 47th stood the splintered trunks of High Wood. General Pulteney, commander of III Corps, had ruled, against the advice of the divisional commander, that the tanks should enter the wood to assist in its capture, a decision that is only comprehensible when it is known that he had never come sufficiently far forward to take a close look at this dreadful obstacle dominating his front. Of the four tanks to hand, one ditched at the outset, the leader of the others reached the nearest German trench, which it raked with its machine guns, before a shell set the hull on fire. The other two were unable to find a way through the broken trees and sought a route towards the east. In the confusion, they broke back into their own lines to fire on men of the waiting London Regiment.

The consequence of this setback was that the flank and rear defences of High Wood were not assailed. As soon as the British barrage had passed, the machine guns on the reverse slopes opened a rapid fire on the 50th Division advancing briskly from the west. Caught in enfilade, the 50th was driven back. There it remained while the assault battalions of the 47th struggled vainly at the edge of the trees. About 1100 hours, the brigadier of the 140th Brigade—on the right of the 47th Divisional front—brought his trench mortars into position to open rapid fire. In seven minutes they fired 750 bombs and while the last of these were still in the air the Londoners advanced again on the wood with grenades and rifles in every expectation of a grim fight.

But suddenly the garrison had had enough. Exhausted, some demoralised, stained and filthy, the Bavarian soldiers stood up by sections, platoons and finally companies to surrender. Two months and one day had passed since High Wood lay open to General Horne for the taking. Now at last it passed into British hands.

General Horne's corps was now next in line to the east. As a consequence of Rawlinson's change of plan, he had the

The central sector of the front, with the skeleton of High Wood in the background, after it had been cleared by units of 47th Division

Imperial War Museum

crucial task of capturing the Gird Trench and Gird Support covering Guedecourt village, 4,000 yards north-north-east of his trenches. East again was Cavan's XIV Corps, directed to open the right hand side of the corridor as the Canadians and III Corps were to open the left.

Cavan's corps had three divisions in the line: left to right, the Guards, the 6th and the 56th. Two tanks were available to go forward with the 56th on the extreme right flank to assist in the capture of Bouleaux Wood. The assault battalions were not confident as zero hour approached; many knew that the guns had not cut the wire lying in hollows in front of the German positions. Helped by the tanks they scrambled into the nearest German trenches but were caught on the wire whenever assaults were launched across the Ginchy-Combles road. One of the tanks was hit by a shell while firing into The Loop, 300 yards from the edge of Combles. The other caught fire after it was bombed by a party of the *28th Reserve Regiment.*

Pulverising bombardment

The 6th Division faced the notorious Quadrilateral, held by the *21st Bavarians.* Several efforts had been made to capture this system of fortified posts following the fall of Guillemont and Ginchy but all had failed. Fresh troops, the pulverising bombardment arranged to open the offensive — more powerful than the Royal Artillery had ever fired in its long history — and the presence of the tanks raised hopes that it would fall on September 15. The fresh troops — the 6th Division — did not fail to leave their trenches promptly. The artillery had pounded the target area, but, as on every previous occasion, the majority of the shells had exploded before or beyond the cunningly sited galleried machine gun emplacements. One tank alone reached the rendezvous, from which it blundered into the 9th Royal Norfolks, waiting quietly for zero hour, opening fire on them by mistake. A company commander bravely approached the flustered crew to point out the error. Without waiting for zero hour the tank advanced along the railway line, fired into Straight Trench above the Quadrilateral and then retired, damaged. At zero, the infantry of 6th Division advanced, the creeping barrage of doubtful value as it was split by lanes left open for the absent tanks. Four battalions assaulted and lost heavily; two followed and their casualties joined those already thickly scattered along the machine gun arcs of the Quadrilateral. Having broken the 6th Division's assault, the Bavarians fired south to deny movement by the 56th Division into Bouleaux Wood, and northward into the flank of the Guards.

The eyes of the Guards' commanding officers were on the village of Lesboeufs and the triangle of roads leading northwest from it to Guedecourt. This was their objective, 3,600 yards from their trenches. Such tanks as had reached Ginchy either broke down, were quickly damaged, or disappeared in an irrelevant direction. Like the 6th, the Guards' infantry advanced alone at zero. But the creeping barrage was unbroken and perfectly timed. Thirty yards behind their own shells, four assault battalions advanced steadily over the cratered ground. As soon as they drew level with the Quadrilateral, however, the right flank came under heavy fire; the left was meanwhile being caught in enfilade from Pint Trench and Lager Lane. Next, Straight Trench opened fire. The leading companies began to double forward, charging into the German trenches. Behind came elements of the support battalions. Dug-outs and shelters were searched and then the survivors took stock. Three-quarters of the officers had been killed, two thirds of the soldiers. The senior commanding officer, Lieutenant-Colonel John Campbell of the 3rd Coldstreams, held a council to reorganise the force and to decide how far they had advanced. Mistakenly they believed, and signalled to the rear, that they were on the final objective.

Some time before 1100 hours Campbell realised his mistake and led a second advance. They had lost their own barrage and at once attracted German shells. The ground was torn beyond recognition: no stone of Lesboeuf's stood sufficiently in silhouette to guide them. When at last they stopped, they were a little over half way to the village; they had advanced just far enough to open the right flank for the breaching operations of XV Corps.

Horne had three divisions of XV Corps in the line: the New Zealanders, the 41st and the 14th — the latter two in or just forward of Delville Wood. Helped by their tanks, ardent in advance, the infantry of these formations stepped quickly into the first German position, the more readily as the foremost platoons were actually inside their own barrage. The machine guns in High Wood hit 80 to 90 New Zealanders during the advance but by 0700 hours the first objective was completely captured. German shelling added to the confusion in the captured positions.

When the advance was resumed, the New Zealanders were hampered by uncut wire. Machine guns from the direction of Flers began to engage all groups moving in the open. Yet despite continuing losses and the progressive break-up of units, the infantry swept on so that, a little before 0820 hours, two small bands of the 12th East Surreys reached the wire covering Flers village. Of the two officers present, both subalterns, one was killed while crossing; the other scrambled on to search out the remaining Germans.

About this time a German field gun, concealed nearby, opened fire. Detachments of the West Kents, Surreys and Hampshires still behind the Flers wire drew together while one or two young second-lieutenants discussed what they should do. Then a tank appeared, D17 under command of Lieutenant Stuart Hastie. Slewing round on its caterpillar tracks, the tank advanced, 'fire spitting from its guns'. Three other tanks were seen to be raking the eastern defences of the village. In a spontaneous movement, the infantry parties ran forward to follow D17 into the ruins.

Overhead, aircraft of 1st Brigade, Royal Flying Corps, saw a triumph and reported it to Horne's headquarters at 1100 hours. The aim of the offensive had been achieved in a morning: a complete breach had been opened in the German line.

Good liaison

During the morning, the corps' commanders were in their headquarters, from which they could speak by telephone to Rawlinson at Fourth Army or forward to their divisional commanders. Thanks to the daring determination of the Royal Flying Corps' pilots and observers, the corps and army commanders had more timely and accurate information of events in the line of battle than the divisional generals. Thus Cavan knew quickly that Colonel John Campbell and the foremost Guards were not at Lesboeufs. He knew that the 6th and 56th Divisions were checked before the Quadrilateral and at Bouleaux Wood, and made several attempts to help them on with the corps' artillery. Similarly, Horne at XV Corps headquarters took action to exploit his success. He spoke to General Lawford of the 41st Division at 1120 hours and told him to push on at all costs. The corps' reserve, 21st Division, was told to begin moving forward its leading brigade. Before noon, then, action was being taken to exploit success.

Unfortunately for the British, the situation in the breach was deteriorating. While the German *First Army* headquarters ordered every reserve unit forward of Bapaume to be committed to seal the breach, corps and army artillery switched the majority of their guns on to the area of Flers and the approaches to it through Longueval and Delville Wood. In the ensuing shellfire, four of the six commanding officers surviving were killed or wounded and with them many of their seconds-in-command, adjutants and company commanders. Early in the afternoon, the brigade-major of the 122nd Brigade, Gwyn Thomas, came forward to Flers to reorganise the fragments of units.

He arrived just in time. The lack of any communication in the little garrison — perhaps 80 strong — had induced a sense of uncertainty and isolation. Major Thomas took a company of engineers into infantry service, drew in two companies of the Middlesex and part of the brigade machine guns to establish a defence along the line of the third objective. The posts on the left were united with the New Zealanders. To the right of the village, Brigadier-General Clemson came up with about 200 men and returned for the remainder of the Middlesex. He and Thomas were anticipating their army commander's wishes for, already, Rawlinson had issued orders to reorganise and consolidate ready for the attack next day.

The sky darkened with rain clouds; rain fell intermittently through the night. Next day, there was insufficient infantry to mount a full assault and time was spent in exploiting whatever local opportunities offered. The gun and howitzer batteries moved forward: the bulk of the cavalry moved back. All day the German guns maintained heavy fire on the sector of attack. The clouds hampered the counter-battery work of the aerial observers. The Germans moved in five relief divisions.

The rain continued, British reliefs were delayed and the date for a renewed assault was successively postponed, eventually cancelled. A heavy counterattack fell on the French which, though repelled, employed the last of their immediate reserves.

The battle of Flers-Courcelette was thus a one-day affair in so far as it was a battle of promise. It was a novel operation because tanks were used for the first time. It was a remarkable action for the valour and endurance of those engaged.

THE TANK STORY

Foreseen before the war by H. G. Wells and other fiction writers, it is possible that the advent of armour was delayed by the mistrust and apathy of the military authorities. Here *Kenneth Macksey* discusses the delays that held up the introduction of the revolutionary weapon, the tank

On June 1, 1915, Lieutenant-Colonel Ernest Swinton heard that his appointment as 'Eyewitness' to the British army in France was to be terminated. That same day he submitted a paper to GHQ espousing the cause of 'Armoured Machine-Gun Destroyers'. Pointing out that it might be possible to blast a way with artillery through the German trenches he wrote: 'this is not at present within our power'—but he was adamant that the employment of 'petrol tractors on the caterpillar principle, . . . armoured with hardened steel plates proof against the German *steel-cored, armour piercing and reversed bullets,* and armed with—say—two Maxims and a Maxim 2-pounder gun' would enable machine guns to be engaged on advantageous terms.

Swinton was following up the idea he had proposed in 1914 and which, by various and devious channels through GHQ, the War Office, the Admiralty and industry were beginning to take shape in the concept of a new type of fighting vehicle. Not that fighting vehicles in themselves were an innovation: from the third millenium BC there had been chariots and a succession of vehicles armoured by hides, wood or metal, and for the past 20 years or more most of the ingredients from which a heavy motorised fighting vehicle could be assembled had been in existence either on the drawing board or as actual hardware in the hands of practical operators. The original spark ignition engine, devised in 1885 by Gottlieb Daimler, had been developed to the stage at which over 100 horse-power could be produced by a relatively compact power plant; various types of caterpillar tracks or footed wheels were in commercial use—particularly in the United States, where machines built by the Holt Company were in use helping to open up undeveloped territory. The British firm of Ruston Hornsby had also made a notable contribution but had then sold its patents to Holts in 1912. Armoured cars were in action on all fronts, manufactured by Austrians, Germans, French, Italians, British and Russians for use on open ground, though not where the trench systems made movement by wheeled vehicles almost impossible. Holt tractors were being employed as heavy gun tractors by the British in France.

One of the first tanks to go into action, a Mark I of C Company, ditched near Bouleaux Wood. Note the shell hole in its side, and the two wheels at its rear. The latter were an aid to steering

If armoured fighting vehicles were to play a part in trench warfare they had first to be defined, then designed and constructed, and finally put in the hands of leaders and men who understood their characteristics and who had the strength of purpose to persuade less enlightened individuals to make use of the new weapon. To the engineers, the feasibility of building a caterpillar fighting vehicle had never been in doubt, but already there had been frequent misunderstandings on the part of those conventionally minded General Staff officers who were responsible for devising means to break the trench deadlock. How could it be otherwise? In their semi-ignorance of science, the General Staffs in most armies regarded the technologists with ill-concealed suspicion: even the development of modern artillery and machine guns had taken several decades to push through in the teeth of opposition from those who worshipped the creed of physical combat. It could not be expected that professional General Staff officers would submerge their differences with the technologists overnight and allow them to produce a completely untested weapon system on the say-so of rabid enthusiasts who had nothing to offer by way of a practical demonstration of the feasibility of their ideas. A convincing working model was required, but first an agreed specification was fundamental to design.

The 'Trojan Horse'

By June 1915 the Landships Committee, set up by Winston Churchill in February under Mr Eustace Tennyson d'Eyncourt, the Director of Naval Construction, had gone beyond the original concept of a kind of 'Trojan Horse' transporting a trench storming party of 50 men into the German lines. With a better understanding of conditions at the front, the committee now realised that a machine big enough for this purpose would be highly vulnerable to artillery fire and extremely difficult to move to the front through narrow village streets and across weak bridges. At this same point Swinton's dialogue with GHQ began to make progress, for whereas he had at first been rebuffed by Sir John French's chief adviser on military engineering 'with a few sarcastic words

sufficient to strangle at birth any invention', he now got in his word with the newly-formed Inventions Committee of whose President, and others, he was a personal friend. A series of papers evolved, each demanding more than its predecessor as Swinton's thoughts were stimulated in discussion with experienced front line officers. By June 9 a specification had appeared which, not illogically, tied in closely with those being separately thought out by the Landships Committee. They were for a machine with:
- A top speed of not less than 4 mph on flat ground;
- The capability of a sharp turn at top speed;
- A reversing capability;
- The ability to climb a 5-foot earth parapet with a 1-in-1 slope;
- A gap crossing ability of 8 feet;
- A radius of action of 20 miles; and
- A crew of ten with two machine guns and one light QF gun.

Meanwhile the committee game was being played with verve and enthusiasm in England, where the Admiralty and War Office tossed the Landships Committee about, from one to the other. As the former began to retract from Churchill's early commitments and the latter got more interested, the Minister of Munitions, Lloyd George, became involved when questions of industrial commitment arose. Yet another shuttlecock was the RNAS Armoured Car Division which had pioneered mechanised warfare in Flanders and elsewhere, and had then been drawn into staking its survival on Churchill's sponsorship of landships. The men of No 20 Squadron had been the trials team for the early experiments and soon moves were afoot to transfer them to the army.

It was Swinton's specification, backed by the approval of GHQ in France, which gave real impetus to the technical enthusiasts in England. One moment the latter were dreading a direct order to stop all activities: the next, at the end of June, the Landships Committee had been converted to a joint Service venture with the War Office Director of Fortifications in the chair. Churchill, at this time, was under immense political pressure as a result of the Dardanelles fiasco, but continued to lend support at critical moments. In any case the drive was now coming from lower orders

—above all from the Secretary of the Landships Committee, Lieutenant Albert Stern, an RNVR officer whose civil occupation had been that of a city banker but whose wartime experience had been with the RNAS armoured cars. Stern, with a boiling force of personality and the requisite ruthlessness for cutting red tape, along with a useful technical insight, was the essential middleman to control the inhibitions of politicians and bureaucrats, and to protect and encourage the designers and engineers while they created the new weapons.

The designers too were men of remarkable creative talent. Apart from D'Eyncourt and the members of his Committee, there was Major Thomas Hetherington, who had been Transport Officer of the Naval Armoured Car Division and who had run the naval experimental section established in the *Daily Mail* Airship Shed at Wormwood Scrubs. Then there was William Tritton, Managing Director of the firm of Foster's which had done original work on howitzer tractors and which, in July 1915, contracted for the development of a tracked machine. Responsible for the technical development was Lieutenant W. G. Wilson—an officer of somewhat unstable temperament, but, with Tritton, a first-class creative, practical engineer. A host of existing projects and prospective tracked models along with power plants and armament had to be investigated, rejected or accepted for further evaluation. Then they had to be tried out before a final design could be settled to satisfy Swinton's specifications which, for want of anything else, now represented the official requirement.

A complex armed vehicle

Holt tractors seemed to offer the best possible foundation for design after a succession of other contenders from the Big Wheel solution to Pedrail tracks and a Killen-Strait tractor had failed to make the grade. Even so, variations on the Holt theme also came to grief either because they were too weak or seemed unduly complicated and time consuming just when the need for rapid development became more urgent after each successive failure on the Western Front. When Swinton was writing his specifications, the French offensives in Artois were grinding to an awful halt and the Russians were being routed in Gorlice. But the General Staff specification in itself made complications inevitable, not only because it had shelved the concept of using a 'Trojan Horse' and, instead, demanded a complex, armed vehicle which would be a fighting platform, but also because the requirements for obstacle crossing were well beyond the capability inherent in Holt tractors. These, in the first instance, had been designed for working only on relatively unchurned ground and certainly not the cratered moonscape then being stirred up along the length of the Western Front.

When a development contract was placed with Foster's on July 24, it was fairly clear what existing components might be available for a production machine. There would be a Daimler 105-hp engine, hardly powerful enough in the event but which was already in quantity production: there was plenty of armoured plate and no great shortage of machine guns, even if the actual types were not the most suitable. Swinton's idea of a 2-pounder pom-pom had to be dropped as it was not available. Luckily, however, the navy offered sufficient 57-mm (6-pounder) guns, along with ammunition, as a substitute. The missing link—quite literally—was a suitable track plate and suspension system. The Holt track system was neither robust enough nor did it provide sufficient ground clearance to meet the specifications. Claims that another American type of track—the Bullock—might serve had to be deferred until a set could be shipped across the Atlantic. Meanwhile, Tritton and Wilson put their heads together and, on August 11—only three weeks after receiving the order—a prototype, to be known as the Tritton, began construction. It was modified, after persistent thought and discussion, by a succession of improvements which eventually turned into a tracked metal box called 'Little Willie'. 'Little Willie' was intended to have a rotating turret which would mount the pom-pom: its track was to be the Bullock, when it arrived, carried on a low slung suspension, but from the start it was clear that this 10-foot high vehicle would be top heavy, have very little ground clearance and only a slim chance of crossing an 8-foot gap. As a test bed it would be invaluable—as a fighting vehicle it would not do, and already Wilson was sketching the design of a machine with radically different lines. This was to be a rhomboidal shaped machine with the tracks carried right round the hull, but it would be so high that all hope of a rotating turret had to be dropped in favour of mounting the guns in 'sponsons' blistered onto the sides of the hull. In August it was renamed 'Big Willie'.

In July Swinton had come back to London to become acting Secretary of the Dardanelles Committee of the Cabinet. The Dardanelles operation was about to have its last fling at Suvla and would soon be over; thus those who wanted to win the war in the West were recovering the initiative and so trench fighting machines were also on the upward grade. There is little doubt that Swinton gave them as much attention as he did his proper job, using the powerful contacts inherent in his job to further their progress. Indeed, Hankey, for whom Swinton was acting, had brought him in specifically to speed things up—and this in itself was enough to give the members of the Landship Committee an attack of jitters in case the new broom would sweep their work away. As a matter of fact they were unaware that the specification to which they worked had been Swinton's handiwork. Fortunately the first meetings between Swinton and D'Eyncourt and then with Stern and the other members of the team were wholly amicable. Each came to appreciate the others' virtues, and with Swinton at the hub of decision and well-versed in the travails of the War Office, a vulnerable chink in the designer's bureaucratic armour was filled. From now on Swinton could manipulate the government committees while D'Eyncourt and Stern handled industry and Wilson.

The great day was approaching when the Tritton would take its first hesitant steps. On September 8 it crawled on the factory floor at Lincoln. On the 10th it crawled again—right off its Bullock tracks—and again there was track failure on the 19th when a trial before Swinton, the Landship Committee and the head of the Inventions Department of the Ministry of Munitions were there to watch. But these were practical men who understood that no brand new design is likely to work first time and the sight of a wooden mock-up of Wilson's 'Big Willie' gave each one of them hope of better things in the offing.

Birth of the 'Tank'

Thus far, the trials had proved what all had guessed—the incipient weakness of the track. But such was the genius, enthusiasm and drive of Tritton and Wilson that they had solved even that problem in three days by building and satisfactorily testing on the bench an entirely new, light-weight pressed-steel plate. Here was the missing link and this, as Stern was to write, was 'the birth of the tank'.

Everything now had to be concentrated upon making a viable fighting vehicle—the choice falling upon 'Big Willie', which had still to be built. On September 29, GHQ was represented at a meeting in London at which detailed specifications were settled —10-mm of frontal armour with 8-mm on the sides, a crew of eight men (of whom no less than four would be needed to co-operate in steering and gear-changing), a speed of 4 mph and acceptance of the Admiralty offer of 57-mm guns. That same day Stern asked Tritton to press ahead with the construction of 'Big Willie'—and there may have been some in the GHQ party who ought to have been thankful, for already it was clear from all their offensives culminating with Loos that artillery was not the answer to the trench deadlock.

'Little Willie' continued to operate as a test bed, all hope of it being a combat vehicle having been abandoned. However, on December 3 it proved, in a running trial, how much more reliable the new track was—but not until January 16, when 'Big Willie' ran for the first time, was there real reason to celebrate.

Thus far only those intimately associated with the production of the new vehicles had seen them. The strictest secrecy shrouded every operation and even prevented Foster's workmen from being awarded War Badges to prove they were engaged in work of national importance. Bereft of status and, in cases, the recipients of 'white feathers', the men began to leave, though Foster's were not at first allowed to give proof of the nature of their work in order to arrange for an issue of badges. Essential though secrecy was to prevent the Germans getting to hear, it was also a threat to the future introduction of the weapon. Until those in authority and those who would have to use the machines had seen them, they could neither be expected to understand their characteristics nor to give backing for priority in finance, production and manning.

The time for a demonstration to the representatives of both the government and the army had arrived. Already, however, GHQ was better educated about the possibilities of fighting machines, for in France, as a mere regimental officer after resigning the appointment of First Lord of the Admiralty, was Churchill, and Churchill had taken it upon himself to write, for the Commander-in-Chief, a long paper entitled 'Variants of the Offensive', which, among other things, drew a rather inaccurate picture of the state of tank development. Haig had read it on Christmas Day and sent a Major Hugh Elles to England to find out more about tanks. Elles duly reported favourably, though at first GHQ thought only in terms of an order for 40.

But GHQ were not represented at the key demonstrations which were held under conditions of great secrecy at Hatfield Park on January 29 and February 2, 1916. At the first, which was by way of being a rehearsal for the second, only those who had been closely associated with the initial experiments were present: for them it was the justification of their efforts. To the second came the great—Kitchener, the Secretary of State for War, Lloyd George, the Minister for Munitions, McKenna, the Chancellor of the Exchequer and many others in power—those personalities, in fact, who could most help or hinder the decision to enter full-scale production and service.

'Pretty mechanical toys'

The demonstrations put both 'Little' and 'Big Willie' through their paces over a stiff obstacle course which, apart from German fire and a bottomless bog, fairly represented the worst terrain that the Western Front could produce. Already at these demonstrations the vehicles were being called 'tanks'—the name which Swinton had given them for security cover, and by which they were to be known evermore. From the first they made a deep impression, though much play has been made of Kitchener's remarks to the designers that the tanks were 'pretty mechanical toys' and that 'the war would never be won by such machines'. Those close to Kitchener said that he did this as a cover so that the trials would not get talked about, but it could also be that, by a provocative remark, he could delve deeper into the minds of men who were, after all, trying a 'hard sell'. The fact remains that immediately afterwards, Kitchener asked Stern to go to the War Office as Head of the Department which was to see to the production of tanks (a logical request since, in December, the Ministry of Munitions had declined to make them)—and it was only later that Lloyd George stepped in to take Stern into the Ministry of Munitions, whose proper responsibility it was to build weapons. No matter: by February 12, Lloyd George had signed a charter of Stern's dictation in which it was settled that an initial order for 100 'Big Willie's' should be placed.

An impression has sometimes been given that the authorities, in the shape of Kitchener, Haig and others, were generally opposed to the introduction of tanks. Yet whenever this was the case it was rarely without a reason—either because the tank enthusiasts had failed to explain some vital point adequately, or

because those same enthusiasts were expecting miraculous results from a totally untried device. When moving into the unknown some sense of caution is entirely desirable. In fact the tanks, by the standards of progress registered by many another technical innovation in the past, positively galloped ahead. In February Swinton was writing the foundations of a tactical doctrine: The simplest and surest way of destroying entrenched machine guns was 'by rolling over the emplacements and crushing them'. If that did not suffice they could be crushed by moving close to 'pour in shell at point blank range'. For communications to the rear, 'one tank in ten should be equipped with small wireless telegraphy sets', while others might lay telephone cable as they advanced and yet others depend upon visual signalling. The tanks would be very vulnerable to artillery fire and therefore must be supported by counterbattery fire.

Thereafter Swinton described in detail the way tanks should be prepared for action, transported to the front and integrated with the infantry so that each would combine with the other in making best use of the special attributes—but at this stage Swinton saw no further than the original concept that tanks were there to help the infantry make a hole in the German lines. 'It seems, as the Tanks are an auxiliary to the infantry, that they must be counted as infantry and in an operation be under the same command.' Although Swinton envisaged the German lines being penetrated as deep as the artillery zone in one day, his vision stopped short of outright exploitation which still, in the minds of the majority of soldiers, remained the prerogative of cavalry.

At this point, just when the British were crossing the dividing line between dreams and reality, the French, quite unknown to the British and in total ignorance themselves of British endeavours, were placing an order for 400 *chars d'assaut* of their own. Here, the efforts of their 'Swinton', an artillery colonel called Jean Estienne, to experiment with a tracked armoured vehicle had been twice foiled in 1915. Only in December 1915, after the total failure of the French offensives, was he given permission to seek a solution in conjunction with the Schneider Creusot factory. But the French were nothing like as thorough as their allies. Picking on a Holt tractor suspension as the best caterpillar system available, they immediately ordered an armed and armoured box to be perched on top without so much as em-

Above: The Daimler-Foster artillery tractor. This was the basis of the original 'big wheel' armoured vehicle idea. *Right:* The Killen-Strait armoured tractor, which failed to win approval as it could carry little armament and could not cross trenches. *Below left and right:* Prophetic—the de Mole 1912 landship

The hope for the future: armoured trench-crossing mechanical monsters

Above left: Almost but not quite there—'Little Willie', built by the Foster works. It was unarmed, but embraced all the principles of later tanks, such as tracks running the whole length of the fully-armoured body. The type was originally envisaged with a revolving gun turret on top, but as the silhouette of the vehicle would then have been too high, the idea was dropped. 'Little Willie' had track frames 12 feet long, weighed 14 tons, had a crew of five and a top speed of three and a half miles per hour (one and three-quarters across country). *Above:* The Holt caterpillar tractor, which first suggested the idea of the tank to Colonel Ernest Swinton. The design was American, and Swinton saw the type in France, where it had been adopted by the Royal Artillery as a heavy gun tractor soon after the beginning of the war.

Left: The old and the new: cavalry and the vehicle destined to replace them, the example here being C19 of the Heavy Section, the Machine Gun Corps on September 15, 1916. *Below:* The first real tank, 'Mother'. Experiments had shown that earlier tank designs had too high a centre of gravity and too short a track length to cross broad trenches, so Tritton and his collaborator Wilson reverted to the 'Big Wheel' idea, but stretched out to a rhomboidal shape to keep the centre of gravity low and to give the tracks as much length on the ground, and so grip, as possible. After the abandonment of the turret idea, sponsons were fitted to the sides to accommodate the two naval 6-pounder guns carried as main armament. Steering was by differential braking of the tracks, and the vehicle could cross a 9-foot trench with a 4½-foot parapet

John Batchelor

barking on a trial to see if this would result in a combat-worthy machine. Thus they engineered a vehicle which was little better than the original Tritton—and which, incidentally, looked very like the Tritton in some respects. But even though they had taken a hazardous short-cut, the French were still a good six months behind the British with no hope of entering action until 1917. The British, meanwhile, were digesting Swinton's tactical doctrine and thinking in terms of tank action in the summer of 1916.

When Haig spoke to Swinton in London on April 14, he not only expressed general agreement with the proposed tactical doctrine but was anxious to obtain as many of the machines as possible by June 1—in time for the opening of the Somme offensive. This, of course, was asking for the moon. Production had hardly begun and the men to crew the tanks had yet to begin training—particularly since training could not realistically start until the first machines had been delivered, which would be in June. The earliest any might be expected in France was August 1 —and that was the height of optimism.

Meanwhile the British crews were being recruited—a major problem in itself from a nation to whom mechanical vehicles were still rather in the nature of a possession of the rich and the sporting. Since the first home of the new force was to be sited where the Motor Machine-Gun Service had its depot and that Service was in process of reduction, it was inevitable that these experts found their way into the new establishment. It was also sensible that, from a security point of view, their rôle should be disguised under the title of Armoured Car Section of the Motor Machine-Gun Service instead of, as originally, the Tank Detachment. It was hoped that many of the RNAS, who had been involved with the experiments, would transfer to the army, but faced by loss of status, a reduction in pay and an imprecise description of their future work, they drew back. From the motor trade, however, and with the assistance of the editor of *The Motor Cycle*, Mr G. Smith, many well-qualified tradesmen were recruited—though their knowledge of soldiering was precisely nil.

Training in driving (using 'Little Willie' at first), gunnery and rudimentary tactics went on throughout the summer in which the artillery's palpable ineffectuality was demonstrated daily at Verdun, on the Somme and anywhere else where men dared to rise above trench level. Pressure from GHQ to send out the tanks before they were ready was increased, and training had to be curtailed in order to meet a deadline to be in action on September 15, 1916.

The first batch of 50 machines was in France by August 30 and from then on could only prepare for a battle whose nature was absolutely beyond the comprehension of their crews. Enthusiasts they might be, but few had seen action before or were trained soldiers. One tank commander wrote: *I and my crew did not have a tank of our own the whole time we were in England. Ours went wrong the day it arrived. We had no reconnaissance or map read-*

ing . . . no practices or lectures on the compass . . . we had no signalling . . . and no practice in considering orders. We had no knowledge of where to look for information that would be necessary for us as Tank Commanders, nor did we know what information we should be likely to require.

Picture the difficulties facing these men in their unlit steel boxes, filled with fumes and exposed working parts, jerked to and fro as its unsprung suspension heaved them across country, deaf from the din of engines and armament and practically unable to communicate among themselves or with the infantry outside. The commander could do little by way of assistance to his gunners to find and destroy targets and had to concentrate on driving the tank by hand signals to the man who changed the gears and the two men, one to each track at the rear of the tank, who worked the levers which 'braked' the track to change direction. It was remarkable that they moved at all, let alone fought, and particularly so when it is remembered that almost constant maintenance and adjustment was required of the machinery.

And once in France and embarked on a slow journey to the front, the crews found themselves alternately the victims of outlandish security measures or objects of intense curiosity under constant demand to give demonstration of the tanks' ability, with a consequent wear and tear on machines which were going to be difficult enough to keep going for the few miles up to and over the start line. There was total distraction of crews in their efforts to prepare themselves and their charges for action. Many were exhausted before they fired a shot in anger.

Nevertheless, on the night of September 13, those tanks which were fit crept forward, guided by white tapes, to their battle assembly positions, creating astonishment in all those who heard them spluttering and groaning in the dark. Next night they moved again to their battle positions and now they entered, for the first time, a genuine area of war-torn ground the like of which the training area simulations in England had not quite reproduced. Here many of the 30-ton machines, grossly underpowered and unsophisticated as they were, broke down as drivers, tense with anxiety, made errors. Gradually, the initial force of 50 was whittled down to a mere 36. But at dawn on the 15th those few were ready and, in the half-light, a new era in warfare opened.

Further Reading
Edmonds, J. E., *Military Operations: France and Belgium 1916* (Macmillan)
Liddell Hart, Sir Basil, *The Tanks* (Cassell 1959)
Stern, A., *The Log of a Pioneer*
Swinton, E. D., *Eyewitness*
Williams-Ellis, C. and A., *The Tank Corps* (Country Life 1919)

Infantrymen and their new aid, the machine that could crush the almighty power of the emplaced machine gun, barbed wire and well-sited trench

Imperial War Museum

THE FRENCH TANK FORCE

On April 16, 1917, the first day of the Nivelle offensive, the French first used tanks in battle — seven months after the British first fielded them on the Somme. *Richard M. Ogorkiewicz* discusses the origins and early development of French armour

The creation of a tank force in France came shortly after that in Britain. It developed independently of the technological advances being made in Britain, and in a less dramatic but more complex way.

As in Britain, the idea of the tank was not conceived in France by any one man but emerged more diffusely, in response to the contemporary military situation, out of the existing technological possibilities. In fact, there were at least three sets of ideas which contributed to the development of the first French tank and hence of the first French tank units.

The initial set of ideas arose out of the development of the armoured car, the first of which had been exhibited as early as 1902 at the *Salon de l'Automobile* in Paris and although progress up to 1914 was very slow, once war began more and more armoured cars were built. Thus, by August 1914 the French Ministry of War had already ordered its first 136 armoured cars and within a month they began to be attached to French cavalry formations. However, these early, improvised armoured cars could operate only on roads, and in consequence, when the opening, mobile stages of the war were succeeded by more static warfare, during which the roads were cut or blocked, their usefulness quickly came to an end.

The short period of operation of the first armoured cars was, however, sufficient to

Brown Brothers

Below: Chars Schneider move up to the front.

95

arouse interest in the possibility of developing them further, so that they could be used beyond the confines of open roads. The most significant move in this direction was taken by the French armaments firm of Schneider, which took out a patent for an improved type of armoured vehicle in January 1915 and then began to consider the design of another armoured car, fitted with tracks instead of wheels.

The French technicians' interest in the use of tracks for armoured cars was prompted by a visit to England in January 1915 by Brillié and another Schneider engineer to examine the potential of the American-built Holt tractor for hauling heavy guns. As a result of this visit, the Schneider Company purchased two tractors from the United States which were tested at its works at Creusot in May 1915. From these tests came the idea of using the lighter of the two tractors, the 45-horsepower 'Baby Holt', as the basis of a tracked armoured car capable of moving off the road and crossing obstacles. In July, Schneider engineers began to work on the design of such a vehicle and in August they produced a layout drawing of its chassis, which was essentially that of a lengthened and widened 'Baby Holt'. However, a month later further work on the design of the new type of fighting vehicle was interrupted by the temporary ascendancy of other ideas.

The new ideas were prompted by the immediate tactical problem of cutting through the belts of barbed wire with which the opposing armies protected their trenches. The wire obviously had to be cut before any infantry attack could succeed and this fact turned thought to various wire-cutting or wire-crushing devices. The leading proponent of this trend of thought was J. L. Breton, a parliamentary deputy who, in November 1914, submitted designs for a mechanical wire-cutter mounted on a wheeled agricultural tractor. His designs were favourably received by the technical branch of the Engineer Corps and, after some experiments, the Ministry of War placed an order in August 1915 for ten of the Breton wire-cutters for further trials. But it soon became clear that the performance of the Bajac wheeled tractor on which the cutter was mounted was inadequate and in consequence Breton was put in touch with Brillié in order to explore the possibility of mounting his wire-cutter on the 'Baby Holt' currently being tested at Creusot. This was deemed to be possible and the Ministry of War went so far as to place an order with Schneiders for ten armoured tracked tractors fitted with wire-cutters. However, further trials conducted

Left: Schneider tank. The girder fitted to the front of the vehicle was designed to force barbed wire under the tracks to be crushed. *Below:* Schneiders in action

DAZY

Brown Brothers

with the 'Baby Holt' from December 1915 to February 1916 showed that the wire-cutters were superfluous, since the tractor could crash through barbed wire by itself. This realisation coincided with the emergence of yet another set of ideas and the development of tractor-mounted wire-cutters was seen to be a blind alley and came quickly to an end.

Sanction from Joffre

The third set of ideas for the tank's development came from Colonel Estienne, an artillery officer who had already made a major contribution to technology warfare. Estienne's idea for a tracked armoured fighting vehicle began to take form in the latter part of 1915. In a letter to Joffre on December 1, 1915, Estienne asked for an interview to explain his idea of a tracked armoured vehicle which would facilitate the infantry's advance. At the time, GQG were daily receiving suggestions on how to achieve a decisive victory, most of them fit only for the waste paper basket. But a proposal bearing the signature of a widely-respected officer deserved — and was accorded — some consideration. On December 12 Estienne was summoned to present his ideas to Janin, the general responsible for equipment at Joffre's headquarters. Eight days later he was on his way to Paris to explore, with Joffre's tacit approval, the possibility of constructing the proposed vehicle.

The favourable attitude of Joffre and other French generals ensured that the ideas would be quickly translated into practice. Thus, within four weeks of writing his letter, Estienne was able to get in touch with Brillié, whom he managed almost immediately to interest in his ideas. Brillié, in turn, having studied the earlier schemes for the tracked armoured car and for the wire-cutter vehicle, was quickly able to produce the layout of a vehicle corresponding to Estienne's ideas. In consequence, on December 28, 1915 Estienne was already able to present to Janin a more concrete scheme which planned for the construction of 300 to 400 vehicles. Again Joffre responded quickly and favourably, recommending to the government department concerned that trials be pursued without delay. Then, on January 18, 1916, he received Estienne's personal report which was then submitted to his staff who received it favourably. In consequence, on January 31, 1916, Joffre wrote to the Under-Secretary of State for War asking for 400 vehicles built along the lines proposed by Estienne.

The responsibility for the supply of the vehicles was vested in the army technical services. These operated slowly and were not too well disposed towards a project which did not originate from them. Nevertheless, on February 26, 1916, the Ministry of War placed a firm order with Schneiders for 400 vehicles. It is interesting that this order was placed only two weeks later than the original British order for tanks and involved four times as many tanks. But the production of the French tanks took longer and the first was completed much later than the first British tank.

The specifications of the vehicle which Schneiders eventually produced did not differ very much from those originally laid down by Estienne. For security reasons it was at first referred to as an artillery tractor and was aptly called the *tracteur Estienne*. However, after Estienne adopted *chars d'assaut* as a generic name for what in English began to be known as tanks, they were called *chars Schneider* or less frequently, *chars CA*. The main difference between the new vehicle and the original specification was that it had a short 75-mm gun instead of a 37-mm gun, and a crew of six instead of four. In principle, it amounted to an armoured box-hull on a modified 'Baby Holt' chassis. The hull had 11.5-mm plates at the sides and rear but at the front

Above: French tank soldier—collar patches of 81st Heavy Artillery Regiment on service dress tunic beneath the leather combat jacket

Below: **Schneider**—*Crew:* 6; *Armament:* one 75-mm gun (90 rounds), two Hotchkiss machine guns (3,840 rounds); *Armour:* 11.5 mm max (17 mm later); *Speed:* 3.7 mph; *Weight:* 13.5 tons; *Engine:* Schneider 70 hp; *Length:* 19 ft 8 in; *Width:* 6 ft 6½ in; *Height:* 7 ft 10 in; *Range:* 30 miles an extra plate was later added which brought the total thickness to 17-mm making it virtually immune to all rifle-calibre bullets. In the front right hand corner of the hull was mounted the short-barrelled 75-mm gun which could be fired over an arc of 20 degrees to the right of the axis of the tank. In addition, in each side plate there was a large spherical mounting for a Hotchkiss machine gun. Within the hull there was stowage space for 90 rounds of 75-mm gun ammunition and for 3,840 machine gun rounds.

With all its equipment the Schneider weighed 13.5 tons. It was powered by a four-cylinder water-cooled Schneider engine which developed 70 horsepower and gave it a maximum speed of six kilometres per hour. In this respect, the Schneider was comparable to the original British tanks. But it was greatly inferior to them in one other important respect, namely trench crossing performance, because its tracks were very much shorter than the overhead tracks of the rhomboidal British tanks. The limited trench-crossing capability of the Schneider tank was seen to be a particularly serious shortcoming after the British tanks made their début on September 15, 1916. Once the Germans knew of the existence of tanks they widened their trenches to make them more effective as tank obstacles and this, in turn, made the French revise their ideas on the employment of tanks.

Estienne's original idea was that tanks should be used in surprise mass assaults on enemy trenches. The tanks were to attack ahead of the infantry and after crossing the first line of trenches one half of them was to keep the enemy down by their fire so that the infantry could follow through the gaps which the tanks opened in the enemy defences and take the trenches. But the possibility of achieving complete surprise was lost as a result of the use of tanks by the British army — a

Imperial War Museum

Below: **St Chamond** — *Crew:* 9; *Armament:* one 75-mm gun (106 rounds), four Hotchkiss machine guns (7,500 rounds); *Armour:* 17 mm max; *Speed:* 5.3 mph; *Weight:* 23 tons; *Engine:* Panhard 90 hp; *Length:* 25 ft 11 in; *Width:* 8 ft 9 in; *Height:* 7 ft 8 in; *Range:* 37 miles

Above: Engine of a St Chamond. With exposed moving parts and hot pipes, the interior of the early tanks was a hazardous place

John Batchelor

use which the French regarded with bitterness as premature – and this coupled with the inability of the French tanks to cross wide trenches, led the French to envisage new tactics for tanks.

Diminished rôle

In general, in the period leading up to the first tank action, less came to be expected of tanks than Estienne had originally envisaged. Thus, the rôle assigned to them became the more modest one of complementing the artillery fire by attacking enemy positions that had escaped the artillery bombardment and which were holding up the advance of the infantry. Moreover, tanks were to be accompanied by units of specially trained infantry who would help them cross obstacles. Tanks were not, however, intended to be tied down to the pace of the infantry when they were able to move ahead on their own.

Before the proposed tactics could be put to the test tanks had to be produced in number and this proved to be more difficult than expected. The first Schneider tank was delivered to the French army on September 8, 1916, but by November 25, when all 400 were expected to have been delivered, only eight were in the hands of the troops. Moreover, they had been built using mild steel, because of delays in the production of armour plate, and were therefore suitable only for training. By mid-January 1917 there were still only 32 training tanks. But by the time the

Ullstein

Brown Brothers

Above: St Chamond tanks in a French wood. *Below:* Schneiders, knocked out by German artillery and stripped by the French for spares. The first two French tanks had poor cross-country capabilities. The Schneider and the St Chamond could only cross trenches 6 ft and 8 ft wide tanks were introduced into action, in April 1917, the French army was better off than the British army was at the same stage as it had more than 200 Schneiders.

The delays in the delivery of armour plate and in the whole tank production programme were due not only to the usual manufacturing difficulties associated with a new product but also to the dispersion of the available effort in two different directions. The second type of tank originated with the technical services who, once shown the way, thought they could do much better than Estienne and Brillié. It became known as the St Chamond tank, named after the firm which designed it and which in April 1916 received an order for 400 vehicles—and all this without any reference to Estienne.

On paper, the St Chamond tank was superior to the Schneider. It had a normal, instead of a short-barrelled, 75-mm gun and two more machine guns; it also had a longer track and an electrical instead of a mechanical transmission which made it easier to drive. However, at 23 tons, it was considerably heavier than the Schneider and consequently performed poorly over soft ground. Moreover, the front of its box-hull projected well over the front of the tracks which greatly reduced its trench-crossing capability. It also experienced more breakdowns than the Schneider and its production was no faster. Admittedly, the first vehicle was delivered at about the same time as the first Schneider but on the eve of the first French tank action in April 1917 there were only 16 St Chamond tanks fit for battle. As it happened, none of them was used, the only St Chamonds to accompany the Schneiders into their first action being four unarmed vehicles which carried supplies.

The production of tanks was accompanied by the formation of the first tank units. The original scheme for their organisation was due to Estienne who submitted it to Joffre in March 1916. It was approved but it was not until July that Estienne was relieved of his artillery command on the Verdun front and attached to Joffre's headquarters to take charge of the formation of tank units—the *artillerie d'assaut*. Following Estienne's original ideas, the basic unit became a *groupe* of 16 tanks: each was divided on traditional artillery lines into four batteries which could be temporarily combined under one command when required.

The organisation of the tank units started in August 1916, at Marly near Paris. Soon afterwards a second training centre was set up at Cercottes, near Orleans, and a tank camp was established near the front, at Champlieu, which became Estienne's headquarters. The first *groupe* was formed at Marly in October and by the end of March 1917 the camp at Champlieu contained 13 *groupes* of Schneiders and two of St Chamonds.

The officers of these units came from various services within the army and some even from the navy; the men for most part came from cavalry regiments whose reserve squadrons were being disbanded for lack of employment. They had all undergone the contemporary type of conventional military training but otherwise almost all were completely ignorant of technical matters. They had, therefore, to learn from scratch how to operate tanks and it was typical of the kind of muddled thinking which surrounded new technological developments at this time that, after a mere two to three months' training at Champlieu, they were thought ready for battle.

Further Reading
Deygas, F. J., *Les Chars d'Assaut* (Charles-Lavauzelle, Paris 1937)
Crow, D. (ed.), *AFVs of World War One* (Profile Publications 1970)
Dutil, L., *Les Chars d'Assaut* (Berger-Levrault, Nancy, 1919)
Duvignac, A., *Histoire de l'Armée Motorisée* (Imprimerie Nationale, Paris 1948)
Macksey, K. and Batchelor, J., *Tank* (Macdonald 1970)
Perre, J., *Batailles et Combats des Chars Français* (Charles-Lavauzelle, Paris 1937)

RICHARD M. OGORKIEWICZ graduated in engineering at London University and after a period working in the motor industry returned to the Imperial College of Science to become a senior lecturer in mechanical engineering. He is the author of two books and numerous articles on the development of armoured fighting vehicles. He has also lectured on the subject in Britain, the United States, Israel and Sweden.

WESTERN FRONT WINTER 1916/17

In a winter which was first exceptionally wet and then unusually cold, both sides were content to rest and recover from the massive slaughters of the summer months. *John Keegan* describes the life in the trenches and the state of morale

OCTOBER

Constant rain in the last half of the month turned the front line into a quagmire, hampering the supply of stores and ammunition and interfering in the work of the artillery. After the bloodbaths of Verdun and the Somme, the French, British and Germans welcomed the onset of winter as a time of recuperation. No large offensives were planned.

NOVEMBER

The bad weather continued. What had been an hour's walk in the summer had now become a gruelling ordeal—men carrying ammunition boxes slipped and fell in the mud; men carrying food supplies failed to reach the front line because they had fallen up to their necks in ice-cold water. Germany's manpower resources were becoming very stretched, and in November she was forced to call up the class of 1918—those youths who were born in 1898. By this means, and through the reduction of establishments, Germany was able to bring about a 20% increase in the number of its divisions by the end of the year.

DECEMBER

Despite the continuing wet weather, the French General Nivelle had his 'last fling' at Verdun on December 15/16. But apart from this, the French tried to maintain a policy of inactivity along the whole front with the object of harbouring resources for a great offensive planned by Nivelle in the spring. Similarly, the Germans were relatively inactive as regards military operations, but otherwise they were extremely busy constructing the *Siegfried Stellung* (Hindenburg Line) in open country to the rear of the trenches.

Left: The German 13-cm field gun, a long range quick-firing gun which was introduced just prior to 1914 to replace the 15-cm long gun. *Range:* 15,748 yards. *Weight of shell:* 22.5 lbs. *Weight in action:* 5 tons 14 cwt. *Muzzle velocity:* 2,280 feet-per-second

Below left: The German 10-cm M1890. *Range:* 11,264 yards. *Weight of shell:* 39.5 lbs.

Below: The French 105-mm M 1913. *Range:* 13,400 yards. *Weight of shell:* 35 lbs. *Weight in action:* 2 tons 6 cwt. *Rate of fire:* 6 rounds-per-minute, 40 rounds-per-hour. *Traverse:* 3 degrees left—3 degrees right

John Batchelor

JANUARY FEBRUARY MARCH

On January 14 a frost at last hardened the ground sufficiently to restore comparative ease of movement over the battlefield, but it did not dry the ground so that the shortest spell of warmer weather brought chaos again. The frost, though preferable, brought its own discomforts and difficulties. It froze the water supply and forced the men to melt ice from shell holes. Most dangerously, the frost damaged the cordite propellant of shells and caused them to drop short. Before the frost froze the wet ground the British made three raids between January 10/12, two of which were successful.

The British continued small scale raiding into February. There was a large night operation on the 17/18th on the north bank of the Ancre, but the Germans were alerted and laid down heavy artillery fire. The British lost 2,700 officers and men and gained between 500 and 1,000 yards, while in simultaneous operations to the north of this Fourth Army won even less ground and lost 1,100 men.

The Germans continued to increase the size of their army, raising the number of combat battalions on the Western Front from 1,289 in September 1916 to 1,422 in March 1917. Morale was still high, and the production of munitions had continued to rise. In the British sector the morale effects of the raids of the winter months were dubious, but the raids did reveal a new standard of skill in the divisions of the Kitchener armies. French morale was still holding up after a relatively quiet winter preparing for the Nivelles Offensive in the spring of 1917.

Above: The German 7.7-cm M 1916 field gun. This new model was longer than the M 1896 and could be fired at very much increased angles of elevation. *Range:* 9,405 yards. *Weight in action:* 2,750 lbs. *Muzzle velocity:* 1,571 feet-per-second. *Elevation:* +38 degrees to −9 degrees 30 minutes. *Traverse:* 2 degrees right to 2 degrees left.

Left: The German 15-cm M 1916 (Krupp) field gun. *Range:* 23,500 yards. *Weight of gun:* 7 tons 3 cwt. *Weight of shell:* 28 lbs. *Maximum elevation:* 46 degrees

Below: The German 15-cm M 1913 long howitzer. *Range:* 9,296 yards. *Rate of fire:* 2 rounds-per-minute normal rate

John Batchelor

Left: British 12-inch Mark 3 rail howitzer, an enlarged version of the 9.2-inch howitzer. *Range:* 14,500 yards (accurate to within 10 yards of target). *Maximum elevation:* 45°. *Traverse:* 120° right or left. *Weight of shell:* 750 lb. *Muzzle velocity:* 1,475 feet per second. Thirty-five Mark 3 howitzers were built and 138 12-inch howitzers of all marks. Total number of rounds fired by all marks—227,000

Right: Field artilleryman in shirt-sleeve order. He is wearing the regulation grey-blue shirt and riding breeches and carries one tool of his trade, a knife for picking stones out of horses' hooves. His boots and leggings, ideal for use in the Flanders mud, were issued to some field artillery units in 1917 but were withdrawn in 1918

Below: British 12-inch Mark 9 railway gun. Only four of these guns were built. The first and second had a maximum elevation of 30° and a range of 28,000 yards. The third and fourth had a maximum elevation of 35½° and a range of 33,000 yards. The traverse of both types was 1°. *Weight of shell:* 850 lb. *Total weight of gun and carriage:* 152 tons. The Mark 9 was combined with one 9.2-inch gun to form a siege battery, manned by four officers and 67 men. The four Mark 9 guns fired a mere 5,000 rounds throughout their use in France

Barry Evans

John Batchelor

Peter Sarson

Above: The crew of a Mark IV tank: **1** Commander. **2** Gearsman. **3** 6-pounder gunner. **4** Lewis machine gunner (and loader for 6-pounder). **5** and **6** Brakesmen. **7** Lewis machine gunner (and loader for 6- pounder). **8** 6-pounder gunner. Moving over rough ground without suspension or any means of shock absorption, and at a maximum speed of 3.5 mph, tank crews were subjected to intense noise, vibration, smell and high tempera-tures (around 100 degrees Fahrenheit) which compounded with cramped space to produce an extremely exhausting fighting environment. *Below, left and right:* The cramped interior of the Mark V tank, looking forward on the right-hand side, and looking behind the engine from left to right. *Bottom:* An exterior view of the same Mark V, showing camouflage painting

John Batchelor

Special Order No 6.

1. To-morrow the Tank Corps will have the chance for which it has been waiting for many months, – to operate on good going in the van of the battle.

2. All that hard work & ingenuity can achieve has been done in the way of preparation

3. It remains for unit commanders and for tank crews to complete the work by judgment & pluck in the battle itself.

4. In the light of past experience I leave the good name of the Corps with great confidence in their hands

5. I propose leading the attack of the centre division

Hugh Elles.
B.S.

19th Nov. 1917.   Commanding Tank Corps.

Distribution to Tank Commanders ..

At 0620 hours on November 20 1917, 381 tanks moved forward from their last assembly points, led by their commander General Elles flying his flag in one of the leading machines in the true style of a 'land admiral'. The wire was easily crushed, German troops in the front lines fled in terror, and a huge hole almost six miles wide and up to 4,000 yards deep was torn in the formidable Hindenburg Line. This was the dramatic birth of large scale tank warfare. Had Haig's armies at last discovered the real answer to barbed wire and machine gun war? *David Chandler. Above:* Brigadier-General Hugh Elles, Commander of the Tank Corps at Cambrai, painted by Sir William Orpen. *Above right:* Elles's Special Order, issued on the day before his Tank Corps went into action

CAMBRAI THE BRITISH ONSLAUGHT

Julian Allen

John Batchelor

Support trench

Communication trench

Fire trench

Outpost

Advanced guard

100 yds

Main body tanks

25–50 yds

Tank echelon
(usually one tank coy:
4 sections of 3 tanks)

Trench cleaners
(4 platoons per tank
section, 36–40 men
per platoon in two files)

Trench 'stop' parties
(4 platoons per tank
section)

**Half battalion
in support**

4 minutes

100 yds

50 yds

Section of three
'wire-crushing'
tanks

Section of three
'fighting' tanks

**Trench
cleaners
in extended
order**

**Trench 'stop'
parties**

Half battalion in support

———	German lines	——— 1st movement
••••••	British objective	——— 2nd movement
⊞	Fascine, 4' 6'' in diameter	——— 3rd movement

Sequence of Attack

1 Advanced guard tanks crush wire, create gap and swing left to rake fire trench with main and secondary armament.
2 These are followed by second tank in each section, which drops fascine, plants flag and crosses fire trench, then swings left to rake support trench.
3 The last tank in each section crushes second wire barrier, drops fascine, plants flag and crosses the support trench towards the objective.
4 All tanks then rally in the vicinity of the objective.
5 Infantry 'trench cleaners' then clear the German lines (2 platoons per trench) from right to left, aided by 2nd & 3rd tanks.
6 Infantry 'stop' platoons secure trenches, set up blocks and improve wire gaps, through which the reserves then pass.

Variation by 51st (Highland Division)

1 'Wire-crushing' tanks dispose of advanced posts, break wire, cross trench (with aid of fascine) and drive on to breach second wire belt.
2 Two flanking fighting tanks cross fascine bridges, then turn right to shoot up the fire trench.
3 The remaining fighting tank passes straight ahead to bridge support trench.
4 General tank rally.
5,6 Infantry, deployed in extended order, carry out normal 'cleaning' and 'stopping' rôle (from left to right).

The dramatic events in the vicinity of Cambrai in November 1917 occupy a special place in the history of the First World War in general and in that of the Royal Tank Regiment (formerly the Tank Corps) in particular. November 20 saw the birth of large scale tank warfare, and for a brief but glorious moment it seemed that a decisive breakthrough had at last been achieved, and that an element of strategic mobility was about to return to the Western Front after three years of trench warfare. In fact the success was to prove more illusory than real, and the ringing of church bells throughout Great Britain on November 23 (the sole time this was authorised before the Armistice) was decidedly premature, for the well-known conditions of stalemate and positional warfare were to reassert themselves within three days of the offensive's opening. Nevertheless, as John Terraine has written: 'After Cambrai there could be no further argument; the decisive weapon of land warfare in the mid-twentieth century had now definitely arrived. A new dimension of war was established. Haig's armies had at last discovered what the real answer to wire and machine guns was.'

Haig had been considering 'an attack of surprise in the centre with tanks, and without artillery bombardment' as early as February 1917. As the autumn of a year more dismal than any of its predecessors set in, the idea hardened into a firm resolve. Haig noted in his diary for September 16: 'I discussed with Byng some operations which he proposed. I told him I would give him all the help I could.' This laconic entry marks the practical genesis of the Cambrai offensive. General Sir Julian Byng, Commander of Third Army, was told that his command would be reinforced to a total strength of 19 divisions, and that the entire Tank Corps would be placed at his disposal. With these forces he was to launch a surprise attack on the German lines near Cambrai on a date – still to be confirmed – in November.

The choice of both place and time was carefully considered. The rolling chalk-based downlands of the Somme region promised far better going than the morass of the Flanders front. It had also been a relatively quiet sector of the front for some time, and the ground was comparatively

free of shell holes. Furthermore, the main line of the Hindenburg defences (to which the Germans had retired earlier in 1917) swung away to the northwestward and then north in a vast sweeping curve, and the capture of the ridge near the village of Bourlon would provide a superb view over the Germans' rear areas almost as far as Valenciennes. A quick surprise attack here might yield useful results. The Cambrai plain had been suggested as a suitable site for a large scale tank raid by Lieutenant-Colonel J. F. C. Fuller, GSO 1 to Brigadier-General Hugh Elles, commanding the Tank Corps, in June 1917. Apart from being well drained, the area was bounded by two canals to west and east, the Canal du Nord, and the St Quentin respectively, and the Allied front included thick woods, more particularly near Havrincourt, and these would help conceal the final preparations. Intelligence reported only two German divisions in the line, with no more than five, and 150 guns, in support. A refined version of Fuller's plan earned Elles' full approval, and was forthwith forwarded to both GHQ and General Byng. Simultaneously, a second plan calling for a similar combined tank and infantry onslaught without a preliminary bombardment over the very same ground was being prepared by Brigadier-General H. H. Tudor, CRA to 9th (Scottish) Division. This scheme reached Third Army headquarters on August 23 via IV Corps. It was a plan based on these two schemes which won Haig's approval at a conference with Byng on September 16.

The timing of the offensive was of the greatest importance to the British Commander-in-Chief. At first it seems he envisaged Cambrai as a purely diversionary attack, intended to ease pressure from the embattled divisions still locked (in September) in the agony of Third Ypres. In fact, however, that terrible offensive was to come to an unmourned conclusion two weeks before the opening of Cambrai. Nevertheless, Haig well understood the need to strive for a success somewhere on the Western Front to set against the dismal tale of failures at Ypres, mutinies in the French army, the catastrophic situation developing on the Russian Front, and, more recently, the massive Italian disaster at Caporetto. There was no idea in Haig's

mind of delivering a war-winning blow at Cambrai – he knew his resources would never permit a massive exploitation even if the attack proved a success – but he was aware of the vital need to give the Allied governments and peoples some evidence of at least one tangible success to compensate in some measure for the horrific casualty lists incurred in earlier failures. His object, then to quote the Cambrai Despatch, was 'a local success'.

Sir Julian Byng, not surprisingly, was more ambitious. Briefing his corps commanders at Albert on October 26, he painted a picture of a three-stage battle opening the way to greater things. In the first phase, some 409 tanks followed by infantry were to smash a five-mile breach through the Hindenburg Line in the sector bounded by the two canals; their initial advance would coincide with the laying down of an unregistered bombardment by 1,003 guns which would provide the Germans with no warning of what was afoot. Next, a 'cavalry gap' would be carved towards the River Sensée, involving the capture of the key communication centre of Cambrai, the domination of Bourlon ridge, and the establishment of bridgeheads over the Sensée itself. Thirdly, the victorious Third Army would sweep north and west up the German line towards Valenciennes.

Haig, as we have seen, was not so optimistic as his subordinate, and insisted on modifications to the plan. First, he laid down a 48-hour deadline for the initial breakthrough; if that was not achieved by the time limit, the offensive would be closed down. Secondly, he insisted that Cambrai should be masked, but not actually captured, in phase two; far more important, in his view, was the physical occupation of Bourlon ridge – and the wood and village of the same name – which would afford a superb view over the German rear areas for artillery observation posts at the earliest moment possible. Thirdly, Haig knew that the exploitation envisaged by Byng was beyond his means. The French, eager to share in such a promising operation, had placed five divisions at his disposal near Peronne, intending to roll up the German line southwards in the exploitation phase, but the British Staff were not too keen to accept this aid. As for Third Army, no less than 14 of its 19

Left: Trees cut down by the Germans across a road in the Flesquières sector — one reason for the check here which ultimately jeopardised the battle
Right: Lt-Gen Kavanagh. His cavalry were to follow through when the tanks broke the German line
Far right: Maj-Gen Harper, 51st Division. He substituted his own infantry/tank drill for Fuller's — another reason for the check before Flesquières
Below: 'Hyacinth', ditched on the first day in the German second line near Ribécourt

Left: A British Mark IV, destroyed by German shell fire
Right: Mark IVs wait to move forward again across terrain (rolling chalk-based downland, comparatively free of shell holes) which promised good going for Fuller's standard tank drill (explained diagrammatically on page 110)
Far right: General Sir Julian Byng, Third Army. He was more ambitious than Haig in his estimate of the break-through possible at Cambrai. Haig had laid a 48-hour deadline for the initial onslaught—if the major objectives were not achieved the offensive was to end

Ullstein

divisions had been bled white at Third Ypres, and both men and resources were almost at exhaustion point. As Brigadier-General John Charteris, Haig's Chief of Intelligence, wrote: 'We shall have no reserves. We shall be alright at first; afterwards is in the lap of the God of battle.' At GHQ there was therefore little hope of a runaway success.

The Hindenburg Line
A word must here be devoted to the Hindenburg Line. The position comprised three lines of double trenches. The front line consisted of advanced posts, then a wide fire trench, with a support trench some 200 yards to the rear. A mile back was the official Hindenburg Support Line, once again two trenches deep, and two miles behind that was a third position, almost completed, known to the Germans as *Siegfried II.* Six belts of wire, the main one 100 yards deep, protected the main positions, and all support and rearward positions were similarly provided for. Holding the Cambrai sector of this strong position were the *20th Landwehr Division,* the *54th Division,* and part of the *9th Reserve Division,* which, together with the *183rd* further south, formed the *Gruppe Caudry* (or *XIII Korps*); this formation formed part of General von der Marwitz's *Second Army* (HQ at Le Cateau), which in turn was under Crown Prince Rupprecht of Bavaria's headquarters. The front line forces were not particularly strong, as Ludendorff subsequently admitted, for the German forces had also suffered considerably at Third Ypres. By a stroke of good fortune, however, the leading elements of the *107th Division,* being transferred from the Eastern Front, began to detrain at Cambrai on November 19, and were placed under temporary command of *54th Division* for use in any (as yet unforeseen) emergency.

General Byng entrusted the brunt of the initial phase of 'Operation G Y' to his III and IV Corps, with the Tank Corps to the fore. Lieutenant-General Sir William Pulteney (III Corps), had four divisions (6th, 12th, 20th and 29th), a cavalry detachment, and the 2nd and 3rd Tank Brigades at his disposal. His task was to engage three divisions in the assault phase, and with them secure the offensive's right flank (aided by VII Corps on

its right). First his divisions would be expected to breach the Hindenburg defences from Crèvecoeur to Bonavis, secure the line of the St Quentin Canal, and then force crossings at Marcoing and Masnières to form a bridgehead, through which the 2nd and 5th Cavalry Divisions of Lieutenant-General Sir C. T. McM. Kavanagh's Cavalry Corps would then advance to bypass Cambrai, sever its railway links, and pour on towards Cauroir, and Iway, to seize crossings over the Sensée. On Z+1 they would be followed by the 3rd and 4th Cavalry Divisions, whilst III Corps infantry formed a defensive flank from Gonnelieu to La Belle Etoile.

Meanwhile, Lieutenant-General Sir Charles Woollcombe (IV Corps), would initially have committed two divisions—the 62nd (West Riding) and the 51st (Highland)—to the battle, supported by the advance of a third—the 36th—on the left or northern flank of the offensive zone. They would be led into battle by the tanks of the 1st Tank Brigade, and it was ultimately decided that the corps would have 1st Cavalry Division under command. The IV Corps' task was to breach the German lines along its sector, capture Havrincourt, Flesquières, Graincourt and Cantaing in the process, and then pass through its reserve divisions and the cavalry for the all important attack on the Bourlon complex (ridge, wood and village)—Sir Douglas Haig's prime objective for the first stage of the battle. It was envisaged that the 1st Cavalry Division would aid in the isolation of Cambrai by establishing contact with the main Cavalry Corps to its right, before wheeling left to attack Bourlon village from the northeast.

Once these objectives had been achieved, Byng would commit his reserve (V Corps—the Guards, 40th and 59th Divisions) to secure the Sensée crossings, and create a bridgehead to the heights beyond. These troops would advance over IV Corps communications. All these associated operations would be supported by some 300 Allied aircraft, four squadrons being earmarked for close tactical support of the assault itself. Finally, on November 17, HQ Third Army notified all senior commanders that the offensive was to open at 0620 hours on Tuesday, November 20.

Meanwhile, feverish but well-concealed preparations were being undertaken at all

levels. One thousand guns were moved up and placed in camouflaged emplacements, and their crews instructed in the means of opening the bombardment without prior registration or ranging. Thirty-six special trains were steadily moving up the 476 tanks, first to the corps mounting area at Bray-sur-Somme, then towards their individual battalion 'lying-up' areas immediately behind the front. One by one, battalions were taken out of the line to train in tank/infantry tactics. The form of these followed the proposals of Fuller: tanks were to operate in groups of three, each vehicle carrying a heavy fascine of wood (weighing $1\frac{3}{4}$ tons), in association with four platoons of infantry, following in file at prescribed distances in two waves. The 'Tank Battle Drill' would be followed by every assault formation except the 51st (Highland) Division, whose commander, Major-General G. M. Harper, a soldier 'of extremely strong views' (according to Woollcombe) imposed a variation which was to have important repercussions on his sector.

Stage by stage the broad intention (but not the date) was revealed to lower formations. The final moves took place from November 17. The tanks (each battalion having a fighting strength of 36 machines supported by a further six) moved forward

Imperial War Museum

Ullstein

by night, crawling along in bottom gear (to reduce the volume of engine noise) following white tapes over the last 1,500 yards, while aircraft flew low overhead and machine guns maintained routine fire tasks further to smother the tell-tale rumble—with success. Camp fires were strictly forbidden by night and carefully controlled by day. On the 62nd Division's front, a false screen of trees and brushwood was erected surreptitiously along the forward edge of Havrincourt Wood, behind which the divisional artillery was sited within 2,000 yards of the German front line. However, the Germans were not so completely fooled as has sometimes been claimed. Although on November 16 von der Marwitz reported that he did not anticipate a major British attack, Crown Prince Rupprecht was not wholly satisfied. Early on the 18th a German raid captured an NCO and five men, who under interrogation revealed that an attack was being prepared against Havrincourt. Consequently, the German *54th Division* was placed on full alert from midday. On the 19th, German monitors picked up a snatch of a telephone conservation—'Tuesday, Flanders . . .' As a result an infantry regiment and several reserve battalions were switched into the Cambrai area, while *Gruppe Arras* was alerted that an attack

on Havrincourt was likely the next morning, and that it might be accompanied by tanks—preceded, however, by a bombardment. From the early hours of the 20th, *Gruppe Caudry* was also stood-to. These moves, however, were mainly precautionary in nature and decidedly limited in scale. In sum, the Germans knew that something was brewing on the Cambrai sector, but failed to appreciate its scale or form. The German High Command was caught unprepared. As Ludendorff wrote: 'We were expecting a continuation of the attacks in Flanders and on the French front, when on November 20 we were surprised by a fresh blow at Cambrai.'

'Zero-hour will be 0620 hours'

By the hour before dawn on Tuesday, November 20, 216 tanks had been moved into carefully camouflaged positions along a six-mile front. A little way back waited a further 96 in support, and each of the nine tank battalions had six more in reserve besides three signal tanks per brigade. At appointed positions 32 special 'grapnel-tanks' waited (charged with tearing large gaps through the German wire), and two 'bridge-tanks' prepared to accompany the cavalry advance. Five divisions of infantry silently formed up behind their tanks, many officers donning privates'

uniforms and carrying rifles. Brigadier-General Elles took up his position in *'Hilda'* towards the centre of 6th Division's front, his tank flying the improvised green, red and brown battle-standard (signifying 'from mud through blood to the green fields beyond'). A final message went to all formations: 'Zero-hour will be 0620 hours.'

Precisely at the appointed minute the guns crashed out, and the first wave of tanks surged forwards into No-Man's Land, each 'main body' vehicle being followed at 25 to 50 yards by the infantry platoons. As the guns successively raised their sights to keep the shell-line 300 yards ahead of the advance, a two-mile smoke-screen soon blinded the defenders of the Flesquières sector, and a half-mile screen filled Nine Wood, supplementing the prevailing autumn mists. Good progress was soon being signalled on all sectors. 'The German outposts, dazed or annihilated by the sudden deluge of shells, were overrun in an instant', wrote D. G. Browne in *The Tank in Action*. 'The triple belts of wire were crossed as if they had been beds of nettles, and 350 pathways were sheared through them for the infantry.' Reaching the German fire-trench, the tanks carried through their drill, passing over fascines to attack the support trench in similar fashion while the infantry poured into the German positions to clear them with grenade, bullet and bayonet. The *Blue Line* was occupied by 1000 hours.

Progress was astoundingly rapid for officers and men used to measuring progress in yards. For the tank crews, the advance was exhilarating but far from comfortable. 'When it lurched it threw its crews about like so many peanuts,' recalled Captain D. E. Hickey, 'and they had to clutch on to whatever they could when we were going over uneven ground. The rattle of the tracked machinery produced the illusion of tremendous speed.' In fact, an average speed of 2 mph was deemed good going, but the lurches, restricted view, appalling din and fumes of the roaring engines placed a heavy strain on the tank crews, all wearing chain-mail masks as protection against metal splinters from inside of the hulls.

These apparitions crawling out of the mists of a November morning in such large numbers terrified the leading German

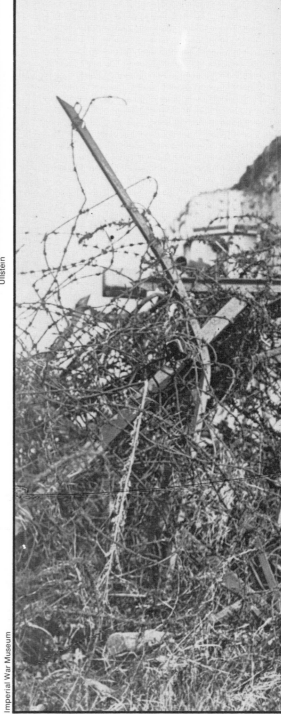

formations. Many turned to flee. 'Without exaggeration', wrote a German officer of the scenes behind the lines, 'some of the infantry seemed to be off their heads with fright.' It seemed as if the entire front was collapsing, as the tank second wave passed to the front through their rallying comrades, and headed for the *Brown Line* — the Hindenburg support positions. On many sectors the rate of advance was maintained unchecked. Away on the distant right, 12th Division had reached the *Blue Line* as early as 0830 hours, and within an hour all III Corps' initial tasks had been achieved. In front of Ribécourt, however, *'Hilda'* had become firmly 'ditched' and a frustrated Elles had to return to his headquarters, where he found time to send a telegram to Colonel Ernest Swinton (the creator of the Tank Corps) in London: 'All ranks thank you. Your show. Elles.'

General Harper's peculiar tactics

All this had been achieved with insignificant loss — except on the Flesquières sector of 51st Division's front, where, as we have already recorded, tank casualties had been heavy. Here officers were already complaining that an excessive interval had developed between infantry and tanks. Why was this? The arguments continue to this day, but it would seem that Major-General Harper must bear personal responsibility. This officer had substituted his own infantry/tank drill for Colonel Fuller's standard version. By Harper's method, the 'advanced guard tanks' were brigaded together, and ordered to push straight ahead over the fire-trench to achieve the maximum possible initial penetration, leaving the 'main body' tanks to support the infantry clearing operations. Even more important, Harper laid down an interval of 'not less than 100 yards' between tanks and following infantry, and insisted that the latter should advance, not by platoons in file, but by sections in extended order. The cumulative effect of these changes was that the lead tanks got far ahead of the infantry, and became easy targets, while far to their rear the Highlanders, in deployed sections, found far more difficulty in struggling through the wire than their comrades on other sectors, who passed through in file immediately behind their tanks, and thus kept in close touch with them.

Here was one reason for the check before Flesquières — which ultimately ruined the effectiveness of the battle. But there were other reasons too. There was no denying that Flesquières constituted the strongest sector of the German position opposite IV Corps. Placed as it was on a reverse slope, its protective ridge forming the head of a re-entrant, leading down to the Grand Ravine valley, which was in turn flanked by the villages of Havrincourt and Ribécourt, it can be understood why General Harper doubted the advisability of a straightforward frontal assault on such a position, with or without tank support. Other unfortunate coincidences created further difficulties. The master plan enjoined a pause to consolidate and regroup for the forces operating against the flanks of the Flesquières salient after gaining their *Blue Line* objectives, and this encouraged the development of a certain loss of momentum in the centre. Furthermore, for some reason the effectiveness of the bombardment by the Allied artillery and aircraft against the German artillery positions neighbouring the village left much to be desired, many of the German guns remaining in action against the exposed forward tanks.

The garrison of Flesquières sector, commanded by Major Krebs, consisted of three battalions, two machine gun companies, and five field gun batteries, supported by four batteries of howitzers and five of heavier guns. Parts of *213 Field Artillery Regiment* were also placed under the command of *54th Division* as they materialised from Cambrai with the leading troops of *107th Division*. General von der Watter, moreover, had specifically and effectively trained his gunners to engage moving targets over open sights. These guns, therefore, proceeded to mete out destruction to 'D' and 'E' Battalions of the Tank Corps. Some accounts claim that 16 tanks were knocked out *before* they even reached the Flesquières wire; the modern consensus would seem to suggest only seven. This notwithstanding, there is no doubt that by last light on November 20 no less than 39 tanks had been destroyed or disabled (two temporarily) on the sector — sufficient, as it proved, to ruin the success of the first day's fighting and even to blunt the effectiveness of Third Army's entire offensive by its side-effects.

Opposite page. Top left: A Mark IV ditched outside Bourlon, the northern-most limit of the British advance. Bourlon Wood was taken on the third day, but despite desperate attacks over the next four days the village itself never fell
Above: A Mark IV clears barbed wire, one of the most important functions of the new tank arm. Preliminary artillery barrages (there was not one at Cambrai) consumed up to 4,500,000 shells to achieve the same end
Left· Fontaine, near Bourlon. German troops march round an abandoned Mark IV on the third day

Haig and Byng called for new efforts, but tempers were becoming brittle. 'If you don't take Fontaine, General Harper', Sir Charles Woollcombe declared, 'God help you!'

The celebrated story of 'the gunner of Flesquières' to whom even Haig paid homage in the Cambrai Despatch, has become the subject of great contention. Some versions speak of a German Major who single-handed operated an abandoned field gun to devastating effect before being killed himself. 'The great bravery of this officer aroused the admiration of all ranks' (Haig). The Germans, however, have never officially recognised the existence of this heroic officer, but *Oberleutnant* Zindler's eye-witness account claims the honour for *Unteroffizier* Krüger of the *8th Battery*. This NCO was stationed 500 yards east of the village, and the historian Becke claims that it was his gun that knocked out seven tanks, and that his body was found beside his gun.

Thus there were many factors that contributed to the 51st Division's failure before Flesquières. However, it cannot be disputed that the division's reserve brigade was never sent into the battle on the first day. It was also unfortunate that an attempt to launch 18th Brigade of the 6th Division against the flank of the position from the neighbourhood of Premy Chapel also foundered. Both circumstances are capable of explanation; *Plan GY* laid it down that the Highlanders' reserve was to be used only against *Siegfried II* – which had not been reached on this sector; and 18th Brigade Headquarters, well forward in the battle zone, was found only after a long search, and daylight was fading before an attack could be extemporised. By that time the rain was pouring down, so it was decided to call the effort off.

One consequence of these setbacks was the failure to take Bourlon and its key ridge. An important rôle in this operation was entrusted to the 1st Cavalry Division (IV Corps). This force was under orders to pass up the Grand Ravin to Ribécourt, flank Nine Wood, press along the St Quentin Canal, and finally swing northwest to attack Bourlon. The cavalry commander, Major-General R. L. Mullens, on receipt of an erroneous message from the Cavalry Corps at 1130 hours to the effect that Ribécourt was still dominated by the Germans, adjusted his orders to incorporate an advance through Flesquières. This was obviously impossible, and by the time 2nd Cavalry Brigade, leading the division, had extricated itself from

the rear area of the blocked 51st Division and reassembled in the Grand Ravine, several hours had passed. Similar difficulties prevented any participation in the proposed 18th Brigade's attack, which was in any case hampered by command problems of its own. Thus 1st Cavalry Division spent a frustrating day; the only achievement was a useful raid by 'A' Squadron, 4th Dragoon Guards, which bypassed Cantaing and routed a German headquarters near Chateau-la-Folie. This was the most dramatic penetration of the 'Cavalry Gap' on the first day.

Meanwhile, on the left flank of IV Corps, the 62nd Division had made great progress up the Canal du Nord, capturing both Havrincourt and Graincourt, and ultimately 186th Brigade reached the Cambrai-Bapaume highroad. Parts of 36th Division made equal gains along their sector to the 62nd's left. As for the fortunes of III Corps later on November 20, these too, had continued to be blessed with success. The Hindenburg Support Line had been substantially breached by midday. On the extreme right, 12th Division commenced the formation of a defensive flank along Bonavis Ridge, whilst the 70 surviving 'runners' of the III Corps tank battalions led a further advance to the St Quentin Canal. Prominent in these operations were the men of 29th Division, who reached Nine Wood and Marcoing by midday. Further to the right, the canal bank was occupied, but not before the Germans had successfully demolished the main crossings. This caused some delay in establishing the 'cavalry gap' demanded by the plan; long lines of horsemen were already

Above: A British Mark IV brings in a captured German 5.9-inch naval gun east of Ribecourt. *Below:* British tanks, two of them carrying fascines, move on the German lines.

This page: 3.7-cm. German anti-tank gun *(bottom),* manufactured by Rheinmetall. *Weight in firing position:* 385 lbs, including 24 rounds of ammunition. *Weight in travelling position:* 1,020 lbs. *Weight of shell:* 1 lb. *Barrel length:* 21.5 calibres. *Muzzle velocity:* 1,125 ft./sec.; later 1,420 ft./sec. *Range:* 2,866 yds. *Elevation:* −6° to +9°. *Traverse:* 21°. *Crew:* 3 men. *Centre picture:* German prisoners march past British anti-aircraft guns: the RAF lost air superiority at an early stage. *Below:* German anti-tank rifle, a model disliked by the troops because of its strong recoil and because the barrel quickly became unbearably hot. *Weight:* 35 lbs. *Barrel lenght:* 4 ft. 3 ins. *Muzzle velocity:* 2200 ft./sec. *Maximum range:* 70 yds. *Calibre:* 13-mm.

John Batchelor

Imperial War Museum

moving up from Villers Plouich towards Marcoing, and from Gouzeaucourt towards Les Rues Vertes, but the canal line had still to be breached. This was, in fact, achieved about 1530 hours by 'B' Squadron of the Canadian Fort Garry Horse, which passed over an intact footbridge and routed a German battery, but in the end this intrepid formation was forced to stampede its horses and return to the bridge on foot under command of Lieutenant H. Strachan, who won the VC that day. Meanwhile, near Noyelles, the Reserve Squadron of the 7th Dragoon Guards also made a brief excursion to the north bank over three trestle bridges, but these relatively small scale successes, together with the exploit of the 4th Dragoon Guards already related, were the sum total of the cavalry's achievements on November 20.

The breakthrough is held
Apart from these setbacks, however, almost all objectives set for the 'break-in' phase of the battle had been achieved. A huge breach—almost six miles wide and up to 4,000 yards deep, had been torn into the Hindenburg Line; even *Siegfried II* had been severely breached on the Marcoing sector. This achievement had cost some 4,000 British casualties, but over 4,200 German prisoners had been taken, besides 100 guns. Much would clearly depend on the outcome of the next day's fighting. Overnight, however, the Germans were taking steps to check the rot. The intrepid survivors of the Flesquières garrison were withdrawn; the *107th Division* continued to come up from Cambrai, proving an in-

valuable source of men for patching the crucial sector between the Bapaume road and Masnières. They were still very anxious about the situation, being unaware of how many of the British reserves had already been committed to battle. 'Fortunately,' recorded the German High Command, 'the enemy was himself taken by surprise by the extent of his success.'

The renewed battle on November 21 from the British point of view is one of increasing exhaustion and a general reduction in forward momentum. In the early hours 51st Division had at last occupied a deserted Flesquières, and 154th Brigade passed through to attack Cantaing—captured, along with 300 prisoners, by 0030 hours. A number of tanks and part of the 5th Dragoon Guards shared in this success, which extended the breach driven into the *Siegfried II* position to a width of well over two miles. However, the desperate weariness of the infantry—and the tank crews—made a full exploitation impossible. Petrol, water and even ammunition were all in short supply. So the theme for November 21 was one of 'consolidation' rather than of dramatic gains. There were, indeed, a few setbacks. On left of IV Corps, a German counterattack retook Moeuvres from 36th Division. That evening, however, Sir Douglas Haig decided that the battle should continue, although his original time limit had been reached without the gaining of all key objectives—most especially the Bourlon position and the exploitation of the 'gap'—and despite the increasing evidence that the Germans were fast recovering from their initial surprise and be-

ginning to bring up reinforcements. However, the bolder course won. 'After weighing these various considerations, I decided to continue the operations to gain the Bourlon position.' Byng was accordingly ordered that IV Corps, supported by V Corps, was to continue its attack, whilst III Corps' offensive was to be 'shut-down' to a holding action on the right. The lure of Bourlon Ridge thus continued to exert its strong—and deadly—fascination over the Commander-in-Chief.

The next week's events were dominated by a herculean struggle for Bourlon. It was predominantly an infantry slogging match of the usual kind. For the British, the new phase opened badly with the loss of Fontaine on November 22 as German counter-attacks slammed home against the tired 51st and 62nd Divisions. However, in rear the Guards Division and two fresh brigades of 36th Division were preparing to mount an attack to regain Moeuvres, while the artillery poured a relentless fire into Bourlon Wood and village.

Next morning (November 23), 100 tanks led 40th Division against Bourlon ridge, with 432 guns giving fire support. Bourlon, however, was now the responsibility of *Gruppe Arras* which had two divisions in the line and a further two (including the *3rd Guards*) moving up in support; there were also now 200 German guns to help contest the sector, while the arrival of Baron von Richthofen's famous 'circus' implied a serious challenge for control of the air over the battle zone. Meantime *Gruppe Caudry* had received two new divisions, and *Gruppe Busigny* had taken over the left of

Peter Sarson

Opposite page. Top left: A fascine-laying Mark IV. The fascines, carried on the unditching rail and released from inside, were 4½ feet in diameter, 10 feet long and 1½ tons in weight. *Top right:* The rôle of the 32 special grapnel-tanks. *This page. Above and above right:* A closer view of Fuller's tanks battle drill (shown on page 110), showing in more detail the relationship between infantry and fascine-laying tanks

the German line to relieve its battered neighbour of all distractions.

The struggle for Bourlon reached its peak on November 23, when Major-General Sir John Ponsonby's 40th Division reached the crest of Bourlon Wood, but failed to penetrate the village beyond. In the space of 72 hours this single division was to lose 4,000 casualties. The Germans were suffering too, but Moser (commanding *Gruppe Arras*) noted that 'our artillery and aeroplanes are gaining the ascendancy more and more'.

Haig and Byng called for new efforts, but tempers were becoming brittle. 'If you don't take Fointaine, General Harper,' Sir Charles Woollcombe declared to the commander of 51st Division, charged with a new objective on the right of 40th Division, 'God help you!' Despite this admonition, little progress was ultimately made, and 40th Division's flank remained dangerously exposed. Shortages of manpower were being experienced, and Byng authorised IV Corps to use 1st Cavalry Division in infantry rôles. He also brought in the Guards Division to relieve the 51st.

A further major effort was ordered for midday on November 24; the gallant 40th

Division and the dismounted 9th Cavalry Brigade were to be thrown against Bourlon at noon; the Guards were to attack the Fontaine sector, and the 36th and 56th Divisions were to clear German positions between Moeuvres and Inchy.

The battle was ferocious; at first it seemed that 40th Division might take the village, but by 1100 hours they had been repulsed save for one small party under Colonel Wade which clung to a segment of the village for two days. By this time the whole of the Cavalry Division was involved, but by last light the Germans had regained the northern edge of the Wood. Sir Douglas Haig might still publicly talk about a breakthrough by three cavalry divisions, and had managed to detain two divisions earmarked for transfer to Italy. Brigadier-General Charteris (his Intelligence chief) was aware of the true situation: 'Things have not gone well. Our troops are tired, and the Germans are getting up large reinforcements; we have none available.'

Byng continued to fling his weary and depleted divisions against Bourlon, but to no avail. He switched his divisions to and fro, set new deadlines, tried to inspire his commanders and men to new exertions, but it was by now beyond the power of Third Army. Colonel Wade was rescued on November 26, and heavy bombardments were hurled at the Germans, who by now had seven divisions in the line, four of them in the key sector, and their artillery strength was 500.

The last effort, as it proved, was made on November 27. The 62nd and Guards Divi-

sions, accompanied by 30 tanks, advanced yet again against the Bourlon and Fontaine sectors. Casualties were heavy. Fontaine was partly overrun, but a German counterattack, ten battalions strong, proved too heavy, and the Guards Division was driven back to its start line. By this time the 2nd Guards Brigade had been reduced to 500 men. At the day's end, the British line in Bourlon Wood had been driven back to the crest amongst the trees.

After this failure the Commander-in-Chief was prepared to concede failure, and Third Army was ordered to close down its offensive. On November 28, IV Corps headquarters issued a significant order: 'Wire should be got up at all costs today, and wiring on the Bourlon perimeter systematically carried out by pioneers and R.E.' This signalled the end of the British adventure of Cambrai: the old conditions of stalemate had reasserted themselves.

But the history of the Battle of Cambrai still had another, final, act to run. German artillery were now hurling shells against the newly-extemporised British positions in Bourlon Wood. On other sectors, both November 28 and 29 were relatively quiet days—but to some this seemed more menacing than reassuring. These fears were proved correct when, at 0830 hours on November 30, an intense German bombardment rained down on the British lines. Soon alarm signals were being received from many sectors. As one sergeant of the 1st Royal Berkshires reported to his officer: 'SOS gone up in 27 different places, and the Bosche coming over the 'ill in thousands.' The German counteroffensive had begun.

CAMBRAI
THE GERMAN

Ten days after the tank surprise at Cambrai the Germans repaid the compliment with one which was similar in principle but different in method. Without a long artillery preparation, a short hurricane gas and smoke bombardment cleared the way for an infantry attack using new infiltration tactics. This was a foretaste of the offensives which were to smash through the British and French armies in spring 1918. *David Chandler.*

COUNTERATTACK

Below: A German war artist's impression of the first day of the stunning counterattack

A battery of 77-mm's in action.
Shell fire was the greatest single cause of tank casualty at Cambrai,
accounting for over one third of all losses on the first day (65 out of 179 tanks)

Following the eventual stabilisation of the front after the exhaustion of General Sir Julian Byng's dramatic but brief offensive, it was not long before the German High Command was planning a counteroffensive. On November 27, while the battle of Bourlon Wood still raged, Ludendorff conferred with Crown Prince Rupprecht at Le Cateau. Meantime 20 divisions were being massed in the Cambrai area. Ludendorff was convinced that 'there has never been such an opportunity' for a successful blow, and insisted that all should be in readiness by November 30.

The plan envisaged a short, intense bombardment followed by a rapid attack by *Gruppe Caudry* and *Gruppe Busigny* in the general direction of Metz, the village immediately to the south of Havrincourt Wood. If successful, the German generals hoped that this would compromise the whole British salient and compel its evacuation. Meanwhile, *Gruppe Arras* (some seven divisions and 130,000 men strong) would fire heavy barrages and conduct demonstrations designed to distract the British IV Corps (Lieutenant-General Sir Charles Woollcombe), and once the eastern attacks had become well established, Lieutent-General Otto von Moser was to launch an attack with three divisions to the west of Bourlon Wood and drive southwards. Reserve divisions would be held in readiness to consolidate and exploit the gains on both sectors of the German attack. The minimum to be achieved was the recapture of the Hindenburg position, but some officers spoke hopefully of a major breakthrough.

November 28 saw the opening of a heavy bombardment against Bourlon Wood, 16,000 rounds of gas and high explosive shells being pumped into the ravaged area. The violence of this shelling served to convince the British High Command that the major German blow, if and when it came, would almost certainly be launched against the northern part of the salient. Not that warnings of other possibilities were lacking. Major-General J. S. Jeudwine, GOC 55th Division (VII Corps), whose troops were holding a six-mile front facing *Gruppe Busigny,* reported ominous German concentrations in the vicinity of Banteux and Twenty-Two Ravines. Indications of a coming attack included German artillery registration on hitherto unshelled areas, a marked increase in German air activity over the front line, and the measures taken to prevent Allied aircraft reconnoitring in the Banteux area. Yet there was little sense of urgency at either GHQ or Third Army Headquarters, and Byng authorised no preliminary movement by the slender reserves.

The British generals later denied vehemently that they were taken by surprise by both the scale and direction of the German onslaught unleashed on November 30, and attempted to blame junior commanders for lack of proper vigilance. Be that as it may (and subsequent research has not borne out the conclusions reached by the Cambrai Enquiry), in the words of the late Sir Basil Liddell Hart, the Germans 'repaid the tank surprise by one that was similar in principle if different in method'. When the German guns abruptly crashed

out shortly after dawn on November 29, there was no immediate indication of the line of the coming attack. All too soon, however, SOS signals were hurtling skywards and reports of attacks flooding into HQ VII Corps, as wave after wave of German troops (some 12 in all, the rearward lines being led by mounted officers) emerged one after another from the Banteux Ravine at the precise time (0700 hours) that Jeudwine had asked for the heavy bombardment. The focal point of the German attack was the boundary between III and VII Corps, and the brunt of the onslaught was borne by Major-General W. D. Smith's 20th Division and Major-General A. B. Scott's 12th Division—occupying the right of Pulteney's sector—and Jeudwine's over-extended 55th on the extreme left of VII Corps. The southernmost limit of *Gruppe Busigny's* attack was opposite Vendhuille, but the northern extension rapidly grew as, at about 0800 hours, the Germans committed *Gruppe Caudry* to the attack from Bantouzelle to Rumilly, and drove forwards towards Marcoing. Thus III Corps suddenly found three of its four front line divisions heavily, and then critically, involved.

The form of attack was novel on the Western Front. Behind the intense and short bombardment, the German infantry came forward in groups, employing infiltration tactics. Centres of strong opposition were deliberately bypassed by the leading formations, which pressed on towards the rear exploiting the line of least resistance. Low-flying aircraft, strafing and bombing, gave close support, and numbers of artillery batteries advanced immediately behind the infantry. Similar methods had been employed with success in both Russia (notably at Riga) and Italy. They worked well enough in France on this bleak late-November morning, and would be re-employed on a huge scale the following spring with even more telling effect. The speed of the German penetration took many formations completely by surprise. Major-General Sir B. de Lisle (GOC 29th Division) was almost captured at Quentin Mill. Headquarters of 35th Brigade (12th Division) was surrounded, but Brigadier-General B. Vincent rallied his staff and fought his way out back to Revelon Ridge, where he began to form 'Vincent Force' from men of many units in an effort to stem the tide of the German advance, which was overrunning the gun-line, capturing many pieces before they could be withdrawn.

The British line is torn open
Soon the rear area of III Corps was jammed with retreating transport and guns, and here and there the flood was joined by units of administrative troops. Numbers of front line battalions found themselves cut off, and communications were plunged into chaos. Generals desperately tried to find reserves to bolster the collapsing front. But the German advance swept remorselessly forward, and by 1030 hours an eight-mile sector of the British line from Les Rues Vertes to Vendhuille had been driven

in, the maximum penetration bringing the Germans to within two and a half miles of Metz after their capture, in succession, of Gauche Wood, Gonnelieu and Gouzeaucourt. The significance of Metz to the German plan lay in the fact that through it ran the most important route up the Grand Ravine to Flesquières and distant Bourlon Wood.

On the northern sector, meanwhile, another heavy engagement had flared up at about 0930 hours as Moser's *Gruppe Arras* began the secondary attack against IV and VI Corps. The German *49th Reserve, 214th* and *221st Divisions* advanced along a three-mile front running from Tadpole Copse in the west to the approaches to Bourlon Wood, supported by the fire of 500 guns. However, the Germans found themselves facing a maelstrom of artillery fire. In anticipation of just such an attack, Third Army had allocated IV Corps no less than eight division's worth of supporting artillery, together with corps and army heavy batteries, and these now made their weight of fire felt. Thus, when the German *3rd Guards Division* (east of Bourlon) attempted to probe towards Cantaing, the attack was disintegrated by gunfire, and by midday it had made no progress. On Moser's main sector of attack, however, the greatest pressure was felt by 56th Division (VI Corps), 2nd and part of 47th Divisions (both parts of IVth Corps). Despite heavy casualties, the German attacks kept coming forward. One group of eight British machine guns, part of 2nd Division, fired all of 70,000 rounds into the flank of successive attacks at close range

with dire effect. Nevertheless, so well pressed-home were the German attacks, that at 1030 hours IV Corps warned its artillery to be ready to fall back at short notice and took preliminary measures to garrison the Hindenburg Support Line in case it should prove necessary to abandon the front. For a time it seemed impossible that Major-General F. A. Davidson's 56th Division could remain in line, but it did hold despite relentless pressure and a growing shortage of ammunition. The Germans made some ground near Tadpole Copse, but nothing vital was lost. On the right of the 56th, the brigades of 2nd Division (IV Corps) also came in for a difficult time. For a period they found themselves out of contact with Major-General C. E. Pereira's headquarters, but 'A' Squadron of King Edward's Horse provided the GOC with 15 gallopers, who maintained a tenuous link with the embattled front line. Many units sacrificed themselves during these desperate hours, and many deeds of great gallantry were performed. The net result was that *Gruppe Arras's* attack proved abortive on November 30. The *Official History* justly describes this as 'an outstanding British achievement in the war on the Western Front'.

It must be recognised, however, that this local success was made possible only at the cost of absorbing a very high proportion of Third Army's resources in terms of both men and guns. Haig urged Byng 'to use his reserves energetically' as GHQ took steps to move four divisions from other sectors towards Bapaume and Peronne as a safeguard against a German breakthrough.

Below: Germans pose confidently on the wreckage of a British tank which a few days before had sent them running in terror. *Inset:* Another wrecked Mark IV, this one at Rumilly, captured by the Germans on the first day of their counterattack

Bayer Hauptstaatarchiv, Munich

But Byng had soon played almost all his cards; as we shall see, the whole of the Cavalry Corps was eventually committed in support of VII and III Corps, as well as 61st Division to man the Hindenburg Support Line. By 1100 hours it had also proved necessary to transfer the Guards Division from IV to III Corps command.

The major area of crisis remained on the eastern sector, where confusion was threatening to convert defeat into disaster. A series of circumstances staved off this danger. Brigadier-General Vincent's intrepid force on Revelon Ridge was first joined by 20th Hussars, who at once entered the fight in a dismounted rôle. Next to appear was 1st Guards Brigade from Metz, the first echelon of Major-General G. P. T. Fielding's division to be sent up from a rest area to patch the staggering line. The 1st Guards Brigade did more: extemporising a counterattack towards Gouzeaucourt, by 1130 hours it had succeeded in clearing the village, while to the south large numbers of British cavalry extended the *ad hoc* line. The recapture of Gouzeaucourt was consolidated by the arrival of 36 tanks of 'A' and 'B' Battalions, switched to the south after the abrupt cancellation of their movement order to the Somme. Then 5th Cavalry Division, after a considerable approach march from Peronne, passed through the Guards towards Villers Guislain, only to be halted by severe German fire. Snow was of the opinion that it would have been far better to unleash the cavalry against the overextended southern flank of the narrow and still disorganised German corridor extending from the east of Gouzeaucourt, but Byng insisted on committing the cavalry to frontal operations. This decision may have sacrificed a chance of a telling riposte to the German breakthrough, and the Germans were afforded an opportunity to consolidate their gains. Be that as it may, by dusk some sort of a British line had been cobbled together, linking the shattered right wing of III Corps with the left of VII. By last light, 3rd Guards Brigade had come up, with 2nd in support in Gouzeaucourt Wood. The 20th Division was rallying on Welsh Ridge, and on its left 29th Division was still in firm possession of Marcoing after a day of heavy fighting. Administrative confusion had still to be sorted out, and many men went hungry. Others were more fortunate. 'Our rations captured', noted Lieutenant-G. E. Chandler of 11th Essex (2nd Division), who had spent an exhausting day digging extemporised positions, 'but another division shared with us'.

On December 1 much of the drama of the day's fighting again centred around the events on the southern flank. With the intention of forestalling a renewed German attack, at 0630 hours 3rd Guards Brigade launched an attack towards Gonnelieu. It did not fare too successfully, but the appearance of a single tank at a critical moment near Green Switch Trench caused many Germans to surrender. Better fortune blessed 1st Guards Brigade which, aided by 16 tanks of 'H' Battalion, succeeded in retaking much of Gauche Wood and Quintin Mill. Mounted action by 4th and 5th Cavalry Divisions on the left of the Guards achieved little of positive value, but there were now 74 tanks available in support of III and VII Corps flank.

In the centre matters did not go well, both Masnières and Les Rues Vertes were

lost, but the German impetus was by now nearly exhausted. The same was true of the northern side of the salient, where the immediate crisis was deemed to have passed by the end of December 1. Lieutenant-General Sir E. A. Fanshawe and HQ V Corps was able to relieve Lieutenant-General Woollcombe and HQ IV Corps — the original hand-over planned for the 30th having been postponed.

The Germans had not yet quite shot their bolt, however. After a reasonably quiet day on the 2nd, they advanced once again on December 3 and took possession of La Vacquerie from 61st Division, which had relieved parts of the exhausted 12th and 20th Divisions only the previous day. The same day, it was deemed necessary to withdraw from the British bridgehead on the east bank of the St Quentin Canal and reconcentrate 29th Division around Marcoing. Meanwhile, the German line assumed its final shape, running from south of Quentin Ridge to Welsh Ridge and thence to Marcoing.

Ludendorff stridently claimed 'an offensive victory on the Western Front' but admitted that matters had not developed 'quite as well as I had hoped'. High British staff circles were far from happy with the overall situation. On December 2, Haig visited the front and told Byng 'to select a good winter line' but not to issue any orders on the subject at that point. The problem was to find a truly secure position. Anxiety centred around the continued German possession of Bonavis Ridge; unless it could be recovered, Haig considered that Third Army's position would remain precariously unbalanced, and the whole Marcoing/Bourlon salient would be compromised. Yet there were no fresh troops whatsoever with which to attempt its recapture, and the thought of becoming involved in a battle of attrition through the winter was unattractive to say the least, and, as Haig pointed out to the CIGS, there would be no question of sending further aid to Italy under the prevailing circumstances. A hard decision had to be taken. On December 3 it was decided that the Bourlon salient must be evacuated; the orders were issued next day. On the night of the 4th/5th the evacuation began, the troops falling back to the 'Yellow Line', some 2,000 yards ahead of the chosen final position. Thus blood-stained Bourlon Wood, the Marcoing area, and long stretches of the Hindenburg Line, were all abandoned to the Germans. The operation was completed by the early hours of December 7. To the west of the Canal du Nord, the British line was almost back where it had been on November 19. In the centre, Havrincourt, Flesquières and Ribécourt remained in British hands, the new line here running along parts of the Hindenburg Support Line, but from Welsh Ridge it swung sharply away to the southwest, and the Germans were left with considerable areas of former British territory in their possession. Losses and gains more or less cancelled each other out.

Not unnaturally, the Germans were astounded by these unforeseen developments. 'We are jubilant,' wrote Moser; 'since 1914 the first withdrawal of the proud Briton'. Ludendorff later described it as 'a good ending to the extremely heavy fighting of 1917. Our action has given us valuable hints for an offensive battle in the west if we wished to undertake one in 1918.'

For the immediate future, however, the Germans needed rest and recuperation as much as their opponents. So ended the famous battle of Cambrai. For the British it had proved 'a sombre sunset after a brilliant sunrise' (Liddell Hart).

The cost of the 17 days of triumph and tragedy had not been light. From November 20 to December 8, the 19 divisions of Third Army had lost 44,207 men. Over 6,000 of these casualties, together with the loss of 103 field and 55 heavy guns, had been the cost of November 30. The German *Second Army* (ultimately 20 divisions strong) confessed to 41,000 casualties, and the loss of 145 guns, but probably excluded considerable numbers of lightly wounded. Of their total admitted loss, 14,000 were suffered during the counteroffensive. What had been gained by either side from these exertions? In terms of the Western Front, precious little ground or overall advantage. It is true that two German divisions from the Eastern Front, intended for Italy, had been diverted to Flanders, but the British programme for reinforcing their Italian allies had also been at least partially disrupted. On the other hand, both sides had learnt much of tactical value: on the British side the employment of tanks; on the German the value of infiltration tactics.

As might be expected, there was much criticism in London about the reasons why 'a resounding victory' had been allowed to degenerate into 'a disastrous rout' (Lloyd George). Characteristically, Haig did not flinch from accepting the ultimate responsibility. On December 3 he had written '. . . whatever happens, the responsibility is mine'. At the Cambrai Enquiry, several senior officers, including Byng, tried to blame negligence on the part of the fighting soldier. 'I attribute the reason for the local success on the part of the enemy to one cause and one alone', testified the commander of Third Army, 'namely — lack of training on the part of junior officers and NCOs and men.' Although General J. C. Smuts, consulted by the War Cabinet as an independent assessor, substantially agreed with this assertion, the verdict has been much modified with the passage of time. In the words of a recent historian of Cambrai, Robert Woollcombe, 'the High Command was responsible for the confusion, and the troops for the valour'. Perhaps the ultimate reason for the bitter disappointments of the period between November 30 and December 7 has been most aptly summarised by John Terraine: 'Two years of offensive strategy had diverted the British army's attention from defensive problems.' This was demonstrably true at Cambrai. This shortcoming, together with the weariness of the troops, the shortage of adequate reserves, and the failure of British military intelligence to estimate correctly the strength and intentions of the Germans, accounts in large measure for the final outcome of this celebrated engagement which brought the bitter year of 1917 to an unmourned conclusion.

Further Reading
Liddell Hart, Sir Basil, *The Tanks,* Vol 1 (Cassell 1959)
Terraine, J., *Douglas Haig* (Hutchinson 1963)
Woollcombe, R., *The First Tank Battle: Cambrai 1917* (Barker 1967)

The new tank arm had seized almost all of its 'break-in' objectives on the first day of Cambrai and had opened the way for a massive advance, but on the second day the old conditions of stalemate reasserted themselves and the advance degenerated into yet another slogging match. Why?
General Sir Michael Carver

FALSE DAWN
TANKS AT CAMBRAI

The arguments about the use of tanks at the Battle of Cambrai in November 1917 were to set the pattern for arguments about the use of tanks in almost every battle in which they were employed thereafter. Protagonists and antagonists were to adopt much the same positions and to remain as blind to and contemptuous of the views of their opponents as they were in the aftermath of the battle itself.

The criticisms levelled by the tank enthusiasts in general were, first, that a higher proportion of the total number of tanks available should have been kept in reserve, ready for use after the initial attack on the Hindenburg Line; secondly, that there were no reserves of infantry available for the same purpose, and finally that the cavalry were not only too far back to exploit the opportunity to break out when it was presented, but that, when they were brought up to the starting post, they were unwilling or unable to achieve anything. In sum, the magnificent opportunity created by the employment of tanks in conditions that, for the first time, exploited their potentiality, was thrown away because the higher command had insufficient faith in the tanks to back them up properly with adequate reserves and placed too much reliance on the cavalry.

A fair amount of this criticism is based on hindsight: some of it is distorted and self-contradictory; but in general it is sound. However, it is oversimplified and glosses over many of the real difficulties.

First of all it is important to clarify the aim of the battle—it changed significantly in the process of conception, and this had important effects on the soundness of its plan. Although Fuller's original idea, conceived as far back as June 1917, was for a joint Franco-British attack to capture St Quentin as a preparatory step for a further offensive in the spring of 1918, this was modified in discussion with Elles to a plan for a raid south of Cambrai 'to destroy the enemy's personnel and guns, to demoralise and disorganise him, and not to capture ground'. The area chosen was that on which the Battle of Cambrai was subsequently to be fought.

Fuller's proposal was for a force of three tank brigades of two battalions each, one, or preferably two, divisions of infantry or cavalry with additional artillery and two air squadrons. The raiding force was to form three groups, the principal one intended to 'scour the country' in the area between the Canal du Nord to the west and the Canal de l'Escaut (also known as the St Quentin canal) to the east, a frontage of about six miles, while smaller groups operated on each flank.

It was envisaged that the first line of tanks would go straight through to the Germans' gun positions and attack them: the second would crush the wire and work up and down the forward trench system in co-operation with the infantry: the third would make for points of special tactical importance and would help in the mopping up. Only three hours after the attack had been launched, the force would begin to withdraw, forming a rearguard in co-operation with aircraft to protect dismounted cavalry who, it was imagined, would be escorting large numbers of prisoners back to the British lines.

It is surprising that so eminent and perceptive a military critic as Liddell Hart should have looked favourably on this plan. To launch a major attack on the most suitable ground for tanks on the whole front: to give a dress rehearsal, as it were, of what one would hope to do in any subsequent major decisive action: to abandon it all after only a few hours, having inflicted damage which would certainly not be decisive and which would probably not take long to make good, inevitably leaving a number of one's own tanks on the abandoned battlefield: to commit all these elementary military errors would have been folly indeed.

The idea smoulders on
Fortunately this plan was never pursued, but with its acceptance of a limitation of resources it had a pernicious influence on the plans which developed from it. Brigadier-General Tudor, Commander Royal Artillery of 9th Division, was anxious to try an attack with no preliminary artillery bombardment or registration, relying on survey methods of gun-laying and on the tanks for crushing wire. He persuaded his superiors in IV Corps to look favourably on these ideas as the basis for an ambitious attack 'to advance to Flesquières ridge, swing left and roll up the German line to the Scarpe, with cavalry operating towards Cambrai'. This was whittled down at corps HQ to a more limited operation involving little more than the occupation of the front and support trench systems of the Hindenburg Line between the two canals, and the destruction of the forces, including their artillery, in that area. Three divisions, two cavalry brigades, eight field artillery brigades and Third Army's heavy artillery were considered necessary for this operation, and it was suggested that the Tank Corps should assess the number of tanks needed.

The corps commander, Lieutenant-General Woollcombe, sent this plan up to Third Army on August 23. Between then and September 6 Elles visited the area and found it very suitable for tanks. So much so that he thought that more could be achieved and that the tanks could clear the area up to the eastern canal. General Byng was fired with enthusiasm again

and had visions of his favourite cavalry at last coming into their own. He envisaged that the tank action would lead to a complete breakdown in the Germans' defence, as there were only two German divisions in the area and it was estimated that 48 hours must elapse before any reinforcements could arrive. By that time General Byng saw the whole Cavalry Corps deployed, galloping northwards to the River Sensée and breaking out northeastwards round Cambrai to cause havoc on the German lines of communication.

Cold water was poured on this glorious concept by GHQ, but General Byng was told to continue to plan the operation in detail in complete secrecy. As the Flanders offensive gradually bogged down in the mud, Haig began to look around for other means of keeping the offensive going in order to prevent the Germans from attacking the French, still reeling from their mutinies. His aim was not just altruistic. He was determined to avoid taking over any more front from the French or reinforcing them.

On October 13 the go-ahead for Cambrai was given. Byng was allowed to allot four fresh infantry divisions (of the five he said he wanted) to start training with the three tank brigades (less four battalions) that had been made available. A commanders' conference was held on October 26 at which the plan was divulged, the very day that Haig was told by the War Office to send two divisions immediately to stop the rot on the Italian Front as a result of the disaster of Caporetto.

The final plan for the battle as issued on November 13 was modified by Byng after comments by Haig. The aim of the operation was now to clear the whole area between the two canals right up to the River Sensée, which would involve an advance of about 15 miles as the crow flies. On the right III Corps was to secure and extend the right flank on the high ground west of the Escaut Canal. On the left IV Corps was to seize Bourlon Wood and Marquion, three miles further northwest on the Canal du Nord. The Cavalry Corps was to cross the Escaut Canal, surround and isolate Cambrai and cover the advance north and northeast of V Corps, which was to exploit the success as far as the River Sensée, sending troops to occupy the hills beyond it. Haig would then decide whether to advance towards Douai and Valenciennes, six and 14 miles respectively beyond the river. Haig insisted that Bourlon Wood should be captured on the first day and said that he himself would call the whole offensive to a halt after the first 48 hours, or even earlier, if the results gained or the general situation did not appear to justify its continuance.

This grandiose and ambitious plan was a far cry from the Tank Corps' proposal in June of a three-hour raid, penetrating only a few miles. In the light of it, it is difficult to accuse Haig of having had no faith in the tanks, although he can certainly be accused of expecting too much of his own arm, the cavalry. He might even be charged with having had too much faith in the tanks and of not allotting sufficient resources to see that the initial success expected of them could be exploited.

In the light of the general concept of the battle, as it had finally developed, we must now consider the criticisms made of the part the tanks had to play. The grand total

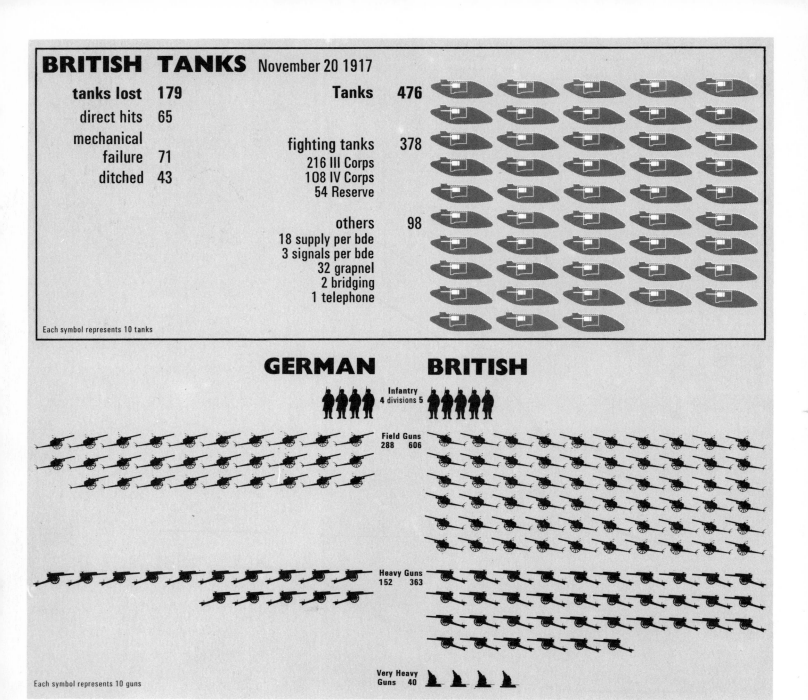

BRITISH TANKS November 20 1917

tanks lost	179	**Tanks**	**476**
direct hits	65		
mechanical failure	71	fighting tanks	378
ditched	43	216 III Corps	
		108 IV Corps	
		54 Reserve	
		others	98
		18 supply per bde	
		3 signals per bde	
		32 grapnel	
		2 bridging	
		1 telephone	

Each symbol represents 10 tanks

GERMAN   **BRITISH**

GERMAN		BRITISH
4	Infantry divisions	5
288	Field Guns	606
152	Heavy Guns	363
	Very Heavy Guns	40

Each symbol represents 10 guns

of tanks was 476. Whether or not more could have been made available is not apparent and nowhere discussed. One must assume that HQ Tank Corps made available every tank that it was practicable to produce, man and maintain on the battlefield. From this total one should subtract 54 supply tanks; 32 fitted with grapnels for pulling away wire on the cavalry's path of advance; nine acting as wireless stations, one carrying telephone cable for HQ Third Army and two bridging tanks. This left 378 tanks, 324 in the frontline and 54 in reserve to replace breakdowns. Thus 324 was the figure available for specific tasks.

If, as has been suggested, as many tanks should have been kept in reserve as were allotted to the initial assault, the number of tanks available for the latter would have to have been reduced to about half of those actually employed. This would have been to put at risk the success of the attack on a 10,000 yard front of the formidable Hindenburg Line. On the right III Corps attacked with three divisions each of which had two battalions of tanks, one company of A Battalion with the 20th

being detached to 29th Division in reserve —the only reserve of tanks. The corps therefore had 216 tanks. IV Corps divided its three battalions (108 tanks) between its two assaulting divisions, 51st Division on its right, facing Flesquières, having one company more than 62nd Division on the left. In both corps approximately two-thirds of the tanks were to be used against the first objective, the first trench system of the Hindenburg Line, and one third, with survivors from the first attack, on the second objective which was generally speaking the support trench system, 3,000 yards further on. Some tanks, especially those directed on to the crossings over the Escaut Canal which the cavalry were to use, were given specific subsequent objectives.

The remarkable success of the initial assault was proof of the soundness and efficiency of the tactical plan and of the organisation of this phase. To have halved or seriously reduced the proportion of tanks to infantry or to yard of front would have prejudiced the chances of success almost as much as it would have done to have reduced the frontage on which the attack was launched.

The operations on the first day, November 20, proved that on firm ground the combination of close co-operation between tanks and infantry with an artillery fire-plan without preliminary bombardment or registration could overcome a defence which was taken by surprise both by the timing of the attack and by the scale of employment of tanks. How much of the success was due to the morale effect of the tanks and how much to the favourable conditions of poor visibility it is not possible to assess. But to suggest that significantly fewer tanks could have been used in the initial assault in order to retain more reserve for subsequent phases is to be wise after the event. In no previous action on the Western Front had attacks penetrated so far so quickly and achieved such decisive results. Too great an optimism as to the effect likely to be produced could have led to failure which would have been to the certain detriment not only of the acceptance and development of the tank, but also to the success of the following year's offensive.

As far as the tanks themselves were concerned, nobody could have expected more of them on the first day. The failures lay elsewhere. If 51st Division had not had peculiar ideas of its own which separated its infantry from the tanks, Flesquières might not have proved the stumbling block it did. The inflexibility of the command arrangements, and the primitive communications available, meant that this stumbling block was not removed, as it could easily have been, by a thrust from the flank or the rear. This prejudiced severely the possibility of achieving the Commander-in-Chief's aim of capturing Bourlon ridge on the first day, an ambitious aim in any case.

The failure of the cavalry

The other major disappointment was the failure to secure, develop and exploit a crossing over the Escaut Canal between Masnières and Marcoing in spite of the existence of a bridge capable of taking cavalry. Had the cavalry been brought up closer behind the attacking troops; had everybody made fewer mistakes and errors of judgement and omission; had the cavalry themselves acted boldly, perhaps the result might have been different. But the fact remains that, even after the barriers of wire had been left behind, the cavalry was both too vulnerable and too weak in fire and shock power on the battlefield to achieve anything when machine guns were present, unless the cohesion of the Germans' defence had totally broken down. The presence of the German *107th Division* carrying out a relief in the Cambrai area was an unexpected asset to the defence, and it is most unlikely that, had the cavalry succeeded in crossing the canal in any strength on November 20, they could have developed operations of any significance beyond it on subsequent days or even perhaps been able to maintain their position there. Nevertheless, in view of the Commander-in-Chief's intentions, and the optimistic assumptions on which the plan was based, the initial positioning and subsequent deployment of the cavalry is certainly open to criticism.

Given the basic failure to secure on the first day the two vital objectives on which the whole subsequent plan depended, what is to be said about the operations on November 21, and the following days? The available strength of tanks is relevant. Of the 378 tanks available on November 20, 179 were out of action by the end of the day, 65 by direct hits, 71 by mechanical troubles and 43 by ditching or other causes. Two hundred were theoretically available on November 21 – perhaps more, both because some of the mechanical troubles were cured, and because the grapnel-carrying tanks had completed their task. It must also be remembered that the decision as to what to do on the 21st had to be taken at an hour on the 20th early enough to enable orders, the distribution of which in 1917 was a slow business, to be issued all down the line, based on the scanty and inaccurate information available when dusk fell. In fact Third Army's orders were issued at 2000 hours, having been previously approved by Haig. In essence they were to complete the tasks which had not been achieved on the first day. Few other commanders would have made a different decision.

With all the advantages of hindsight it is now possible to judge that the decision of Haig and Byng was almost certainly wrong.

Many of their basic assumptions were false, especially as to what cavalry could achieve. They were over-optimistic, not only on that score, but also as to the effect on the Germans of even the unprecedented degree of success achieved by the tanks on the first day. If they had appreciated that they could count on success only where and when they could repeat the sort of operations that day had seen, they might have revised their original unrealistic plan on more realistic lines. The tanks could not cross the Escaut Canal. It was therefore hopeless to expect operations beyond it to be developed successfully. If the plan had been limited to making certain of securing a line west of the canal, including Bourlon ridge, as a jumping off place for a subsequent offensive, it might have succeeded and the ignominious withdrawal caused by the counterattacks at the end of the month been avoided. Even though the initial plan was hopelessly unrealistic, there was still a chance of achieving this more limited aim, if a change had been decided on at the close of the fighting on November 20. It would have meant a pause on the 21st while tanks and infantry were reorganised, and prepared for a second major thrust for Bourlon ridge, while the right flank was firmly held. Even if this had failed on November 21, it should have been possible to develop yet another attack within the next few days before all chance of success disappeared. Admittedly the line reached would have been awkward to hold, overlooked as it would have been between Fontaine and Flesquières by the high ground east of the canal south of Cambrai; but it would have been much easier and less vulnerable to hold than the deep and narrow salient that would have resulted if the original plan had been successful.

However unrealistic the plan may have been and whatever the possibilities of better results than those achieved, the repercussions of the Battle of Cambrai were far more significant than the immediate effects, local in place and time. The remarkable success of the tanks established them as a decisive weapon of war. It is astonishing that it was to be another 25 years, and half way through another world war, before it was finally recognised that horsed cavalry no longer had a part to play on the modern battlefield and that the tank had taken its place.

Further Reading

Dugdale, G., *Langemarck & Cambrai* (Wilding 1932)
Everest, J. H., *The First Battle of Tanks*
Liddell Hart, Sir Basil, *The Tanks,* Vol I (Cassell 1959)
Military Operations: France & Belgium 1917, Vol III (HMSO 1948)
Pree, Maj-Gen. H. D. de, *The Battle of Cambrai* (RA Institution 1928)

GENERAL SIR MICHAEL CARVER, GCB, CBE, DSO, MC, was born in 1915 and was educated at Winchester and Sandhurst. He was commissioned into the Royal Tank Corps in 1935 and during the Second World War he commanded the 1st Royal Tank Regiment in North Africa, Italy and France. Since the war he has held a number of important appointments, including C-in-C Far East, and has published three books—*Second to None, The History of the Royal Scots Greys; El Alamein,* and *Tobruk.* He is married and has four children.

FULLER Prophet of Armoured War

Lieutenant-Colonel (later Major-General) John Frederick Charles Fuller, DSO (later CB, CBE), who is remembered today as one of the most original and influential military thinkers of this century, was born at Chichester in 1878. Educated abroad and at Malvern, he was commissioned from Sandhurst in 1898 into the Oxfordshire and Buckinghamshire Light Infantry and almost at once ordered with it to South Africa. Appendicitis kept him out of the major battles of the Boer War and he spent the later guerrilla phase commanding block houses and reading widely. After serving in India in 1903/6, where he acquired what was to be a lifelong interest in its religions, he was appointed adjutant of a Volunteer battalion, the 10th Middlesex. This adjutancy gave him the chance to put his reading into practice, using real soldiers in tactical experiments, and also to begin writing. By the outbreak of war in 1914, besides having attended the Staff College, he had published articles on mobilisation, infantry tactics, weapon training and entrainment. The latter secured him the post, in August 1914, of railway transport officer at Southampton, from which he was later transferred to Second Army Headquarters at Tunbridge Wells. By the time he arrived in France in July 1915 the worst of the early fighting was over and he had established for himself a reputation as a Staff Officer of more than ordinary powers. Thus it was to turn out, though by no means at his own wish, that he was not to play any combatant rôle throughout the war. His creative and executive reputation grew during 1916, both through continued publication, notably of an article in which he satisfactorily defined for the first time the Principles of War, and through his creation of an Officers' School for the Third Army and then of a Senior Officers' Course for the BEF. He was therefore an obvious choice to fill the new appointment of Chief General Staff Officer (GSO 1) at Tank Corps Headquarters when it was created in December 1916. He came to the post, however, with no preconceived enthusiasm for armour. Indeed, his attitude has been described as 'caustically sceptical' towards tanks, which he regarded apparently as 'an adjunct' to the infantry and not as an arm of their own. His views were quickly to change and he was to infuse the Tank Corps staff with all the confidence he came to hold in the decisiveness of the tanks' future rôle, while himself working out from first principles both tactics and major operational plans. Of these the most important was that for Cambrai. [*John Keegan.*]

Imperial War Museum

Imperial War Museum

DIAGRAMMATIC SECTION OF A FRENCH LIGHT (OR "MOSQUITO") TANK.

When they had recovered from their initial shock, the Germans dismissed the tank as a mere 'terror' weapon and devoted little time or energy to its development. Not so the British and French, some of whose officers clearly saw the possibilities of the new arm and were gripped by a sense of urgency. *Kenneth Macksey*

Top left: The British Gun Carrier Mark I. More a self-propelled gun than a tank, the first Gun Carrier was in service by January, 1917. The model pictured here carries a 60-pounder gun, although other Gun Carriers were fitted with a 6-inch howitzer. In the static war of the Western Front, the appearance of mobile guns caused considerable confusion to the opposing artillery spotters. *Above:* The French Renault 'Mosquito' tank. Equivalent to the British Whippet tank it had inferior cross-country characteristics but a good turn of speed. *Below:* The German A 7 V. A large armoured box on a Holt-type chassis weighing 30 tons, the A 7 V reflected the lack of importance attached to tank development by the German command. *Opposite page. Above:* A British Mark V, male. Successor to the Mark IV, the tank of Cambrai, the Mark V was the first heavy tank that could be driven by one man. It first appeared in 1918, and saw action in July of that year. *Below:* A British Mark IV with a 'tadpole' tail. The tail extension was added to increase the trench-crossing ability to 14 feet, but it proved lacking in rigidity and strength

TANK DEVELOPMENTS

When the surviving handful of tanks were extracted from the Somme mud in November 1916 a rough poll of opinion taken from men at the front might have indicated that there was little future for the new weapon, so slight had been its effect. The Germans, recovering from their initial surprise, were almost unanimous in regarding tanks as a 'terror' weapon designed, more than anything else, to attack their soldiers' morale. Confident in their men's ability they were content to leave the solution of the problem to the artillery and infantry. One wrote that the troops 'soon learnt to know its vulnerable parts and attack it accordingly'. Another saw the tank as 'a comparatively easy prey for the artillery who detailed special guns to deal with it'. But at the British GHQ a more enlightened view prevailed. Here the tanks' initial mechanical failures and the inexperience of the crews were recognised as the inevitable results of untested equipment and organisation. Haig's approval of the new idea was reflected in his demand to the War Office for 1,000 new tanks and the setting up, on October 8, 1916, of a special central organisation in France to develop the fighting capacity of the tanks. Thus, long before the Battle of the Somme had ended, he brought into being the HQ of the Tank Corps and guaranteed the new weapons' future.

To head the new corps came Elles—the same sapper officer who earlier that year had reported favourably to Haig on the experiments in Britain. A few weeks later he was joined by his new Chief Staff Officer, Major J. F. C. Fuller, an intellectual and sceptical infantryman. Once convinced that the tank was a feasible weapon, it was Fuller, by his own example, who urged the other members of the staff not only to collect, synthesise and disseminate every scrap of information about tanks, but also to devise original and improved ways of employing them. Together this team was to turn an amorphous collection of men and machines into a coherent fighting force capable of working closely among themselves and in reliable fashion with the infantry who, incredulously, were beginning to regard tanks more as a help than a hindrance. Throughout the winter of 1917 the new organisation grew, publishing a flow of tactical notes, and issuing a flurry of technical directions to the crews and to the newly founded workshop organisation. The men of the Tank Corps were enthusiastic and quick to learn, but the indoctrination of senior officers and those who would enter battle with the tanks was more difficult. Progress with original ideas was bound to be slow in an army which still had much to learn about the older established weapons. The unimaginative employment of tanks at the Battles of Arras, Bullecourt, Messines and Passchendaele stemmed more from ignorance than bigotry. Even so, every obstacle seems to have been thrown in the tanks' path despite the appeals of the Tank Corps officers. Only lip service was paid to the principle that tanks, like any other weapon, did best when used by surprise and in large numbers rather than in pairs and even singly. More serious from the tanks' point of view was the sight of strengthened German defences, based on deep ditches and defended by field artillery, growing up to make the future task of Allied tank forces more difficult. They were not to know that, by November 1917, the Germans had virtually dismissed tanks as a serious threat. Indeed, the French tanks had also done badly on the Chemin des Dames and the newly arrived Americans were openly saying that there were no military prospects for a weapon of which the Germans had taken full measure.

But those who decried the deficiencies of the original machines overlooked the rapid changes that technology could effect. Even as the first thin-skinned British Mark I's were being delivered in June 1916, it was decided to attempt the construction of a shell-proof tank – an order which eventually resulted in the production of a machine with two to three inches of armour, armed with a 57-mm gun and five machine guns, weighing 100 tons and sardonically nicknamed 'Flying Elephant'. In fact, before trials commenced on this monster, it was rejected in January 1917 as being too costly. By then, however, it was realised that, although shell fire was the tanks' worst enemy, the chances of Mark I's survival were better than Kitchener and many others had first imagined. In fact the most dangerous threat to the Mark I, apart from its incipient unreliability, turned out to be the existing German armour-piercing bullet which easily penetrated the low quality British 10-mm armour plate. Based on battle experience, production of the earlier Mark I, Mark II and Mark III tanks was restricted to only 200 and the main effort concentrated upon building a more reliable and battle-worthy machine. Mark IV, when she began to arrive in France in April 1917, looked, at first glance, very much like her predecessors except that the tail wheels had been removed. She was still underpowered by the 105-hp Daimler engine and still required four men to drive and steer her, but in other ways she was much more formidable. The 57-mm guns were now short barrelled and better suited to use on rugged land than the original, longer naval types. Unfortunately the substitution of the Lewis machine gun in place of the original Hotchkiss and Vickers guns was a retrograde step, though not crippling. Range of action had been increased by carrying additional petrol, but the most important modification was an increase in the maximum thickness of the frontal armour to 12-mm – sufficient to defeat the Germans' armour-piercing bullet and thus to render their infantry wholly dependent on artillery for protection.

The sense of urgency
As the British were improving their original rhomboidal tanks, both they and the French were searching for means to increase both the number of tanks available and their speed across country. William Tritton made his proposal for a 'Chaser' tank in December 1916, seeing the need for a faster tank to exploit a breach, once it had been made in the German lines by the heavier tank. In effect he envisaged armoured vehicles in lieu of the horsed cavalry which had already shown its incapacity to operate in the open. From the Chaser was to come the development, throughout 1917, of the first Medium A's, later known as Whippets. These 14-ton tanks, with a speed of 8 mph (twice that of the Mark IV) and armed with four machine guns, were entering production just as the Tank Corps was being ground into the mud of Passchendaele, but were not to be ready for action until 1918.

The French became active in the construction of light tanks after the comparative failure of their early Schneiders and St Chamonds. On the suggestion of Estienne, in July 1916 an order had been placed with the firm of Renault for a simple, armoured machine gun carrier weighing six tons, capable of accompanying the infantry in the assault. By December the first model – called Renault FT – was ready and in March 1917 an initial order for 150 was placed. Unlike the British Whippet, which was given a good trench crossing capability of seven feet, the FT was struggling when crossing a six-foot gap and at first it was not received with acclaim by those in the French army who believed that an armament of a solitary machine gun was inadequate. Nevertheless, after successful trials in April 1917, coincident with the failure at the Chemin des Dames, the initial order was expanded to 1,000 and large scale production begun of the simplest and cheapest tank yet designed.

Nothing like the sense of urgency which gripped the Allied tank pioneers ever caught the Germans. Principal Engineer Vollmer of the Department A 7 V was instructed to design and produce a tank in November 1916, but because the General Staff remained so confident in the ability of the troops at the front to defeat tanks on their own, little enthusiasm was imparted to the work. Nevertheless, in January 1917 a wooden mock-up of the tank that was to be known as A 7 V had been produced and four days later an order for 100 was placed. But German industry was strictly orientated, as in everything else in 1917, to the demands of the basic military strategy. In the east, where they were on the offensive and the front was fluid, there was no overriding need for a 'storm tank'. Nor was there an immediate need for one in the west since

there the army stood on the defensive, although the possibility that, one day, they would have to attack and break the trenches, and might need tanks, seems to have been overlooked. Partly out of haste, but also because he lacked strong backing, Vollmer could do no better at first than mount a large armoured box on top of a Holt type chassis, based upon the one which had been demonstrated by Mr Steiner of Holts before the war and which, since then, had been lying, disused, in Austria. The 30-ton A 7 V, which appeared in prototype in October 1917, was therefore no more promising than the original French tanks on their Holt chassis. None would be ready for operations in 1917 and only 20 were ever made since an over-strained German industry was already fully committed to the manufacture of conventional weapons. Under these circumstances a project for a 150-ton heavy tank, launched in March 1917, can only be viewed as a distraction instead of part of a well thought out scheme.

In spite of the losses incurred by Allied tanks throughout the attritional artillery battles of the summer and early autumn of 1917, both the British and French tank forces improved in quality and quantity. The British took delivery of nearly 1,000 Mark IV's before November 20 and had about 450 ready for action that day. By then the French possessed some 500 Schneiders and St Chamonds although, in its phase of defensive recuperation, the French army found little use for them. The waste caused by mechanical unreliability overlaid almost every other consideration – even though most Allied machines were remarkably efficient considering the haste in which they had evolved. Nevertheless, any one tank which ran more than 20 miles without breakdown signified the performance of a notable feat even by a well trained crew. All crews had been hurriedly trained and few reached a high standard in 1917. Morale, however, was high. The Tank Corps had been fortunate in its leader in France and in the staff who served him. Not a brilliant man, Brigadier Hugh Elles nevertheless possessed the freshness of youth combined with a calm competence which gave men confidence. By gently fighting their battles at GHQ, he was able eventually to win the Tank Corps a square deal. If, in his GSO I, Fuller, he possessed a man with a caustic wit who rubbed up senior officers the wrong way, he also owned a genius – an officer endowed with genuinely original ideas who visualised a rôle for the tank far beyond its original concept as a mere instrument of assault. While guiding the tactical thoughts, training and operations of the corps through a trying year of innovation, Fuller was always searching for new ways to employ the tanks as the dominant technical weapon in a decisive battle – in a rôle subservient neither to infantry nor artillery. But within the framework of his most sweeping concepts, he made detailed plans like any good staff officer, demanding that tanks should never be launched into battle without thorough and minute preparation.

Thus when it was decided to give the tanks their first big chance in a massed attack, Fuller and his staff were ready with settled and well understood methods for moving tanks secretly and swiftly from one front to another. They had also collected detailed information about every piece of German-held terrain where tanks might have to be used and, in so doing, had created a reconnaissance organisation which always provided the crews with accurate information in plenty of time before action. Meticulous but simple drills had been devised for co-operation between tanks, infantry, artillery and aircraft in the assault – drills which, at Cambrai, were to revolutionise the whole scheme of assault. Where it was known that the tanks would have to cross the immensely wide anti-tank ditch running like a spine the length of the Hindenburg Line, great rolls of brushwood – called fascines – were made ready to be carried forward by the leading tanks to make the crossing possible.

This time when the tanks went into action each crew commander – unlike his predecessors on September 15, 1916 – knew his task, understood the problems to be overcome and knew that artillery, infantry and aircraft were briefed to give specific aid to the tanks. And each crew member was trained to a higher standard than ever before, while the machines were vulnerable only to German artillery and stood a fair chance of reaching their limited objectives without breaking down.

Further Reading
Fuller, J. F. C., *Memoirs of an Unconventional Soldier* (Nicholson & Watson 1936)
Liddell Hart, Sir Basil, *The Tanks,* Vol I (Cassell 1959)
Macksey, K., & Batchelor, J., *Tank* (Macdonald 1970)
Nehring, W., *Die Geschichte der deutschen Panzerwaffe, 1916 bis 1945* (Propyläen 1969)
Ogorkiewicz, R. M., *Armour* (Stevens 1960)

Villers-Bretonneux

As the failure of the *Georgette* operation in the north became more and more obvious, Ludendorff resolved to make one last attempt to gain control of the strategically-important town of Amiens in the south, by capturing the vantage point of Villers-Bretonneux, about ten miles to the east. An element of surprise was vital to the success of this last phase of the *Michael* offensive, and was provided by a detachment of 13 tanks: machines which the Germans had been unusually slow to manufacture since their appearance on the Somme in 1916. The result was the first tank 'duel' of the war. *John Vader.* *Above:* German infantry suffered heavily in this new form of warfare. Crude anti-tank defences pitched against the manoeuvrable British Whippets were useless: two German battalions were nearly wiped out.

THE FIRST TANK-TO-TANK ENCOUNTER

By the end of March 1918 Ludendorff knew that his offensive across the old Somme battlefield had failed. He had run out of steam: the Germans had outrun their communications and their fire power was insufficient to maintain the thrust. Amiens, however, remained as a valuable objective. The Germans' drive had brought them to within a few miles of the plateau south of the Somme, and from the edge of the plateau near Villers-Bretonneux they would be able to overlook Avre, Noye and the vital road and rail junctions of Amiens.

'*Fini retreat—beaucoup australiens ici*', a Digger was reported to have informed a peasant woman during the retreat of Fifth Army, when the AIF 3rd Division was moving forward. 'You Australians think you can do anything,' said an artillery brigadier to Lieutenant-Colonel Lavarack, chief of

the divisional commander's staff, 'but you haven't a chance of holding them.' The morale of the Australians was high, the opposite to what the Germans expected when *Eighteenth Army* issued the order: 'The enemy for the moment has only inferior or beaten troops opposite us.' The Germans too were dispirited, as Captain G. Goes later reported:

The fighting during the closing days of March had left no doubt that the great offensive battle was threatening to become a battle of attrition on the largest scale. Everywhere along the front of nearly 120 miles the infantry had been compelled to have recourse to the spade, and saw the spectre of hated position warfare rising before it. The situation was very much more unfavourable than before March 21: no trenches, no dugouts, streaming rain for days, which had

turned the devastated area behind the troops into a morass, and caused the roads and tracks laboriously rendered serviceable to break up again. More and more reports trickled in of fresh enemy divisions springing up round the fragile salient which had been won; more and more the artillery fire swelled in volume; higher and higher rose the losses of the Germans in dead, wounded and sick, and more and more did the spirit of their attack evaporate.

Preparations were indeed in progress at another place, over in Flanders, for another surprise attack; nevertheless, the Supreme Command decided to try its luck with Amiens once more. Perhaps now, after a breathing space, after the arrival of fresh divisions and the replenishment of the ammunition dumps, the thing could be done.

FRONT LINE APRIL 24
BRITISH SUPPORT POSITIONS
GERMAN ATTACK APRIL 24
FRONT LINE AFTER GERMAN ATTACK
BRITISH COUNTERATTACK APRIL 24/25
LINE AFTER COUNTERATTACK
FINAL LINE APRIL 25

Ancre
Somme Canal
Corbie
Daours
Hamelet
8 Aus Bde
18 Div
Aubigny
Fouilloy
Hamel
Bois de 243 Div
14 Aus Bde
Hamel
Camon
Somme
15 Aus Bde
Bois de Vaire
Bois des Tailloux
Australian Corps
5 Aus Div
Blangy Ironville
25 Bde
228 Div
Warfusée
Glisy
Longueau
Roman road
24 Bde
Villers Bretonneux
4 Guards Div
54 Bde
Boutillerie
Bois de Blangy
Bois l'Abbé
Switch
23 Bde
III Corps
8 Div
Cagny
13 Aus Bde
Gentelles
Cachy
173 Bde
77 Res Div
174 Bde
18 Div
53 Bde
Avre
Bois de Gentelles
Marcelcave
Boves
St. Nicolas
58 Div
175 Bde
Bois de Hangard
208 Div

FRENCH LINE
RAILWAYS
ROADS

0 YARDS   4000
0 METRES   3000

Noye
Fouencamps
Domart
Hangárd
Gd Ersatz Div
Aubercourt
Luce
Demuin
French 131 Div

N

Above: The Australian defence of Amiens. *Below:* British Medium Mark A tank, later called the Whippet. Fast and lightly-armed it was designed to exploit breakthroughs. *Crew:* 3; *Armament:* 4 Hotchkiss machine guns; *Engine:* Two 45-hp Tylor, each driving one track; *Armour:* 5-mm/14-mm; *Speed:* Between 8 and 9 mph. *Right:* First used in March 1918, Whippets caused about 400 infantry casualties in the first 'duel' between tanks at Amiens in April

John Batchelor

They benefited by fine weather during the first two days of April, but it began to rain on the 3rd, and the suspended attacks were renewed in the final offensive which began the following day. But the Allies had been forewarned by captured prisoners. Just before dawn, shrapnel and gas shells were bombarded across the front line and the artillery and back areas, followed at first light by swarms of infantry from *Eighteenth, Second* and *Seventeenth Armies.*

The British army too had had time to re-adjust its front. The sector attacked was held by two understrength divisions, the 14th and 18th, the latter without its artillery. The Australian 9th Brigade was also in the area, and the centre ahead of Villers-Bretonneux was held by its widely extended 35th Battalion, with the other three battalions behind the town in close reserve. They were to face the strongest attack yet made against Australians: five German divisions attacked under good cover across the valleys running parallel to the front.

The fresh *9th Bavarian Reserve Division* drove hard at the Australian battalion

which stopped them with a heavy fire from machine guns and rifles, with good support from the guns. The 14th Division, to the north, suffered a particularly heavy bombardment and was driven back, and the Germans were able to take Hamel and to swing south, threatening to envelop the Australians from that flank; they withdrew to a support position a mile east of Villers-Bretonneux. The AIF 33rd Battalion then moved up to extend the left of the 35th, and 6th Cavalry Brigade was used to fill gaps in the line. The AIF 15th Brigade, guarding bridges, sent some of its men to help support the 18th Division, which managed to stand fast until a second attack, made in mid-afternoon, forced the line to retire. When the Germans reached the 1870 war monument on the outskirts of the town it looked as though the way to Amiens was about to be opened to them.

The Germans' first tank attack
The Germans' hopes were dashed by a remarkable charge by the reserve AIF 36th Battalion, joined in its attack by several British infantrymen on its right, part of

35th Battalion on its left, and later by some Londoners and the cavalry. Attacking on the run with bayonets flashing, the unexpected reinforcements first stopped the Germans advancing from Monument Wood then drove them back to old trenches more than a mile from the town.

The 15th Brigade was brought across the Somme to hold the vital heights north of the town, and the 33rd Battalion again went forward, protected on a flank by the mounted 17th Lancers and aided by a Canadian motor machine gun battery which dealt with German machine guns. By dusk the line east of Villers-Bretonneux was secure, and during the night the 9th Brigade made advances to gain ground which would improve its field of fire, a job which entangled the 34th in some stiff fighting before establishing itself in the old line that had been held by the 35th Battalion. South of Villers-Bretonneux the Germans drove the French back two miles beyond the Avre and were in sight of Amiens. The River Somme ran some five miles north of Villers-Bretonneux, and the Germans, expecting that the Allied line in

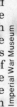

front of the town would crumble, launched two divisions against the New Zealanders and Australians positioned north of the river. The Germans were thoroughly beaten here also. Further north, the Australian 4th Division fought a vicious battle on April 5, this resulting in little change in the line at a cost of some 1,100 casualties among its two brigades. The AIF 9th Brigade's casualties at Villers-Bretonneux were 660.

In a message to General Foch, Sir Henry Wilson predicted further German moves against Amiens: 'In my opinion, the proper course for the enemy to pursue now is as follows: place Amiens town and railway and junctions under his guns so as to deny all serious traffic, then mass an attack of 40 to 50 divisions against the British between Albert and the La Bassée canal.' During the first half of April, fighting raged all the way to the coast, both sides suffering catastrophic losses in several battles, before the Germans again became active at Villers-Bretonneux—disabling some 1,000 reserves behind the town with mustard gas shells. Before the Australians were relieved by two battleworn British divisions they witnessed the shooting down overhead of the German ace Richthofen.

The change over by the divisions was barely completed when the Germans made their first big attack with tanks—13 of them—which broke through the British lines manned, in many cases, by 'boy recruits'. The attack began at dawn on April 24 in the manner to be exemplified in the Second World War—infantry following the tanks and rolling up the line right and left. The tactic was used on either side of the town, across good tank terrain, and the attack was pressed on, regardless of an enormous barrage laid down by Allied guns. Villers-Bretonneux, Abbey Wood and Hangard Wood were lost as the Germans moved forward as far as the junction of the Avre and Luce. One factor in the German success was the presence of fog, which they thickened with smoke; another was that there were no tank defences so that when a tank straddled a trench it could fire on the defenders.

The presence of the German tanks drew out British tanks, of which there were 20 in the area—13 Mk IV's and seven Whippets. The 1st Section, 1st Battalion, went into action with one male, mounting two 6-pounder guns, and two females, mounting machine guns, and although the male was disabled by a shell the crew brought a gun into action and knocked out one of the German tanks. Another surrendered when the concentrated fire from the 58th Machine Gun Battalion put it out of action by 'the splash of the bullets'. More tanks of the 1st and 3rd Tank Battalions assisted the 1st Sherwood Foresters in their counterattack, and a charge by light Whippet tanks

Above: The shattered bodies of German soldiers killed during the hour-long artillery bombardment accompanying the Australian recapture of Villers-Bretonneux. *Below:* Scene of the first German tank attack. German A7V's in the field before Amiens, throwing up clouds of chalk dust scattered the German infantry across the plateau, causing at least 400 casualties as they made two runs through battalions of *77th Reserve Division*. One Whippet was knocked out, three were disabled and three got back from this successful mission which originated when a scout plane dropped a message that the German battalions were resting in a hollow in front of Cachy. It was to have been a tank-infantry assault but, when the 23rd Brigade was ordered to counterattack with armour it had no men available, and when the 8th Division cancelled the order the tanks were not informed.

Lieutenant-General Butler of III Corps considered that the 8th Division was capable of dealing with the situation and decided not to accept the offer of the AIF 15th Brigade's commander, 'Pompey' Elliott, who was fuming to be allowed to strike. The brigade had been stationed about a mile north-west of the town, kept in reserve and ready to counterattack if the town were lost. While the formal messages were being passed, time was lost and the Germans were allowed to dig themselves into Abbey Wood and the heights that gave such an advantage over Amiens, good reasons for the 'tempestuous' Elliott to be 'fuming and petitioning' for action, as the AIF's historian observed.

It was predictable, nevertheless, that the brigadier would get the job, along with another Australian brigade commander, Brigadier-General Glasgow of the 13th, which was given the task of forming the southern pincer; the 15th formed the northern. When the brigade commanders met Butler they were told that he wished the attack to be made by daylight from the south northwards, and Glasgow said, 'If God Almighty gave the order we couldn't do it by daylight.' It was agreed, fortunately, that an attack across an open plateau, in front of machine gun fire, could barely succeed, and that the Australians' plan to attack at night without previous bombardment spoiling the surprise would be a better plan. Rawlinson and Butler decided that the attack should begin at 2200 hours when the moon would be giving some light to the field of action.

The 15th Brigade was to advance southeast across the northern side of the town; the 13th Brigade was to move across the southern side of the town; and the 54th Brigade was to move eastwards on the southern side of the 13th. The two Australian brigades were given the 2nd Northamptonshire and 22nd Durham battalions and three tanks to mop up when the town was recaptured. The artillery was to maintain a standing barrage on well defined targets until an hour after the initial attack began, then the heavy batteries were to lift 500 yards beyond the town while the field artillery lifted 300 yards.

One factor contributing to the early German successes near Amiens was the fog, thickened by smoke bombs. But the attacking tanks soon drew the British Mark IV's and Whippets into action, and a 'duel', the first of the war, began. *Above:* A captured Mk IV advances past a flamethrower

Before clouds covered the full moon there was too much light: the 13th Brigade was seen assembling south of the woods, and the Germans opened fire with numerous machine guns as the Australian advance moved forward. The flank was stopped until Sergeant 'Charlie' Stokes urged his platoon commander to attack the Germans in the woods – which was not part of the plan. The commander, Lieutenant Sadlier, and Stokes led their men in a bombing attack which quickly destroyed six German posts, allowing the southern pincer movement to go forward, and earning for the platoon commander a Victoria Cross, for the sergeant a DCM. As the brigade moved on it was joined by the Bedfordshire battalion of the 54th Brigade; its other two battalions – 9th London and 7th Royal West Kent – had lost touch, one forced to return to its start line, the other stopped by machine gun fire from shell holes and was finally dug in about halfway to the objective.

The 13th Brigade did not quite reach its objective, but it was in a position to ensure the success of the pincer movement if the 15th did its job. After the holdup at the wood, the 13th's 51st Battalion suffered heavy casualties going through the wire at Cachy Switch, where it was enfiladed by German machine guns. After one gun was captured, Vickers were set up to keep the others occupied and the Australians moved on, occasioning 'a panic which could not be overcome in time, as the reserves failed to come up quickly enough', as the Germans later stated. There were many leaderless Germans wandering aimlessly about who were killed or captured, but the opposition became very strong; an attack from the town endangered the 51st's flank until the

50th came up to drive them back. When these two battalions aligned themselves they were near a railway cutting south of the town, an exit which was eventually to allow some Germans to escape.

The 15th Brigade was late getting away from its start line and there were the usual confusions associated with night operations. One company could not even find the assembly point. The actual start was almost two hours late, so the Germans described this move as a second attack. There was also some confusion about exactly where lay the objectives – the Hamelet road and Hamel road. The first was reached after an uneventful mile tramp, then the Germans, alerted by scouting activity, began to let fly their flares and small arms. The 59th was the leading battalion and when its CO yelled 'Charge!' the command was rapidly passed down the line so that a great yelling, cheering rush was made on the Germans, now visible under the lights of their flares and the glare of burning houses. In their panic, the Germans forgot to lower their sights as the Australians with fixed bayonets rushed the enemy trenches and machine gun nests. At 0130 hours they were at the Hamel road having lost fewer than 150 men.

Two companies pushed on to make contact with the 13th Brigade which they expected to find near the old British front, but the 13th was not within sight or hearing and the 57th's companies returned to the road, where positions were dug facing Villers-Bretonneux. The mopping up battalions found that the town was still too strongly defended and their work was delayed. Not far away the French had prudently accumulated reserves in case the British could not handle the Villers-

Bretonneux situation, yet when General Debeney was informed of the plan to counterattack he promised to co-operate if it were postponed until the following day. When Rawlinson informed him that the action should take place that night he merely offered to send the Moroccan Division in to occupy the reserve line, freeing some of 58th Division's reserve.

Before the artillery was directed on to the railway cutting escape route that lay in the 1,500 yards between the two pincer ends, the Australian brigades began to close in on the town, assisted by four British infantry battalions and three tanks. By noon the town was occupied and the mopping up was left to the Durhams and Northamptonshires. Because of considerable confusion in the German lines, a counterattack by the German divisions ordered for 0700 hours was postponed twice, and then finally abandoned through lack of fresh troops. Just before 1000 hours Glasgow sent in his reserve battalion to close the gap, an operation which met with such fierce resistance that it was postponed until that night, when it was carried out with few casualties. The original British front had not been recovered, but Amiens was secure.

Further Reading
Bean, C. E. W., *Official History of Australia in the War* (Canberra)
Bean, C. E. W., *The AIF in France, 1918* (Angus & Robertson)
Cutlack, F. M., *The Australians: Final Campaign, 1918* (Low, Martson 1918)
Monash, Gen. Sir John, *The Australian Victories in France, 1918*

Right: A German flamethrower crew moves up in support of one of Germany's few tanks

Inset: Elfriede, the first German tank to be engaged and captured by British tank forces. Found overturned and abandoned in a sandpit she was minutely examined by Allied Intelligence

'BIG BERTHA' BOMBARDS PARIS

Designed to coincide with Ludendorff's spring offensive on the Somme, Germany's engineers fulfilled a remarkable briefing: the creation of a colossal gun with a range of nearly 75 miles — aimed on Paris. *Jean Hallade. Below:* 'Big Bertha' under construction in the Krupp artillery department

In spring 1916, while the battle of Verdun was reaching its culmination, an important meeting was held in Berlin in the presence of General Ludendorff, Head of the Supreme War Council. The naval officers commanding the heavy-calibre guns on the Western Front asked him if he would approve the costs and expenditure of material and personnel necessary for the construction of a gun with a range of 62.1 miles (100 kms).

Ludendorff has often been depicted as a reserved and cold personality, with no great liking for advanced technical ideas. And yet the general reacted to this idea immediately. At that time, the front passed within 55.9 miles (90 kms) of Paris, and Ludendorff must have grasped the importance of this project. To be able to damage the morale of the people in the rear areas with a giant cannon, co-ordinated with a large scale offensive, would give striking proof to the world both of German technical capabilities, and of her ability to continue the war.

The project passed rapidly to a practical stage and the navy obtained the utmost co-operation from the Krupp Works' Artillery Department management. At the beginning of the war, Krupps had already astonished the world when the 420-mm mortars built in its foundries demolished the concrete masonry of the forts of Liège and Maubeuge. But between a 420-mm mortar, firing at a maximum range of under 9.3 miles (15 kms), and a piece whose calibre was still to be determined, which could fire a projectile a distance of 62.1 miles, many problems still remained to be solved. Gradually, in silence and secrecy, the navy's Artillery Direction, in collaboration with Krupp, pushed the project to a very advanced stage of studies allowing the construction of the supercannon.

Nine months had elapsed since the Berlin meeting in which the study of this fantastic cannon had been authorised, when a brief telegram arrived from Ludendorff: 'In subsequent work on very long range pieces, please take as your basis a range of 74.5 miles (120 kms) instead of 62.1 miles.' This astounded all those engaged on the project. There was colossal work involved in resuming the study taking into account these extra 12.4 miles (20 kms). Everything already calculated had to be recalculated from scratch. What was the reason for this modification of the range demanded in Ludendorff's telegram? It was due to the fact that a withdrawal to the Hindenburg

Line had been decided by the German High Command, increasing the distance from Paris to the front by 12.4 miles. These new technical problems provoked intense activity at Krupps and soon a model designed by Professor Rausenberger, Director of the Artillery Department, fulfilled all requirements. There now remained only to build the gun.

Immediately the project was given a name. It was called *Wilhelm Geschutz,* 'William's Gun', in honour of the Kaiser. Sometimes it was called 'Long Max', but Parisians later christened it 'Big Bertha'.

To produce their curious device, the Krupps engineers used two calibres: a 15-inch (381-mm) barrel and an 8.3-inch (210-mm) barrel. They calculated, according to their preliminary studies, that it was necessary to nearly double the initial velocity of existing shells. To gain time, or simply because it fulfilled all requirements perfectly, the basis of the giant gun was a 15-inch barrel measuring 55 feet 10 inches (17 metres) in length. First of all they increased the internal diameter of the 15-inch barrel, into which they introduced a new 8.3-inch barrel which projected 36 feet 1 inch (11 metres) forward of the

muzzle of the original gun. The forward part of the gun was then reinforced with a barrel-sleeve. Finally—and this was a great innovation—they screwed on a chase (smooth tube) 19 feet 8 inches (six metres) long at the end of the gun. This chase was not rifled and its perfectly smooth internal bore prolonged exactly the bottom surface of the rifling in the main tube. The gun had a total length of 112 feet (34 metres) and an overall weight of 138 tons.

Once the gun had been made, they had to devise a special powder for it. It had to

Opposite: left to right: The 8.26-inch calibre shell; *Zusatzkartusche* (auxiliary) and *Vorkartusche* (main) cordite charges, both wrapped in silk; and *Hulsenkartusche,* encased in brass weight. During its railway journey, the tube had a length of only 91 feet 7½ inches (28 metres), the smooth extension being mounted later in the firing position. An enormous truck-mounting comprising 18 axles carried the rifled and nondismantable section whose overall weight was 256 tons. The assembly of the 19-foot 8-inch (six metres) smooth tube took place near the spot which the gun was to occupy. This operation was complicated and delicate. The smooth tube was screwed on to the rifled tube with the help of a dismantable gantry moving on two parallel railway lines to the right and left of the main railway line on which the truck-mounting lay. A platform was necessary to receive the truck-mounting. It consisted of a ring-shaped casing, which could be dismantled into six sections for purposes of transportation, on which was laid a turntable mounted on ball bearings. The lot rested on a solid concrete foundation.

'Tomorrow, open fire on Paris'

During the long truce of winter 1917/1918, and despite tentative peace proposals, the Germans did not remain inactive, and they continued with their great project for an offensive along the entire front, supported by long range artillery fire aimed at demoralising the French. The place chosen to install the gun in battery was the forest of Crépy-en-Laonnois near Laon. The railway station of Crépy-en-Laonnois lies on the railway between Laon and La Fère. That is where they sent waggon loads of timber and munitions which were unloaded by French civilian prisoners. Hidden among the trees and copses, men set to work. Trees were felled and immediately cut into logs, while efforts were made to conceal the destruction. Tracks were cut through the copses, sleepers laid, and the lengthening railway lines were immediately covered with camouflage netting to ward off spotting from the air. The earth was dug up in several places. At three points, the construction of concrete platforms was begun. All the areas laid bare by these gun emplacements were covered with wire mesh fitted to the tops of trees and overlaid with a net. Once the trees started to bud, the whole lot would be covered with foliage. This work was begun in November 1917 and continued actively in January and February of the last year of war.

Once the work had been completed, each gun was in position at the end of a railway

spur laid just beyond the place where the railway line cut the road leading from Crépy to Couvron. There remained only to point each gun in the direction of Paris at an angle of 52 degrees and fire the projectile. After a three-and-a-half minute journey, it would land in the middle of the French capital. Such was the formidable German arrangement designed to demoralise Paris the day after the start of the great offensive on March 21. On the evening of March 22, an order from the General Staff was transmitted to the command post situated in the Crépy-en-Laonnois forest: 'Tomorrow morning, open fire on Paris'.

It was 0715 hours on the morning of March 23. Feverish activity had been in progress for several hours on the wooded eastern slope of the Mont de Joie. It was chilly that morning, and a thick fog covered the plateau and its vicinity. The sound of the guns could be heard from nearly all directions, and especially from the southwest. Two days previously at dawn, the formidable German offensive had been launched. Hidden in the middle of the Mont de Joie forest, an enormous tube lifted its muzzle to the sky. Brief orders were given and everyone got out of sight, sheltering in huge concrete shelters or in well equipped trenches close by. It was just after 0716 hours when a tremendous explosion shook the atmosphere, and the guns firing in the distance seemed to redouble in intensity as though in echo.

In Paris it was cold in the early morning of March 23. For some Parisians—and also some Parisiennes, for in the factories women were replacing the men who were at the front—it was time to go to work. The night had been quiet, no Gotha bomber had flown over the capital, and the last alert dated from the previous evening. At 0720 hours an explosion shook the 19th arrondissement. In front of No 6, Quai de la Seine, there was a hole in the roadway, some windows were broken and the walls in the vicinity had received splinters. Even though it passed practically unobserved, this explosion was a fantastic event: a shell fired over 74.12 miles away had just struck the capital. For just under three years, Paris had been untroubled by daylight bombardment. The few people who believed it was an attack thought it was an air raid, probably a single aircraft flying above the fog and dropping a bomb, without an alert being sounded.

Twenty-five minutes later, at 0745 hours,

be absolutely perfect, as each round required about 550 lbs (250 kgs) of powder packed into a chamber nearly 16 feet 5 inches (five metres) long. And then there remained to make a shell. With such a powder charge, erosion was considerable inside the tube every time a round was fired, and the artillery specialists rightly considered that the gun would wear out rapidly. In that case, accuracy of aim and range would decrease as the firing went on. They calculated that the gun could fire only 65 times, after which it would have to be rebored. They thus achieved the astonishing solution of numbering each round from one to 65 and increasing the weight of the shell by 33 lbs (15 kgs) between the first and the 65th round.

With little hesitation, they decided on railway transportation. It was not a simple business to move a piece of this size and

The incredible had happened: 'William's Gun', or 'Big Bertha' as she was unlovingly called by Parisians, could bombard Paris from 74½ miles away. Here a first model is being tested a second missile fell, this time in the 10th arrondissement, striking a building in the Gare de l'Est. Now, people seriously believed it to be an air attack, but why had no alert been sounded? At last, at 0915 hours, the sirens sounded, warning the population to seek shelter. Three more projectiles had dropped and this time there were fatalities.

The first casualties

At 0815 hours at No 15, Rue Charles V, in the 4th arrondissement, a man had been killed—the first victim of this long range gun. A quarter of an hour later, again in the 4th arrondissement, Rue Miron, four people had been wounded. It was, however, at 0845, Boulevard de Strasbourg, the part facing the Gare de l'Est, that the greatest disaster of the day occurred: a shell killed eight people and wounded 13. As soon as this serious incident had occurred, and even though sightseers continued to scrutinise the sky looking for German aircraft, the trams of the Gare de l'Est-Montrouge line refused to take on any more passengers and returned to their depôts. A few minutes later, the alert was sounded. Public services were no longer functioning, people sought refuge, the shops closed and the streets became deserted.

Gradually, anxiety grew. People started asking questions about these strange detonations which were occurring practically every quarter of an hour, and the end of the alert was very long in coming. To complete the people's disarray, the official services of the War Ministry, which by 1000 hours still did not know what it was all about, or refused to recognise the truth, issued a communiqué which did not improve the situation. 'At 0820 hours, a few enemy aircraft flying at very high altitudes succeeded in crossing the lines and attacking Paris. They were immediately engaged by our fighter aircraft, both those from the entrenched camp and those from the front. Bombs are reported as having been dropped at several points and there are some

casualties.' It was true that fighter aircraft had indeed taken off, but the explosions continued to take place every quarter of an hour.

After the fourth explosion, the rate of one shell every 15 minutes was maintained up to 1345 hours when the 21st round fell once again in the 19th arrondissement, at 57 Rue Riquet, without causing any casualties. Why was there a one-hour interval between the 21st and the 22nd and last round? A mystery! Possibly there may have been a technical difficulty with the gun or in the ammunition supply.

After midday, the thick fog which covered the Crépy-en-Laonnois region, began to disperse, its marvellous camouflage being replaced by the first rays of the sun, and consequently firing was interrupted because in the distance French observation 'sausage' balloons were rising on their cables, and it was unwise to divulge the site of the battery which must already have been approximately marked by sound despite every precaution. The last round was fired towards 1441 hours to burst at 1445 hours in the suburbs near Pantin station. On the slopes of Mont de Joie, the long tube which had been protruding into the sky since the morning returned to its horizontal resting position.

What was the opinion of the official services in the various ministries early that afternoon? The advocates of an air attack, as against shelling, were fast losing ground. It was 1430 hours when the telephone rang in the editorial office of the paper *Le Temps* which was due to be run off the presses within a few minutes. It was requested that publication should be delayed for a few minutes because an official communiqué was being prepared at the War Ministry. At 1500 hours—barely a quarter of an hour after the last shell had arrived—the telephone rang once again at the paper. The editor heard the duty officer tell him: 'Are you sitting down? Yes? Well, hold on to the table because the news is sensational!' And then he dictated

The bombardment of Paris was not restricted to guns alone: after an interval of three years, German bombers once again flew over the capital of France. *Below:* A statistical résumé of the German aerial effort over Paris. *Bottom:* The incredible velocity and trajectory of the shells fired by the original Paris gun

	Took off	Lost	Killed	Wounded	No.	Weight (lbs)
JANUARY 30	30	1	61	198	267	31460
MARCH 8	60	1	18	41	92	
MARCH 11	70	4	173	132		
MARCH 24	1				2	
APRIL 1	7				21	
APRIL 11	1		27	72		1543
MAY 22	1		1	12	22	
MAY 23	1		10		50	660
MAY 27	15	1			4	
MAY 30	6		3	3	17	
MAY 31	6					
JUNE 1	3			28	14	
JUNE 3-7	1					
JUNE 15	1		3	5	9	990
JUNE 26	1				6	660
JUNE 27	3	2		18	26	
SEPT 15	50	2	7	30	85	

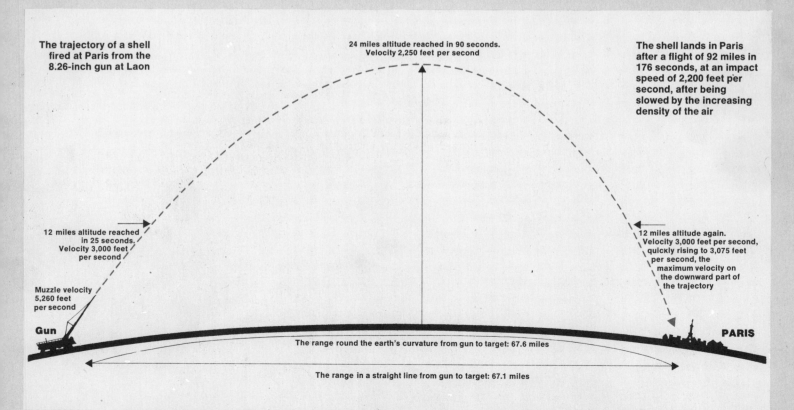

The trajectory of a shell fired at Paris from the 8.26-inch gun at Laon

24 miles altitude reached in 90 seconds. Velocity 2,250 feet per second

The shell lands in Paris after a flight of 92 miles in 176 seconds, at an impact speed of 2,200 feet per second, after being slowed by the increasing density of the air

12 miles altitude reached in 25 seconds. Velocity 3,000 feet per second

12 miles altitude again. Velocity 3,000 feet per second, quickly rising to 3,075 feet per second, the maximum velocity on the downward part of the trajectory

Muzzle velocity 5,260 feet per second

Gun

PARIS

The range round the earth's curvature from gun to target: 67.6 miles

The range in a straight line from gun to target: 67.1 miles

this communiqué: *The enemy has fired on Paris with a long range gun. Since 0800 hours this morning, every quarter of an hour, 9.5-inch (241-mm) shells struck the capital and its suburban area. There are about ten dead and 15 wounded. Measures to counter the enemy piece are now in course of execution.*

Thus was the fantastic exploit officially recognised. There was an error in this communiqué. The calibre of the shell was actually 8.3-inches (210-mm). As for the paper *Le Temps,* it thought it advisable to reassure its readers and avoid panic by adding that the front was still 62.1 miles (100 kms) away.

Twenty-two shells fell on this first day, 18 on Paris and four on its suburbs. They killed 16 people and injured 29. The following day, to the surprise of the Parisians who believed the gun had already been destroyed, firing was resumed and a first shell fell at 0645 hours in the Rue de Meaux (19th arrondissement), killing one person and injuring 14, most of them slightly. Twenty-two shells fell on Paris and its suburbs on that day, the last one (which wounded two people) at 1300 hours at Pré-Saint-Gervais.

Were there two guns?

This day was marked by a new event: shells started falling at very short intervals. For instance, it was noted that one shell fell at Pantin at 0917 hours and the next one at 0920 hours in Rue de la Lune in the 2nd arrondissement. These two rounds, only three minutes apart, could not have been fired from the same gun. From that moment, it had to be considered that there was not just one long range gun, but at least two. On that Sunday March 24, 1918—Palm Sunday—a shell that dropped at 1145 hours near Blanc-Mesnil Church, killed four and injured seven churchgoers leaving after Mass. On Monday March 25, only six shells were fired on Paris, five between 0649 hours and 0740 hours and the sixth in the afternoon (at 1548 hours in the Père-Lachaise cemetery).

For some unknown reason, firing stopped for three days. No shells were fired on March 26, 27 or 28. Once again legends began to circulate among the Parisians

Right: The centre of Paris, showing the places in which German shells landed in 1918

SHELLS FIRED FROM GERMAN LONG RANGE GUNS MARCH 23-AUGUST 9. PARIS SHELLED 44 TIMES (367 ROUNDS USED)

(12) NUMBERS OF ARRONDISSEMENTS

Montmartre · La Chapelle
BATIGNOLLES MONCEAUX (17) · BUTTE MONTMARTRE (18) · La Villete · BUTTE CHAUMONT (19)
Grave du Nord
Porte de Neuilly · Gare St Lazare · OPERA (9) · Gare de l'Est · ENCLOS-ST LAURENT (10)
Arc de Triomphe · ELYSEE (8)
PASSY (16) · BOURSE (2) · TEMPLE (3) · MENIL-MONTANT (20)
Eiffel Tower · LOUVRE (1) · HOTEL DE VILLE (4) · POPINCOURT (11)
PALAIS BOURBON (7) · Place de la Bastille
Auteuil · Invalides
LUXEMBOURG (6) · PANTHEON (5) · Gare de Lyon
VAUGIRARD (15) · REUILLY (12)
OBSERVATOIRE (14) · GOBELINS (13) · Place d'Italie
R. Seine

250 PARISIANS KILLED
620 PARISIANS INJURED
0 — 1 MILE

Left and below: The original 8.26-inch calibre German Paris gun. It is shown mounted on the carriage used at the naval gun-proving grounds in Germany. The weight of the shell fired by the 8.26-inch gun rose from 229 to 262 lbs with a 15½ lbs charge, and that of the later 9.13-inch gun from 273 to 307 lbs with an explosive charge 19¼ lbs in weight

Dazy

Roger Violett

146

Opposite page: Ruins of the church of Saint-Gervais in Paris, where 75 people died on Good Friday 1918. *Inset:* Strict attention to detail marked the installation of the 'Berthas'. This site, in the forest of Crépy-en-Laonnois, was heavily camouflaged by netting tied across the treetops: in spring leaves would spread over the netting, and mask the activity underneath. *This page:* The platform of the first gun. It consisted of a circular casing, mounted by a turntable on which the gun could traverse

about the gun exploding or its destruction by French artillery, because it was true that the French artillery had begun firing in its turn in the direction of the Crépy-en-Laonnois forest, less than 30 hours after the firing of the first round.

On Friday March 29 — Good Friday — only four shells were fired by 'Bertha', and only one fell on Paris, but with dire results. On that day, a considerable crowd filled the old Church of Saint-Gervais, Rue Miron. There were no longer any seats, and many were the women and children who had come to pray for those falling in the terrible battle in progress for the past ten days. It was exactly 1633 hours, a priest who had given a short sermon had just descended from the pulpit and a concert given by the *Petits Chanteurs à la Croix de Bois* was going to end the ceremony, when suddenly, in an unnerving silence, the air was shaken by a dull explosion. A frightful shock followed by an appalling noise shook the church. A vast surface of the vaulted roof and part of the left hand side of the nave collapsed. Cries and shrieks of pain soon rose from the pile of rubble and masonry that entombed what remained of the congregation. A shell had just struck the church; there were 75 dead and 90 injured, some of whom subsequently died. An enormous crowd gathered outside and was with great difficulty pushed away from the building by a police cordon. This single shell accounted for more victims than any other day.

The firing continued with more or less intensity during April. The bad weather helped the Germans, as the French reconnaissance planes were greatly handicapped by a month of execrable weather. In the whole 30 days only April 12 was sunny.

On May 1 the shelling of Paris stopped:

French guns were causing casualties. French artillery continued its firing until May 3. For 26 days 'Bertha' was silent.

Before dawn on May 27, the Crown Prince launched his divisions towards the Chemin des Dames in a southerly direction. In less than ten days, on June 4, the Germans found themselves at Château-Thierry, and an advanced spearhead crossed the Marne. This was to be their last victorious offensive. While the German infantry overran the French positions on the dawn of May 27, a first shell fell on Paris at 0630 hours. Fifteen shells, seven for Paris, and eight for the suburbs, the last one of which fell at 1828 hours, fell on the Paris region killing four and injuring 20.

The 'Bertha' was back, and the 'psychological' firing was resumed at the same time as the new offensive was launched, but another mystery appeared: the shells were no longer coming from the Crépy-en-Laonnois forest but from much further to the west and slightly to the south, from the wood of Corbie, near Beaumont-en-Beine, 68.3 miles (110 kms) from Paris, giving an appreciable improvement in the wear and tear of the tubes. Another fact emerged with this resumed bombardment. The splinters picked up showed the calibre had been changed. It was no longer 8.3-inch shells that were falling on Paris but shells of a calibre of 9.5 inches. It has been suggested that during this period, the Beaumont-en-Beine gun was not the only one, but that a remaining piece on the Crépy-en-Laonnois slopes had also fired.

Five weeks were to elapse without a single shell dropping on Paris. It is certain that the wearing out of the guns was rapid and as soon as they could the Germans endeavoured to bring their pieces closer in order to reduce the powder charge. They had already gained 9.3 miles (15 kms) by installing their 'Parisian cannon' near Beaumont-en-Beine.

Since their last lightning offensive, the Germans were on the Marne at Château-Thierry. Why not place a giant cannon further to the south, especially since very great progress had been made in the field of installing platforms which allowed a relatively rapid erection? While the

establishment of the concrete platform on the slopes of Mont de Joie had required over seven weeks, the entirely metal one which the Germans had just built for firing in all directions gave them the opportunity of rapidly mounting a firing emplacement for their giant cannon very close to Paris and only 58 miles (93 kms) from the capital. The site was found in the wood of Châtel, not far from the Oulchy-le-Château—Château-Thierry highway, six miles (ten kms) to the north of the latter. When the gun arrived in the environs of Fère-en-Tardenois, the French artillery was already pounding the region. This was to be the third series of firings which lasted two days. On July 15, 15 shells exploded in Paris. They killed three and wounded four. The next day, July 16, firing was resumed at 1030 hours and ended at 1720 hours, but in seven hours only four shells were fired. The position was too untenable because of the French artillery, and the Germans evacuated their position to return to their original one.

For three weeks, since July 16, the 'Berthas' had been silent, when suddenly on August 5 at 1005 hours at No 19 Rue Danton in Vanves, a shell killed two and injured eight. The fourth and last series of firings lasted five days. The last shell of the 17 fired that day fell at 1930 hours in Avenue de la Grande Armée. From the rate of firing, it would seem that a single piece alone was in action, as the shells kept arriving in Paris every 15 to 20 minutes from the departure base in the wood of Corbie near Beaumont-en-Beine which the French artillery once again started to plaster. The next day, August 6, Paris and its suburbs received 18 rounds, the first one at 0857 hours, the last one at 1850 hours. On August 7, 12 shells were fired, killing five and injuring 40, while on August 8, six more shells were despatched, one man being reported killed.

But the end was near. On August 9, the first shell fell at 0916 hours in a field near Dugny. Ten other shells followed. They killed three and injured seven. On Friday August 9, 1918, the 367th and last shell fell in Rue Saint-Denis at Aubervilliers.

It was over. The advance of the Allied troops had overtaken the German gun, and it had returned home. The last of the giant cannons which killed 256 and wounded 620 had fallen silent for ever. No Allied Armistice Commission was ever able to find any trace in Germany of these guns. Everything had been demolished with oxy-acetylene cutting torches.

Further Reading
Hallade, J., *Mystérieux canons dans l'Aisne* (Paris 1968)
Poirrier, Jules, *Les bombardements de Paris* (Paris 1930)
Thierry, M., *Paris bombardé par avions, Zeppelins et canons* (Paris 1920)

JEAN HALLADE was born in 1922 and studied at the Institution Saint-Charles in Chauny. In 1943 he joined the Resistance and, after the Liberation, he volunteered for the army. He is passionately interested in history, especially in the naval and air aspects of the two world wars, and his publications include articles in specialised papers and three books, *Wings in the Storm; Mysterious Guns on the Aisne;* and *The Resistance was at the Rendezvous.*

«ARCHIE»

The growth of air power in the First World War was matched by the parallel development of guns to deal with aircraft, from the early improvised mounts of 1914 to the precursor of the Second World War '88' in 1918

Below: **The British 13-pounder.** *Weight of shell:* 13 lbs. *Elevation:* +80°. *Traverse:* 360°. *Muzzle velocity:* 1,700 feet per second. *Rate of fire:* 6 to 10 rounds per minute. *Vertical range:* 13,000 feet. *Horizontal range:* 8,200 yards. *Weight of gun:* 2,150 lbs

Below: **The British 3-inch,** mounted on a Thornycroft 3-ton J Type lorry. This was a successful improvised gun, to take a shell made up of an 18-pdr case and a 13-pdr projectile. *Calibre:* 13-inch. *Weight of shell:* 12.5 lbs. *Elevation:* +90°. *Traverse:* 360°. *Muzzle velocity:* 2,500 feet per second. *Rate of fire:* 15 rounds per minute. *Vertical range:* 18,000 feet. *Horizontal range:* 10,450 yards. *Weight:* 12,500 lbs

ANTI-AIRCRAFT GUNS OF THE FIRST WORLD WAR

Right: **The German 7.7-cm.** *Calibre:* 7.7-cm. *Weight of shell:* 15 lbs. *Elevation:* +70°. *Traverse:* 360°. *Muzzle velocity:* 1,520 feet per second. *Rate of fire:* 6 to 10 rounds per minute. *Vertical range:* 14,000 feet. *Horizontal range:* 8,650 yards. *Weight:* 3,675 lbs.

Below: **The French 75-mm.** *Calibre:* 75-mm. *Weight of shell:* 15.8 lbs. *Elevation:* +70°. *Traverse:* 360°. *Muzzle velocity:* 1,735 feet per second. *Rate of fire:* 15 rounds per minute. *Vertical range:* 16,400 feet. *Horizontal range:* 9,850 yards. *Weight:* 8,800 lbs.

Left: **The German 8.8-cm,** forerunner of the famous anti-aircraft and anti-tank '88' of the Second World War. *Calibre:* 8.8-cm. *Weight of shell:* 21 lbs. *Elevation:* +70°. *Traverse:* 360°. *Muzzle velocity:* 2,575 feet per second. *Rate of fire:* 10 rounds per minute. *Vertical range:* 12,600 feet. *Horizontal range:* 11,800 yards. *Weight:* 6,700 lbs.

By the end of 1918, the design philosophy of the first tanks of 1916 had reached its culmination: its zenith, the Allied Mk VIII, was about to enter production. But the new designs about to see fruition were of more significance: track runs were lower, hull profiles more compact and the idea of a superimposed turret reintroduced. Thus the formula for future vehicles was laid down. It only remained to be seen if the tactical lessons had been learnt

Above: The last word in British tank design philosophy, the Anglo-American **Mark VIII** heavy tank, the International. This was the heaviest tank produced in the war, and also set new standards in crew comfort. Only four prototypes had been finished by the Armistice. *Weight:* 37 tons. *Crew:* 8. *Armament:* two 23-calibre 6-pdrs with 208 rounds and seven .3-inch Browning machine guns with 13,484 rounds. *Armour:* 16-mm front, 12-mm and 10-mm sides, sponsons and turret and 6-mm roof. *Engine:* Ricardo V-12 (British) or Liberty V-12 (American), 300-hp each. *Speed:* 7 mph max. *Step crossing:* 4 ft 6 ins. *Trench crossing:* 16 ft. *Range:* 50 miles. *Length:* 34 ft 2½ ins. *Height:* 10 ft 3 ins. *Width:* 12 ft 4 ins. *Left above:* The **Carro Armato Fiat 2000**, Italy's first venture into the design of heavy tanks. Only two were built. *Weight:* 40 tons. *Crew:* 10. *Armament:* one 65-mm gun and seven machine guns. *Armour:* 15-mm minimum, 20-mm maximum. *Engine:* Fiat 6-cylinder, 240-hp. *Speed:* 4½ mph.

Left below: The French **Char de Rupture 2C**. Designed in 1918, ten of these monsters were built between 1920 and 1922. *Weight:* 70 tons. *Crew:* 13. *Armament:* one 75-mm gun with 125 rounds and four machine guns with 10,000 rounds. *Armour:* 13-mm minimum, 45-mm maximum. *Engines:* two Daimler or Mercedes 6-cylinder, 250-hp each. *Speed:* 8 mph. *Range:* 107 miles. *Length:* 43 ft 2 ins. *Height:* 12 ft 8 ins. *Width:* 10 ft. *Below:* Germany's equivalent of the British Whippet, the **LK II**. *Weight:* 8¾ tons. *Crew:* 3. *Armament:* one 57-mm gun (another version had two machine guns). *Armour:* 8-mm minimum, 14-mm maximum. *Engine:* Daimler 4-cylinder, 55-hp. *Speed:* 8 mph. *Range:* 40 miles. *Length:* 18 ft 8 ins. *Height:* 8 ft 2 ins. *Width:* 6 ft 5 ins. The LK II was decidedly underpowered, and the limited traverse of its armament would have been a liability; but in the event, only prototypes had been built before the Armistice. Similar in design to the British medium tanks, it had no all-round protection

John Batchelor

THE SAMBRE

The Allied advances of August and September 1918 had by no means knocked the German armies out of the fight. But suddenly in October and November the German armies started to crumble. *Douglas Orgill. Above:* Into battle 1918-style

As the month of October opened in 1918, the shadows were falling fast across the whole of the German war effort. Yet on the Allied side of the lines, too, observers sensed a certain chill. The end of the war, to military eyes, was not yet clearly in sight; there were firm indications that the German armies were far from broken; and the dreadful possibility of a spring and summer campaign in 1919 was still heavy in the minds of the Allied staffs. In addition,

it was now autumn, and not the season in which to fight a dragging, bloody campaign. In September the Allied Commander-in-Chief, Marshal Ferdinand Foch, had planned a three-pronged offensive. In the south the Americans, with Gouraud's French Fourth Army on their left, would attack towards Mézières; the French centre would advance beyond the River Aisne; and in the north the British armies, supported by the French left, would drive forward to Cam-

Südd Verlag

CROSSINGS

brai and St Quentin. The forces available for this ambitious offensive were far from overwhelming, and at the British end of the front were barely adequate. Holding a line from St Quentin to Armentières was Haig's group of four British armies. These were Rawlinson's Fourth Army, Byng's Third, Horne's First, and Birdwood's Fifth. Between them, they comprised 52 divisions (including two American divisions and all reserves) and three cavalry divisions.

Opposing them were 63 German divisions, 30 of which were held in reserve—although the ratio in terms of man for man was not quite as high on the German side as it looked, since the prevalent influenza and heavy battle casualties had reduced some German nominal divisions to a shadow of their former strength. Further north still, holding the line from Armentières to Ypres, was King Albert's Flanders army group, consisting of Plumer's Second British

Army of 10 divisions, 12 Belgian divisions and 9 French reserve divisions.

On the battlefield Plumer faced the battered countryside of Flanders, where the tide of battle had ebbed and flowed for four years. This was a zone of deep devastation, which also embraced the front held by Haig's four armies. A senior officer who saw it that autumn reported later that . . . *from Vimy Ridge to the eastern outskirts of Amiens and thence through St Quentin northwards by Cambrai to Douai, in an area of over 1,000 square miles, there was hardly a house to be found intact, no village which had not been gutted; the surface of the ground was torn and blasted by shell-fire, the vegetation withered by poison gas, the roads had been destroyed, the railways torn up, and all the bridges over the many rivers and canals blown down.* In addition, the autumn rain turned the whole area, Passchendaele-style, into a desolate sea of mud. Behind the French forces in Champagne, too, there was another stretch of destroyed roads and desolated countryside, while the Americans had at their rear the old battlefield of Verdun. Armies need food, ammunition and stores: the delays inevitably entailed in the bid to rebuild an adequate communications system now made themselves felt on all the three fronts of Foch's offensive.

As October opened, King Albert's army group was about two miles from Roulers, yet it would be a fortnight before the town finally fell. Cambrai, too, had been enveloped to north and south by the First and Third Armies, but the Germans still clung to the greater part of the town. Further down the line, Gouraud had made an initial advance of about six miles, but had achieved little progress during the first nine days of the month. The worst delay of all was on the right wing of the triple offensive, where Pershing's Americans, crowded on to a narrow front where the staffwork was not good enough to operate them properly, were hopelessly wedged in the forest of the Argonne. The transport problem here was so bad that vehicles piled up in masses, unable to move forward or back, and troops in the line were going hungry and short of ammunition. The two wings of Foch's great attack, in fact, were stalled, while in the centre the French—who, like every other combatant, were none too keen to incur heavy casualties in what might be the last weeks of the war—waited willingly for the situation to sort itself out. These were disappointing days for Foch, as Haig was swift to note. Haig's diary entry for October 3 recorded that . . . *Foch's staff are terribly disappointed with the results of the American attacks on the west of the Meuse. The enemy is in no strength in their front, but the Americans cannot advance because their supply arrangements have broken down. The divisions in the front line are really starving, and have had to be relieved in order to be brought to where the food is.*

Haig himself, however, was well aware of the need to press on, and Foch had no need to repeat his stern principle of 'attaquez, attaquez, tout le monde à la bataille'. The British Commander met Foch at his headquarters at Mouchy le Chatel at noon on October 6, and announced that, provided enough guns and ammunition could be moved forward, he proposed to attack around Cambrai next day. He also asked for some more American troops to help push the assault along. 'I told F.', he said, 'that with three fresh American divisions it would be possible to reach Valenciennes in 48 hours.' Foch had already tried this gambit on Pershing, however, asking him for troops from the stalled American offensive to reinforce French armies. The answer from the American commander had been a brusque, unequivocal 'No'. Pershing was going to work out his own problems, and his mind was fixed exclusively on the problem of the Argonne.

Foch: disappointed in the results of the American operations on the west bank of the Meuse

Generals Byng and Currie. *Right:* Allied attacks that brought the Germans to breaking point

Haig, however, had grasped what needed to be done. The Allied delay had given the retreating Germans a little breathing space. Moreover, Ludendorff, who had seemed to be broken forever by the September storming of the Hindenburg Line, was now slowly recovering his nerve. He was fighting intelligently to hold the Allied armies out of Germany at least until the following spring. This meant a long stand on the line of the Meuse. Thus the American standstill in the Argonne played into his hands while he slowly withdrew his right flank from Flanders. The threat to his plan would be a British advance through Cambrai to Maubeuge, which would do much to cut off the German armies on both left and right flanks. This was precisely the advance which Haig now intended to make.

Meanwhile, the German army was told

of Germany's bid to secure an armistice, but in terms which emphasised the value of a stern continuance of the present struggle. An order of the day from Wilhelm II on October 5 reminded his troops: *For months past the enemy has been striving against your lines with powerful efforts, almost without a pause. You have had to resist by fighting for weeks on end, frequently without rest, and to show a front to a foe vastly superior in numbers. Therein lies the immensity of the task which has been given you, and you are fulfilling it . . . Your front is unbroken and will remain so. In agreement with my allies I have decided to offer peace once more to our enemies; but we will only stretch out our hands for an honourable peace.* To any German soldier who read beyond the bombast, this message must have had alarming undertones.

On the British front, Ludendorff was withdrawing grudgingly to a position partly along the line of the Selle which was known to the Germans as the *Hermann* position. In general, this line was intended to protect an area from the River Scheldt, south of Valenciennes, to the River Oise, just west of Guise, but it was very far from ready. Its chief strength had been given it by nature alone: the River Selle was an unpleasant obstacle for assaulting troops.

Second Cambrai: another tank 'duel'
At dawn on October 8, Byng and Rawlinson, with the Third and Fourth Armies respectively, launched the second battle of Cambrai, along an 18-mile front, and supported by 82 tanks. These were all the Tank Corps had managed to make fit for battle, after the extensive casualties and breakdowns which had somewhat inhibited its rôle since the great armoured stroke at Amiens on August 8. The troops had been skilfully assembled in the dark in difficult, shell-smashed and trench-ridden country. Not without difficulty, however, and the XIII Corps, on the left of the Fourth Army line, were badly harassed by shelling and air attack as they formed up. When they advanced, however, it was to success: some indication of gradually deteriorating German morale was given by ordinary line infantry who fought only briefly before running away. The machine gunners, however, as always stuck to their task, firing until the last moment.

One rare, noteworthy event marked the day. The Germans counterattacked with tanks—captured British Mark IVs—in groups of four or five. This happened on the left, near Awoingt, and two of the German-crewed machines were knocked out—one by a 6-pounder shell fired by a British tank, and the other, appropriately, by a round fired from a captured German field gun laid by a British tank section commander. The other German tanks then turned back into their own lines. This was the second tank-versus-tank action of the war, the first having been fought in April near Cachy. The German command, however, was never able to use tanks on anything like the scale of the Allies. At no time during the war did the German tank force exceed 40 machines—15 of their great slab-sided A 7 Vs, and 25 captured British models. At no time, too, did they succeed in using more than 25 in a single operation. The British command was also unwilling to use tanks in an exploiting as well as a break-in rôle, though this, admittedly, might well have been beyond the mech-

Bottom: Renault 37-mm tank. *Weight:* 14,300 lbs. *Armament:* 37-mm gun, with 237 rounds of ammunition. *Dimensions:* Length 16 ft 5 ins; width 5 ft 7½ ins; height 7 ft. *Engine:* 35 bhp. *Speed:* Cross-country 2.2 mph; on roads 4.8 mph. *Range:* 22 miles. *Armour:* Front 16-mm; sides 8-mm; top 8-mm; belly 6-mm. *Turret:* Either round (22-mm) or panelled (16-mm). *Crew:* 2 men. *Below:* A column of Renaults at Suvigney

National Archives

John Batchelor

Top left: A road in the Somme area. Their advance left the Allies with the previous battle zone to their rear, complicating their supply problem. *Above:* Early mechanisation. A French tractor in the Meuse area. *Left:* Members of 110th Regiment in Varennes-en-Argonne

anical resources of the Tank Corps in October 1918. All that was offered for exploitation was cavalry – and it had already been demonstrated many times that cavalry on a modern battlefield was doomed; an easy victim for the ubiquitous wire and machine guns, and inhibited by the simple fact that it could not lie down and take cover. No decisive cavalry charge, in fact, could be made until the last machine gun had been captured. This was a prerequisite which could never be achieved; the British Official History observes sombrely that 'every effort was made by the higher commanders to pass the cavalry through to play havoc with the enemy's communications; but only a few patrols got much farther than the infantry's front line . . .'

However, with the tanks helping in what was now their traditional support rôle, the

XIII, II American, and IX Corps of Fourth Army moved forward to within a mile of Le Cateau by nightfall, while the Germans in front of Third Army finally pulled out of the battered city of Cambrai. The disciplined retreat planned by Ludendorff began to exhibit signs of panic, as troops and lorries and horse-drawn wagons jammed the roads and bridges in front of the River Selle. German battalion accounts of the day's fighting sound a note of despair. Battalions, it was said, averaged only 150 officers and men, and in some of them only 'severe measures' had held the formations together in the line. Strong measures were also taken rather higher up the line of command. The German army group commander, Boehm, was abruptly sent on leave, and was later reduced to the command of a single army. The army group itself was broken up, the German *Second*

Army going to Rupprecht's *Gruppe* based to the north, and the *Eighteenth* to the Crown Prince's *Gruppe* to the south. 'The troops,' said one official account, 'were completely used up and burnt to cinders . . .' There was, too, increasing evidence of the infection of revolution in the German army: the men whom Ludendorff had earlier noted as shouting 'blacklegs' at reinforcements moving up into the line were steadily growing in numbers and influence.

The next problem for the British command was to force the line of the Selle, the river on which the town of Le Cateau stood. Supply difficulties now dictated a pause in the onward movement: Rawlinson's Fourth Army, which was to make the assault, needed a week to establish its preparations on a proper footing. Rawlinson was covered on his right by Debeney's First French Army, and on his left by Byng's Third

Army, with Horne's First Army on Byng's left. Between October 11 and 16 some small improvement was made in the British positions. Horne, in particular, battered his way up the Sensée Canal—an advance which was sure to inhibit the German defence of the Selle in the next few days. At 0530 hours on October 17, Rawlinson struck again, in mist so thick that it reminded Fourth Army of its earlier triumph in the fog on Ludendorff's 'Black Day' of August 8. His attack was on a ten-mile front, supported by almost 50 tanks. The programme set for Fourth Army took two days to achieve instead of the one which had been planned, for the Germans fought well, counterattacking at well-chosen points, and heavily shelling British assembly areas. Le Cateau was emptied of Germans by the evening of October 17, but the American 27th and 30th Divisions,

attacking a hillcrest railway line south of the town, met an unexpectedly ferocious response, and it was not until October 19 that Rawlinson's right wing closed up to the line of the Sambre Canal, and then stopped—five miles beyond the Selle. On October 20, also against desperate resistance, seven divisions of the Third Army and one of the First crashed their way across the Selle west of Le Cateau. The advance of all three armies began again three days later, and 15 miles were gained between the Sambre Canal and the Scheldt. A breach six miles deep and 35 miles broad had been punched into the German front, and thousands of prisoners were streaming into the cages. It had been a stunning victory, achieved in a strangely unspectacular manner, though at high cost. In the struggle for the Selle, the 24 British and two American divisions en-

gaged had taken 20,000 prisoners from 31 German divisions opposing them, and had captured nearly 500 guns. About 50 men from each British battalion in the assault had been killed or wounded.

The strong German resistance had, nonetheless, given Haig food for thought. He warned Wilson, Chief of the Imperial General Staff, that the Germans were not yet done, recording in his diary on October 19:

I visited the War Office soon after 10 am and saw Wilson. He gave me his views on conditions of armistice. He considers that the Germans should be ordered to lay down their arms and retire to the east of the Rhine. I gave my opinion that our attack on the 17th inst. met with considerable opposition, and that the enemy was not ready for unconditional surrender. In that case, there would be no armistice, and the war would continue for at least another year.

Later that day, to the Prime Minister, Lloyd George, Haig gave his considered view of the state of the Allied armies, summing it up later as:

French army: worn out and has not been really fighting latterly. It has been freely said that 'the war is over' and 'we don't wish to lose our lives now that peace is in sight'.

American army: is not yet organised: it is ill-equipped, half-trained, with insufficient supply services. Experienced officers and NCOs are lacking.

British army: was never more efficient than it is today, but it has fought hard, and it lacks reinforcements. With diminishing effectives, morale is bound to suffer.

And yet Haig was too pessimistic. The Battle of the Selle had seen the end of Ludendorff. His policy of retiring to a shorter holding line was manifestly being eroded by events, and Wilhelm II knew it. Ludendorff put his own head on the block when, in an astonishing act of insubordination, he issued an order saying that President Wilson's armistice proposals were 'a demand for unconditional surrender, and thus unacceptable to us soldiers'. On October 26 he was summoned to the presence of the Kaiser.

'There followed,' Ludendorff recorded later, 'some of the bitterest moments of my life. I said respectfully to His Majesty that I had gained the impression that I no longer enjoyed his confidence, and I accordingly begged most humbly to be relieved of my office. His Majesty accepted my resignation.' General Wilhelm Gröner, an expert on railway transport, replaced Ludendorff as First Quartermaster General.

As the British command prepared for what was to be the last great British thrust, the German slide was accelerating. The First Army reached Valenciennes, and the Fifth brushed aside feeble German rearguards to reach the Scheldt Canal. Plumer's Second Army, under King Albert's overall command in Flanders, had crossed the River Lys on October 19, preparing for a new move forward to the Scheldt. The next combined offensive was to be a drive by four armies, over a 40-mile front from Guise to Condé. The forces to be employed were the British Fourth, Third and First Armies, and Debeney's First French Army on the right. They were ordered to 'resume the offensive on or after November 3 with a view to breaking the enemy's resistance south of the Condé Canal and advancing in the general direction Avesnes-Maubeuge-Mons'. This advance would threaten Namur, the seizure of which would imperil all the German armies in western Belgium. Taken in conjunction with a resumed American advance through the Argonne to Mézières and Sedan, it would completely wreck any German attempt to establish a secure line on the Meuse. If it succeeded, the path into Germany would be growing broader and more inviting. Nevertheless, the attack would be made over difficult country, with an especially unpleasant feature in the shape of the Sambre Canal. This obstacle was 70 feet wide over a good deal of its length, and at least six feet deep. Along part of it the Germans had opened locks, flooding the low ground, though in general to a depth of only a few inches. Here the British Expeditionary Force had assembled four long years ago on its arrival in France. Mons was a charismatic word to every British soldier.

A little before dawn on November 4, the Battle of the Sambre began. 17 divisions of the three British armies attacked, with six in reserve. It was significant evidence of the inroads made by battle upon the limited resources of the Tank Corps at this stage of the war that only 37 tanks were available to support this mass of infantry. Rawlinson, on the right of the British line (with Debeney on his own right), was confronted by the canal at a point where it was both wide and commanded by good German defensive positions on the other side. He attacked with two corps—the XIII on the left and the IX on the right. The more difficult part of the canal was allotted to Braithwaite's IX Corps, which put the 1st and 32nd Divisions into the assault, with the 46th in reserve. Each division was allotted three tanks of the 10th Tank Battalion—an armoured support which can only be described as derisory.

The opening hours for Braithwaite's corps were grim. The assaulting battalion of the 1st Division was the 2nd Royal Sussex. Its

Above: German A 7 V tank. These were used alongside captured British Mark IV's. *Below:* François Flameng's painting of tank warfare

Musée de l'Armée

objective was a lock, with a group of houses on the far side, and a subsidiary stream a hundred yards short of the main canal. However, as the Royal Sussex battalion moved determinedly into the attack, a major setback was discovered—apparently the planks and bridging used in rehearsal were in fact a little too short for the actual obstacle of the subsidiary stream. Meanwhile, as the main body of the battalion began to pile up on the near bank, the German gunners found the range, and salvo after salvo, laced with streams of machine gun bullets from the houses beside the lock, tore into the struggling infantry. With tremendous courage and determination, the commanding officer of the Royal Sussex, Lieutenant-Colonel D. G. Johnson, led his infantry into the shell-storm to protect the bridge-carrying parties of the Royal Engineers, them-

selves commanded by Major G. de C. E. Findlay, of the 409th Field Company. While men dropped, hit and dying, into the stream, the bridges were eventually pushed and shoved into place, to be instantly crossed by the revengeful Royal Sussex, their machine gunners firing the heavy Lewis guns from the hip, cutting down German defenders running frantically from the houses beside the lock gate. Nearly 150 Royal Sussex and sappers lay dead or wounded behind them. For their part in this decisive action, Johnson and Findlay each received the Victoria Cross.

The other assaulting battalion of the 1st Division, the 1st Cameron Highlanders, were more fortunate, getting bridges across the canal in the first few minutes, and closing with the Germans on the far side in bitter hand-to-hand actions in the early morning mist. The 32nd Division, on the